white bees

a memoir

Amy Jo Wilde

*May you
seek to find
white bees in your
own life.*

Aj Wilde

ISBN: 9780615904719

Printed in the United States of America
First Printing, 2013.
All of the characters, dialog, and experiences
in this book are truthful and correct to the best
of my knowledge and records. A few names have been
changed. Compressed storytelling has been used in
a few instances when records were not
available to validate memories.

Summary: Amy Jo Wilde, born with a bilateral cleft lip and
palate, bravely takes on her trial with optimism, protected
by the *white bees* and finds the power of God in the beautiful
pattern of her life.

Cover Model: Sierra Thornley
Cover Design: Amy Jo Wilde
Author Photograph: Emma Justine Wilde
Editing: Katie Carter
Proof Reading: Proof Positive, http://proofpositivepro.com/
Author Website: www.amyjowilde.com

For My Mom

...for all the reasons why...

Note to Reader

In 1973 there were 3.14 million babies born in the U.S., of which 4,486 were born with a cleft palate. In March of 1973 I was one of those babies, and was lucky to be born into an incredible and supportive family.

Everyone has a story, this is mine.

white bees

Timeline of cleft lip and palate treatment milestones:

- **Lip Repair** — Birth / 5 days
- **Lip Revision** — 7m
- **Palate Repair** — 18m
- **Hearing Evaluation** — 2y
- **Lip Revision** — 3y
- **Speech Therapy** / **Pharyngoplasty** — 4y
- Pharyngoplasty — 5y
- **Ear Tubes** — 8y
- **Braces** — 9y
- **Cranial Facial Surgery / Bone Graft** — 16y
- **Rhinoplasty / Lip Repair** / Dental Treatment — 15y
- Dental Treatment — 18y
- **Rhinoplasty** — 20y
- **Eardrum Reconstruction** — 28y
- **Rhinoplasty / Lip Revision** — 35y
- 40y

Specialists:
- Reconstructive Surgeon
- Audiologist
- Speech-Language Pathologist
- Otolaryngologist
- Orthodontist
- Dentist

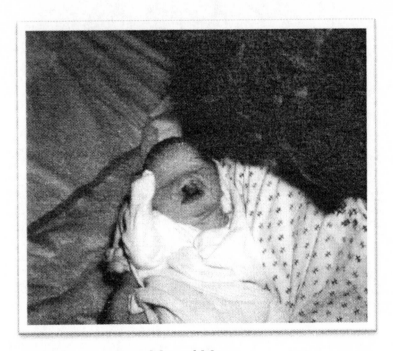

Me and Mom

March 11th, 1973

CHAPTER ONE

My mother has loved me from the very start.
I must have felt her faith as she took me in her arms the
day I was born and looked upon my tangled face and into
my new blue eyes with courage and complete
understanding, knowing the road ahead would be laced
with trials and mixed with grace.

High school wasn't supposed to start this way. The same way all of my other school years had started — wearing my same face that brought the painful responses I pretended not to see. Above my basement bedroom, I heard Mom opening and shutting cupboard doors, the weight of her feet flexing the creaky floor in the rhythm of a new morning.

I turned my head and inhaled the honest scent of my pillowcase, the fibers holding traces of salt water from nights I carried my burden alone. Not everyone stared at me with critical eyes. Mom stared right into my heart, my being, my soul. She didn't ask if I was being teased or if I wished I were perfect. I'm not even sure the idea crossed her mind. Instead, she told me I was confident and beautiful, with way more friends than she'd ever had. She said I amazed her. And I believed her.

I pulled my right leg to my chest and hugged my knee, then dropped my hand to trace the inch-long scar on the inside of my ankle from an IV I'd had as a new baby. Mom couldn't remember which surgery caused the scar. But she'd said it had started as a small pierce from a needle and, once healed, had stretched as I'd grown. For some reason moving my finger back and forth over the raised scar brought me peace.

My younger sister stirred in her twin bed four feet from mine. She lobbed one arm up and out from under the covers and onto the nightstand where her thick glasses rested. With the other hand, she cleared the tangled hair away from her face. She situated the glasses on her nose and asked, "Is it already time to get up?"

I leaned up on one elbow, looking past her silhouette to our bedroom window. "Yup, it's morning, Toots, even though it's still dark outside. Jeannie is already up. I call the shower next."

"What's that sound?"

"That squeaky sound?"

"Mmm hmm."

"Just Mr. Sorensen. You know, letting his dog, Max, out to pee. His gate squeaks."

"Oh. How'd you know that?"

"I've been paying attention all summer. Listen. In a minute you'll hear it again when he goes back inside. I've memorized the whole process."

Jeannie, older than me by eighteen months, threw open the door connecting our two rooms. "Hey, I lost the back to one of my pink triangle earrings. Do either of you have a pencil eraser I can use?"

8

"I do," Toots said. "But don't use my favorite pencil. Just use one of the regular orange ones over there on my desk."

"I only need half. Thanks, Toots. You're a lifesaver."

I released my hand from my ankle, stretched both legs down to the end of my bed, then pointed my toes until my feet arched and my calf muscles burned. I'd waited fifteen years to be transformed into beautiful. The "big" surgery, the cranial facial surgery I'd been waiting for, was supposed to have happened before I started high school. Instead, it hung on the horizon teasing me with time until the bone in my face matured. The surgery was partly for me, but mostly for the people who had to look at me. I wanted the surgery for the kid in the grocery store line who tugged on his mom's shirt, pointing at my face while she shushed him. I wanted it for the bully who unleashed his verbal torment on me in elementary school, strangling my confidence, and I wanted it for those so distracted by my lips that they never heard the words that crossed them.

I swung my legs out of the bed, flipped on the lights, and saw the outfit I had laid out the night before: acid washed jeans, a sweater, and dangly earrings—all with tags still on. A rush of energy inflated my mood. I showered, dressed, scrunched and winged my hair, then worked the pastel pink and aqua eye-shadow around my bright eyes. My face didn't seem ugly to me, just different. My upper lip looked as if someone had pinched the left side until it ballooned over to the right side. Two prominent scars traveled from the inside of my nose all the way through my lip, leaving white lines cutting through the bright pink coloring. My bottom lip was just like Mom's, full and perfect. However, I didn't get her small, tidy nose. Mine had character. Not necessarily the good kind of character, more like blocky, not-enough-cartilage, smooshed character. Yet, when I was all alone getting ready in front of the mirror, I could see traces of normal beneath the deformities. I could see the beautiful shining through, peeking out, as if it didn't care one bit what I looked like. To me my scars were constant reminders of how far I had come since the day I was born, the day Mom saw my bilateral cleft lip and palate for the first time—with no warning. She didn't push me away in fear and shock, instead, she tucked me in close—right next to her heart, sure that God had a plan in store for both of us.

I slipped on my new shoes and took the stairs two at a time up to the kitchen, feeling my confidence take hold.

"Well, good morning! Don't you look cute."

"Thanks, Mom."

"Now look here, I made this nice big batch of pancakes, so you get a plate and load up. I'm just making up some hot maple syrup."

"Aw, wheat pancakes again? Why can't we ever have white ones?"

"Whole grains are good for your body! I ground up this wheat early this morning."

My rowdy brothers made it to the kitchen next, piling their own plates mile-high with six pancakes each. Jeannie, who was a senior, grabbed her breakfast on the run when her friends honked for her out front. I finished my breakfast, checked my outfit again in Mom's full-length mirror, pushed open the front door, swung my backpack over my right shoulder, and climbed into the old, green Ford truck with Dad.

"Well, A-mouse," Dad said, backing the truck out and calling me by the nickname he had given me years earlier, "your first day of high school is finally here. From this day forward your grades count toward getting into college."

"We don't actually do any work on the first day, Dad."

"Well, a*ctually*, I don't *actually* think any kid is *actually* going to do any *actual* work today," teased Dad, emphasizing a word he loved to use, but didn't think had any business being in the English language.

"I just hope I can remember where all my classes are. The high school is so big. I wrote my locker number on my hand. I'm nervous I'll forget it."

"The good news is you get to do this all over again tomorrow."

Dad, a teacher at the high school, said goodbye and parked his truck in his space—the one with his name painted in white letters. The cement walk to the front doors swarmed with students. I held my head high and prepared for the knocking stares. I had a trick though; I pretended I didn't see them looking at what was wrong with me and assumed they were in awe with my outer fashionista and wanted to copycat my style. When I reached my locker, Katie, my best friend in the whole wide world, wasn't there yet. I turned my body toward the locker and quickly checked to make sure the stuffing in my bra was secure. I'd used just three cotton balls, but I planned to work up to six by the end of the year. I hung up my backpack, organized my new Bic pens and Trapper folders on the small metal shelf, aired out my damp, palm-sweat covered class schedule, and turned to the growing mass of students. Right away my eyes found him.

The bully stood far enough away that I could watch him and not get caught. I dropped my eyes momentarily to the floor, cringing inside. He had grown at least four inches since I'd last seen him three years ago in elementary school, but he still wore his trademark short haircut, heavy denim jeans, and plaid shirt. I hated his proper clothes that made him appear polite. After elementary he'd gone to a junior high on the other end of town, and I'd prayed he would be gone from my life for good.

I watched him change the weight from his left foot to his right, and my mind instantly replayed the hurtful words from years earlier in elementary school: "Hey, FAT LIP!" he would shout while kicking sand at me. In my heart I wanted to believe he wasn't talking to me, I'd never heard those words before. I would look away from him, ignore his shouting, and let my eyes follow the meandering wave of the chain link fence. When I didn't acknowledge his banter, he'd increase the volume, adding salt to his words: "You can't hide from me! I can still see your smashed-in dog face!" I knew the kind of dog he was referring to, the ugly kind that were kept penned up in a dog run. The bully's brash laugh traveled like a megaphone across the hot blacktop, loud enough that the other students could hear. I missed Mom like crazy when he tormented me, and ached for her to fill me up with her faith. My thoughts returned to the present, and I leaned against my locker, wondering if the bully had any clue how much he'd wounded me by magnifying my pain. A part of me believed I deserved his crushing cruelty, but a bigger part knew his words could never define me.

I shut my locker, careful not to slam it, and then ran my hands over my hair to make sure the shell of hairspray was holding everything together.

"Kates! You made it just in time," I yelled over the reminder bell. "Holy cow! You look so cute!"

"Right back at ya! See you at lunch, right?" she asked as she scooted past me and merged into the stream of students making their way to class.

"I'll save you a seat!" I answered, and then glanced toward where the bully had been standing. He was gone. His energy lingered, though, and as I crossed where he had been minutes earlier, I could almost feel his hurtful words trying to whip any ounce of assurance from me that I had gained during the past summer: The summer of staying out late, playing kick the can and capture the flag in Katie's backyard, laughing till our sides hurt, running as fast as we could, then sitting in the cool grass and talking till midnight. The summer that made me forget all about my messed up face. The best summer of my life!

Amy Jo Wilde

CHAPTER TWO

Embrace the authentic spaces of life that effortlessly reveal your truest form. These are the times you will look back on in aging: laughing while youth, energy, and friendships are remembered.

The summer before high school, the *best* summer of my life, I wanted three things to happen: my boobs to grow, to spend all my time with Katie, and, most importantly, I wanted to forget about my treasure chest of insecurities, my self-proclaimed "layer eleven".

I never told anyone about my layer eleven. It was the place I put all the mean words kids shouted to me—laughing with their friends as if I was some sort of disfigured freak. It was where I put the anxiety of surgeries, the social pressures to look perfect, and compounded stress from years of not looking like the other kids. It was even where I put the very name of the condition I was born with, cleft lip and palate, because just saying it was like admitting something *really was* wrong with me. I locked up all the poison emotion there, in a safe place in my mind, so I could focus on my positive, happy layers.

The best summer of my life included being inseparable with a group of neighborhood girls and guys that shared my same Sunday School class: Katie, Moose, Christy, Wendy, Stephen, Michelle, and the new guy, Clint. "The Rebels" became our club name after we all wore our Hard Rock Café t-shirts to church, ran off three Sunday School teachers in a row, and convinced the last, Mr. Caine, to go buy doughnuts during class and bring them back to church for us to enjoy. Some of the adults in the neighborhood still give us that distrustful look for stealing (never happened), staying out past our curfew (happened), or the unthinkable "mooning" incident (may or may not have actually happened). I don't blame them for judging us; from the outside looking in, one would have thought we were nothing but trouble. By our standards though, we were just a tight-knit group of teenagers singing "Happy Trails to You" each night before we went our separate ways back home.

"What did kissing feel like? Tell me everything!" I begged Katie the second week of summer.

"Well, it all started when Clint asked me if I wanted to watch a movie with him," Katie started. "So we went down into his basement, and he picked out a movie he thought I'd like, but I didn't even see which one it was, honestly! Then we sat down, he scooted over next to me, and he put his arm up around the back of the couch. Oh, wow, and he smelled *so* good. Like soap mixed with cologne!"

"OK, go on... wait. First, tell me, were you nervous? Oh, I seriously can't believe this happened to you!"

"Yes! I was nervous! So after we watched the movie, he turned and looked at me and then just sat there with this goofy smile on his face—and I looked at him and realized something might just be about to happen. Then he leaned in and kissed me!"

"Oh, Katie. Your first kiss! How did you feel? Did you even know what to do?"

"Well, I'm pretty sure it was just a kiss on the cheek, but he kind of missed and got half of the left side of my lips, too..."

"Are you telling me that it was *not* just a kiss on the cheek?"

"I guess, I mean...I don't know! Ahhhh!!!!"

"OK, start from the beginning again, but this time more detail! Oh, Kates! You will always remember the summer of 1988. The summer you got your first kiss," I said as I noted to myself that my best friend, Katie —at fifteen–and-a-half years old — would never have to say, "sweet sixteen and never been kissed." Even if it *was* just a half-kiss.

Katie later told me, while sitting cross-legged on her bed sorting through her earrings, that if I wanted to become a good kisser the best thing I could do was practice on the back of my hand. Of course, I had to believe Katie. She had experienced the real thing. I tried it once, after going to bed. I turned my pillow up on its side and placed my right hand up to eye level. I closed my eyes and leaned in, missing my hand completely. I tried again, with my eyes open so I could hit the target, and it just felt all dirty and very, very dry. So that was that. I made two vows that night: *never* tell anyone I practiced kissing on my hand and *never* practice kissing on my hand again. I wanted so bad to have a real live kiss like Katie, but my lips weren't exactly my best feature, and listening to her stories were just about as good as the real thing.

I don't remember my life without Katie or when our friendship began. Our backyards connected with a little pathway between our two houses. Some years, the path was worn right down to the dirt, and each time that happened her dad planted new grass. The grass never grew, though, because the footprints were too constant. Everyone should have a best friend like Katie: loyal, generous, and a true spitfire. Katie—older than me by just one and a half months—had, long brown hair; nice teeth; eyes that coordinated with whatever she happened to be wearing—from hazel to blue; *and* the skill to master any sport, including a deathly round of tetherball.

Clint and Katie instantly became boyfriend and girlfriend after the famous half-kiss. I wanted the same thing that Katie had; I truly ached for a boyfriend to bake cookies for and share kisses with. But I never had any boys who liked me. I pretended I didn't care. That way, nobody could accuse me of having my feelings hurt over being silently rejected. Katie had what I had wished for my whole teenage life: a boy who liked her and whom she liked back. Simple, beautiful chemistry.

Thankfully, a few weeks after the half-kiss, the romance cooled and things went back to normal. I was the first to admit that I liked it better that way.

The leader of our group, Moose, had a large bubble nose, spiky hair, and the most infectious laugh I had ever heard. He was the biggest kid when we were in elementary school, so the name Moose took over for his real name, Michael. The Rebels spent many hours during the summer in his

18

basement, an unfinished masterpiece of two-by-fours that created a loose and very cool framework for a teenage hangout. We watched movies, lit cologne on fire (very exciting!), played his acoustic guitar, and on occasion listened to the forbidden sounds of heavy metal. Nobody in the Rebels group called me ugly, or even thought it, they only saw the real me. Being with the group was easy and addicting.

"Guys, I have a plan. Everyone listen up," Moose firmly said one blistering afternoon on the sidewalk of 150 East. "We have a problem." He positioned himself for a stately speech on the curb, though it was a mere half-inch taller than the sidewalk. "The gossip in the neighborhood has gotten out of control," he started, "and people are starting to talk about us. We need to stop this mindless crap, and now. First, we need to figure out where the gossip leak is coming from. I think we can all agree that it's probably Mrs. Carter and Mrs. Edgewood, right?" he questioned, looking at all of us for approval. I nodded my head quickly and found myself all too eager to do whatever plan he had rallied us for. "Let's give them some bait and see if they turn it into gossip."

The Rebels listened as Moose laid out the plan. Our reputations would be marked based on what these ladies said about us. "Here is what we're going to do: when they leave their houses to go to 7-Eleven to refill their giga mugs of soda, we'll set up a decoy situation that will make them think we really *are* rebellious, OK?" I nodded again. "Katie," he continued, looking directly at my best friend as if the whole plan hinged on her, "you and I are going to fake a make-out right in front of Michelle's house."

In plain sight? I thought. *Moose you are brilliant! Katie! So lucky!* Michelle's house was the only one of our houses on the main drag, and Moose was right; it was the logical spot to set up. "Wendy, Michelle, Christy, and Amy, you guys hide over next to the end of the street and give us the signal that they're turning the corner by shouting, 'Action!'"

It was no secret that Mrs. Carter and Mrs. Edgewood refilled their mugs twice a day, just like clockwork. Katie and Moose practiced the fake kiss once or twice, amid laughs from all of us watching. Christy, Wendy, Michelle, and I found our hiding spot behind some untrimmed fitzers, where we had a clear view of the street. Stephen and Clint were stationed at the lookout post on the other side of Michelle's house, and if the plan started to fall apart, Stephen was prepared to whistle and warn Moose and Katie to stop.

"They're coming!" Christy shouted once we saw the large Suburban pulling out of the driveway two houses from where we hid.

"Get down, everyone. Shhhhhh. Low as you can." whispered Wendy, who was practically sitting on top of me as we all smooshed together into our hiding spot.

"Action! Action!" I passed on to Michelle, trying to contain my laughter. Michelle, in turn, shouted the signal to Moose.

And then the moment happened: the fake kiss, the rubbernecking heads, the brake lights, and finally, the Suburban and the two women were out of sight. We cheered long and loud for a winning act and a successful ploy.

The theory played out exactly as suspected, and by Sunday the rest of the neighborhood had heard about the kiss. By the weekend we realized Moose was right; gossip did indeed fill the streets, and it didn't take much to nudge it alive. Moose wouldn't stand for any more rumors, and he determined that we would be known as the "Gossip Busters" from that day forward—a name that was not nearly as cool as the Rebels.

As the new Gossip Busters, we took action right away. We came up with a very catchy chant, and then, in the dark of the night, walked over to the gossip ladies' cul-de-sac and sang the song at the top of our lungs. Come to think of it, none of it really made sense. But in the moment, the idea of banning gossip by singing obnoxiously late into the night was simply brilliant. Until, of course, the neighbors yelled at us to stop and followed up with what sounded like a bit of a threat. We finished our song that night like we always did everything—in grand fashion. Then we promptly changed our name back to the Rebels.

When the sun was high in the sky we piled high into Stephen's brown, piece-of-junk car and drove to the dam to swim and enjoy the sun. There weren't enough seatbelts, so I'd volunteer to ride in the trunk. Who else was skinny enough for the job? Only me. When we got to the beach, we would burst out of the car, lay down our towels, and turn on the boom box, which took 8 D-size batteries. Moose would chuck rocks at the seagulls that tried to steal our lunches, and together we would spend the day being lazy and drawing shapes in the sand. Wendy would run after them, her blonde shoulder length hair catching sunshine as she moved.

"Tell me again about the notebook," I asked my sister Jeannie, in desperation near the end of summer. "You know, the one that makes your boobs grow." I had almost forgotten all about my messed up face during the warm months, but my non-existent boobs—they were a real concern. Jeannie had the biggest boobs in our family, including Mom—evidence that the notebook worked.

"OK, but this is the last time, so listen good. If you want a bigger bust size, you must believe it!" she would tell me while showing me her secret notebook hidden in her bedroom with "32B 32B 32B 32B" written line after line after line. She'd heard a rumor that one of her friend's cousins had kept a notebook of their ideal bra size, and before going to bed this girl would imagine her chest as a 32B. Eventually it worked! She *became* that bra size. Jeannie adapted the system shortly afterward. The whole idea of just *thinking* my boobs bigger was intoxicating and before my sister could finish telling me what to do, I was two steps ahead of her detailed instructions, in a daze of glory, already visualizing my growing chest. In my mind I could almost hear people saying, *"Wow! You look so* different, *so* mature!" I imagined myself smiling, nodding along—not telling them my secret but knowing they were *so* right.

"How long will it take?" I asked, wondering if the effect would happen by morning.

"It is different for everyone. My friend's chest started to grow in two months."

"Oh. OK." *Two months. That is so long! I am*

going to write in the notebook morning and night.
Then they will grow in one month.

I wrote down 32A one hundred times in my notebook before hiding it in my desk drawer. Jeannie had said all I needed to do was, "Meditate. Write my fantasy size. And believe!"

After two weeks there was zero change. I swore I was doing it wrong. So I asked Jeannie to tell me the process again, and she acted like she had no idea what I was talking about—pure denial. I took matters into my own hands that day and doubled the number of times I wrote my dream size in my notebook. I even added the famous, "We must, we must, we must increase our bust!" mantra to my workout. Nothing seemed to help. Impossible!

"If you want your boobs to look big, all you really have to do is stuff your bra with cotton," Jeannie confessed to me when it looked like I wasn't a strong candidate for the notebook system. "Get it wrong though, and you will have a set of lumpy boobs and everyone will know it's just cotton balls."

"OK, great, will you show me?" I asked, as I watched her put on her foundation to cover her sprinkling of freckles.

"First thing you need to know is that you can't reuse cotton. Ever. It is a one-time deal, so don't go trying to recycle."

"All right, what else?"

"In a pinch you can use Q-tips and take the cotton off of them to fill in small gaps," she said, brushing through her long blonde hair. "You have to use about twenty Q-tip tops though." Ah, pure genius. I knew I would be just fine in this life if I just followed what she did.

The last day of summer the Rebels, the Clead sisters, and the rest of the neighborhood all met in Katie's backyard for a game of capture the flag. The air was still warm long after the sun went down, almost as if it too was resisting the end of a great season. When the game was over and everyone else had gone home, we Rebels ended the night like we did all the rest: by singing at the top of our lungs, hoping we would wake the neighbors with our farewell to summer party.

It had worked. The summer before high school I forgot all about layer eleven. All about my face. All about the surgeries. All about comparison, mean stares, and trying to fit it—all because I didn't have a chance to remember any of it.

CHAPTER THREE

Who can possibly define where beauty comes from? A baby doesn't know if she was born into the world with such a title. She only knows that she must fight for her first breath and each moment of persevering thereafter.

"Two boys said 'hi' to me on the way to class!" I rambled to Mom the first day of high school as I leaned my elbows up on the kitchen countertop. I knew that some of the students passing me in the halls were judging my face, even if they didn't mean to. I probably would have stared at me too. Nobody laughed at me though, at least not that I could hear. Mom stayed busy chopping onions and adding spices to the dinner she was making, holding one hand flat against her hip while another hand stirred and added ingredients. Her hair was a modest, short style, with a crown of permed curls that framed her face. Her makeup was equally understated, consisting of nothing more than rouge to brighten her cheeks. She didn't lean on fashion or trends to build her confidence, hers came from trusting God. She talked to Him every day just like a best friend.

"*Oh?* Tell me more," she encouraged as she switched on the noisy fan above the stove to catch the onion fumes (which only *seemed* to work).

"Well, everyone was pretty cool! Lots of girls liked my outfit." I said, thankful I hadn't made eye contact with the bully in the hall, and even more thankful that we didn't have any classes together. I finished telling Mom the details of my day, rushing to get everything in before the rest of the kids came through the door.

Mom had all six of us by the age of thirty-six: Jeannie, came first, then me just a blink later, then my brother Todd, sister Toots, brother Justin, and finally Darin. Dad was there at the hospital when I was born, hoping I might be a boy baby. But he didn't get a boy, or a perfect little girl. Instead he had to adjust to taking care of a baby with so many needs— looking far different from any baby he had seen. From then on, each of the following times Mom went into labor, Dad avoided being in the delivery room. I understood why, too. I felt the sting of guilt for ruining the moment of my siblings birth's for Dad. Like it was my fault he didn't dare be there.

Dad sat down for dinner at the head of the table and popped the paper open in front of his face—then dropped one side momentarily while he scratched his head with the mess kit military fork he used to eat supper with.

"Dad is going to start on the new shower in a few days," Mom announced.

"He *is*? You *are*?" I answered, looking towards Dad, my mouth still full of food.

He slumped the paper down in front of his nose and replied, "Got the shower all ordered up, and it is going to be *real* nice. All white manufactured marble with no tile so Jeannie can't bust through it."

My sister Jeannie had broken the tile in the shower months earlier doing some amazing superhero moves. The idea was not her best, but it had made for a movie-like moment never to be repeated as one-inch tiles smashed to the floor and shattered in every direction after her hand had gone through the shower wall.

I couldn't figure out if my sister was actually that strong or the wall that weak. I determined she was *that* strong. And, yes, a new shower would be oh so nice—every morning we had been taping up a new plastic bag over the seeping black hole. It was starting to gross me out.

The next few days the same pattern played out: running in the door from school to tell Mom all of the greatest moments of my day—eliminating any negative details on purpose, followed by dinner, and finally planning my face distracting outfit for the following day. By Thursday we had a new shower.

After the dishes were cleaned up I made my way to my bedroom to lay out the outfit I would wear for the first Friday of high school. I settled on a Quicksilver shirt in neon stripes, converse high tops, and the same acid washed jeans I wore Monday. I put on the whole outfit to make sure it would look right, then practiced pegging the jeans, just like Katie had taught me. First I folded over the bottom of the leg and then rolled it tightly two times. Then I sat down. The peg-legs held.

I put on my nightshirt and crawled under the covers, high school wasn't so bad after all, I just had to keep my streak of fashion going. As I was ready to drift off to sleep, Jeannie burst through my door. "Amy! Tomorrow you are in charge of waking me up ON TIME!" She was waving a reminder note high above her head. The bold blue words stated, "Wake me up at 5:30 a.m. Don't forget!" She put the note next to my bed and then loudly read it to me before going back to her own bedroom.

"Huh. I guess I won't be the first one in the shower tomorrow," I said under my breath, rethinking my whole morning strategy. I wanted to have time to do my hair in the tiny curls that would complement my outfit and make everyone believe I was beautiful. Now that was all ruined.

CHAPTER FOUR

An older woman who had died momentarily on the operating table floated as a spirit high above her own body. She could not help but wonder who the poor lady was below her that the doctors worked so hard to save. She did not know this woman's face. No, not a single feature seemed familiar.
But the hands, she knew. They were her own.

Outside my window there was no light, just the melting darkness of early dawn. I got out of bed, woke Jeannie up as instructed, and then waited my turn to shower. I needed at least a full hour and a half to get ready, every minute counted if I wanted to look my best. Jeannie took her sweet time shaving her legs and washing her hair, hogging the new shower and all of the hot water. She didn't care my precious time was ticking away. I paced back and forth in my room listening for the shower water to turn off. Five more minutes passed. Ten minutes. My gut burned with deep frustration and anxiety. Jeannie didn't need to put any effort into her appearance. But I did. She could go to school with wet hair and everyone would say she looked amazing. After twenty minutes she turned the water off, but it was too late, I didn't have time to shower. I ran my hands through my bed-head hair, it was a thick mess of curls and spray. I had no choice but to make it work. I got dressed, put on extra deodorant, and re-ratted my hair. White flakes of day old hairspray dotted my bangs. "Dang it!" I shouted to my reflection, "Not today!" I ran to the bathroom to look for another alternative.

"Geez. What's your problem?" Jeannie asked as I pushed past her.

"Nothing. I'm fine."

"Well, you can shower now. I'm done. It's pretty awesome."

"I don't have time anymore," I grumbled.

"Don't have time? How long does it take you to get ready?"

"Dad leaves in an hour and so I don't have time."

"Oh. Sorry. Tomorrow I'll let you shower first."

I doused my bangs with water from the sink, towel dried the excess water out, and finally used the blow dryer and hairspray to add height. When I was all done my hair had a second-day flair to it. I had pulled off the impossible.

"Hey woman!" Katie said as soon as I made it to our lockers, "Love your hair!"

"Really? It looks OK?" I asked, letting out a sigh.

"Better than OK. You are one foxy lady!" She stacked her books on her locker shelf and asked, "Can you meet at my house at seven o'clock to get ready for the stomp?" I had no idea why the casual school dance was called a stomp, but it sounded way cooler than saying we were going to an after-school dance.

"Yeah, I'll get ready right after dinner and come over. Oh, Kates! Tonight is going to be a blast! I think I'll wear my orange short-sleeved top, denim shorts, double-layered socks, and gold earrings."

"I can't believe you already have that figured out. That's totally awesome!"

"Oh, I've known for two days what I wanted to wear," I said before heading to class. I'd been preparing for my first stomp ever since Jeannie told me how fun they were. I knew I had to make a good first impression if I wanted to get asked to dance.

Wendy met me after school to walk the short distance home.

"Wend," I said as soon as our faces hit the bright light of outdoors, "I was thinking we should invent our own sign language. You know, so we can talk to each other in dance class and our teacher will think we are just dancing!" I laughed. "Check this out," I said, looping my hands into fake signs, not paying attention to the giant crack in the sidewalk until I had tripped over it, nearly biffing to the ground.

"Smooooth move, Ex-Lax!" she laughed back, flipping her blonde hair away from her face with the back of her hand.

"That was the sign for 'Don't worry, Be happy'!"

"Oh, I love that new song! *Here's a little song I wrote...*"

I pointed at her, then sang, "*Might want to sing it note for note...*"

"*Don't worry, be happy. Ohhhhh ooooo ooo ooo...don't worry, be happy.*" We sang together, complete with the bogus sign language. Her harmony on top of my basic melody was one of her many gifts—that and making me laugh.

"See you tonight at the stomp, OK?" I said before she turned down her street.

"Christy and I will be there."

"See ya later!" I said, making a giant rainbow in the sky with my hand. "That's the sign for good-bye!"

"No doy!" she laughed running down the hill to her house.

The last time Wendy and I went to a school-sponsored dance was the Christmas Dance in ninth grade, and it was the most horrible dance ever. My hair didn't work out, and the music wasn't loud enough. That night Wendy and I showed up with just three slow songs left, and finally—the worst part—not one boy asked me to dance. The prettiest I could be wasn't good enough, it never was. All the other girls were dancing, but not me. The rejection just smacked me across the face as I stood against the wall by myself—hoping the shadows would hide my desperate plea to be dancing, and hide my face, too.

Tonight felt different, though. For starters, I washed my long brunette hair, then diffused it for volume, then did my famous tiny curls all over. Finally, I added three layers of hairspray for added height and the "crunchy" look. Just the way I liked it. Then I hosed down my bangs with a coating of spray while holding them high above my forehead, punching a shot of cold air on them until they were rock solid. My back-up plan was to put my hair up in a banana clip. Thankfully, no back-up plan was necessary. Before I left my room, I took a few minutes to practice my high kicks and new dance moves. I felt beautiful! Yes, tonight would be epic.

I made my way to Katie's house as soon as my look was complete. I unclipped the chain link gate and pumped my legs up the steep grass incline until I reached the back porch. Through the large sliding glass window I could see Katie in the kitchen having a bowl of Rice Krispies cereal. She opened the door, at the same time asking, "Do you want some cereal?"

"YES!" I said without taking a chance to catch my breath.

The best, *best* thing about going to Katie's house was that she had access to sugar. My house, well, it was sugar-free. As kids, Jeannie and I used to wait by Katie's back door for her mom to toss out empty bags of sugar during canning season. We would hold the bags up to our mouths and let the sugar fall and dissolve on our tongue, savoring the granules like gold. Mom didn't believe in refined sugar, and instead, encouraged us kids to partake in her green drink concoction. "Amy, go out and pick me some dandelion leaves from the back yard," she would say each morning. Her casual request seemed like a joke at first, but she skipped on telling me how good they were, and also, how *abundant* they were! And free—they didn't cost a dime! I would dart across the yard, back and forth, ripping the leaves off the stem, hoping nobody from Katie's house could see me collecting weeds for Mom's special drink. "There now, let's see what else can we put in. Lettuce, spinach, sprouts, ah yes, greens! They're good for you!" she would say, talking to herself as she put load after load of "greens" into her juicer.

Then she would give each of us kids a glass of frothy green to drink before school. I would plug my nose to ward off the taste.

I pulled out a barstool while Katie poured me a bowl of cereal and then slid me the sugar jar across the clean countertop, where I loaded up spoonful after spoonful until the whole top of the bowl became coated in a layer of white. I added milk, although I wouldn't have minded eating it plain, and downed my snack in no time flat.

Katie wasn't ready. Not even close. I had known that might be the case, but the fact that I'd just been treated to a bowl of delicious sugar with some cereal thrown in numbed me just enough that I didn't care.

"Katie, what happened?" I asked walking into her room, a small basement office converted to a bedroom.

"I can't find anything to wear. I've tried on twenty outfits." She wasn't kidding. Piles and piles of clothes lay dead on her bed, vetoed.

"Why don't you wear your black and blue striped shirt and black denim pants?" I asked, knowing it was her one standby outfit.

"Yeah, you're right. That's super cute on me," she said, as she searched for the outfit in the pile of clothes. She found it three layers deep.

"And now, let's go do my hair." I sighed. I wished just once—just *once*—Katie would have been ready to go on time.

Katie's bathroom had a frog theme. Sitting on the back of the toilet were thirteen ceramic frogs, some sitting on tiny doilies, others painted to look like toads, and three in a group that were doing acrobatics. The frogs belonged to Katie's big sister, Heidi, who had a frog fetish. I had all the frogs memorized. While Katie did her hair, I sat and looked at the frogs. Counted them. Dusted them. Picked them up carefully so I didn't break off any legs.

"I think I'm going to start collecting monkeys," I said to Katie as she started to spray her bangs. "When I was nine my dad gave me a small stuffed monkey, and I love that little guy."

"Mmm hmm..." Katie said, concentrating on the art of doing her hair.

"I still have him somewhere. That was the first gift my dad ever gave me, you know, that he bought all on his own without my mom picking it out," I said while watching Katie focus on her reflection. "When he gave it to me I was so surprised that he got something special just for me. The monkey had these little tennis shoes on, blue with white bottoms, and a navy blue ball cap. I am going to keep him forever—or at least until college."

Katie pulled the front of her hair up tight then sprayed, then ratted, then sprayed, then ratted, then smoothed her bangs up and over like a rainbow and got them to stay sky high by holding them just right while coating with hairspray one last time. I couldn't ever seem to get my bangs to go as high as hers. While her hair dried she combed and sprayed her eyebrows, giving them every bit as much volume and style as her hair.

"OK, almost...ready..." Katie said working in slow motion as she turned to get a full view of her hair.

Katie's bathroom was equipped with a fancy three-way mirror. The kind you see in rich people's houses. The edges were adorned in shiny brass, and the whole contraption was far nicer than anything I had access to at my house. The two side panels popped out while the center mirror stayed put, so you could really get a good look at your hair from all angles. With her bangs dry, Katie went to her room to get matching accessories, and I decided to check my own hair for flaws. I stood in front of the mirror and navigated my way around until I could see the back of my head clearly. My hair looked pretty good. There were a few low spots and one or two hollow places, but I quickly fixed them using Katie's brush and spray. When I moved the mirrors back in place, I was startled and lost my thoughts completely for a minute.

Who was that!?

A sting of denial rushed through my veins as I pulled the mirrors out again. I turned them just right until my side profile came into view and inhaled sharply.

Is that really how I look??

My mind flashed to a thousand different places. I knew I looked different, but this—this was horrible. I gulped in a breath of air, my head spinning. The more I turned the two side mirrors the worse the perspective got. My cheeks burned red with shame. From the right I saw my scar stretch from the inside of my nose to the top of my lip, in a swooping fashion, making the side of my lip puff up and stick out. I knew one side of my lip was bigger than the other side, but not *that* much bigger. I

36

looked so...deformed. And my nose – it was so flat on the left side, and what should have been the tip did not line up at all with the center of my lips. My nostrils were flat, misshaped, and uneven in size. Character? My nose belonged *on* a character! The left mirror revealed another scar fading into the small slop of my upper lip. *Wow, does my lower lip really hang so far out like that? Everything looks so twisted.* There was no symmetry or rhythm to the triangle of my face from my nose to my chin. I raised my cheeks into a fake smile and saw the giant space on the left side where I should've had teeth, like someone had taken a sledge hammer to my mouth and knocked all of them out. I was embarrassed and shocked. And my chin. There was so little chin. My profile was sawed and flattened. I rolled my face from side to side, stunned with my internal reaction. It was as if I had been given the perspective of a staring stranger. My face scared me. I snapped the mirrors back in place and looked at myself straight on. "Not so bad now," I said quietly, taking one breath in, then another before I focused on my favorite feature: my eyes.

Katie stepped back into the bathroom. "Ready to go?"

I paused. Suddenly sick.

Why hasn't Katie told me how bad I have looked all these years?

"Yes, I am," I answered, my throat tight, desperate to forget the reality I just saw.

I memorized the mental picture the mirror showed me, and it seared my soul. And oh how it hurt. Dad always told me I was the one person in the family that could find anything. But I found something that I didn't know existed. My hope for a good night felt lost.

All I could do was keep breathing and remember that everything had a purpose. Even shocking moments of pain. I pushed the vision aside and thought only about my feet and how much they liked to dance.

When Katie and I pulled up to the high school, the song was so loud it spilled out of the building and onto the walkway.

Just have fun, be confident, and don't worry about the mirror, I reminded myself.

We met up with Christy and Wendy inside, but to my surprise, people weren't really dancing. They were just standing in circles, talking.

"What is everyone doing?" I asked Katie, who shrugged her shoulders, twisting her neck around to see if there was anyone at the stomp that she recognized. I saw Tracy Clead—whom we always called by her full name—dancing with her boyfriend, Brandon. She threw me a quick wave and smile, then went right on with the swaying, tight bear hug. Tracy Clead was a year older than me and lived on 150 East. She had met Brandon in choir when we were in junior high— they were paired up as partners to sing together and had natural chemistry. She was still completely devoted to him and had no interest in dating anyone else. I watched her laugh and then rest the apple of her cheek on his while they made a small circle on the floor. The image of my face slammed into the back of my mind as I watched them dance, pounding home the fact that I'd never have a boyfriend.

My eyes scanned the outer rim of the stomp, not making eye contact with any of the boys. The slow song dragged on in a miserable key. There was so much pressure to be "picked" to dance, and now that I knew how others saw my face, the typical pressure graduated to a hot and embarrassed burn. The girls standing next to me started to get asked to dance, one by one. Deep inside I felt the lonely cross of rejection—no matter how hard I tried, my flaws were what the boys saw first. I couldn't escape my face. My beautiful, brave face. I panned the few couples dancing close. I only wanted to be out there too, dancing. I used the muscles from my lower lip and pulled it tight toward my bottom teeth, then secured my lip by gently biting it with my two front teeth. It made breathing through my mouth a little more difficult, but at least my lip wasn't sagging. The bully was standing in the corner of the commons area with a group of his friends. I shuddered and fought back the reflex of hate. He had left me alone during the first days of high school, transferring his energy to flirting with the prettiest girls in the school, harassing them with a different kind of teasing.

The slow song ended and the first two measures of *Mony Mony* hit, and I couldn't help it, I had to dance! I didn't want to think about the mirror anymore, or the bully, or anything in layer eleven.

"It's our song, Christy!" I shouted.

"Let's get out there and dance our guts out!" Christy yelled back to me.

"Come on, everybody!" we said in unison.

Pretty soon we had a whole group dancing with us. Incredible! I started doing a crazy move with my arm, and I was really getting into it, burning up the dance floor, when the unthinkable happened.

The worst thing. *Ever.* My so carefully stuffed bra decided at that *exact* moment to give way and bust right open there in the middle of the dance floor. There was cotton falling to my toes! Matted, sweaty cotton. I tried to assess the situation without giving any indication that I was in major peril. I reworked my dance move to a simple wave of one hand up over my head, while I strategically placed the other arm over my chest.

What am I going to do? What am I going to DO?

I could tell that the bra, which was a front clip contraption, had either come apart on its own or broken in half. I danced backward to avoid all eyes and danced my way toward the bathroom.

Please, please, please, nobody talk to me. Please, please, please, don't look at me.

The longest twelve seconds of my life passed, and—finally—I made it safely into the farthest end stall in the girls' bathroom. I whipped off my shirt only to find a sad, tired, broken bra. *Ugh. NOOO!* My heart started to pound. Oh, what bad luck. What very bad luck. People would know my flat chested secret now; there was no way I could go back out there.

Just then the thought occurred to me that I had used a safety pin on my shirt to keep it in place, and right now that safety pin was needed somewhere else! Oh relief! Things would be OK.

I worked in stealth mode. Quietly and quickly I transferred the pin from my shirt to my bra, and within a short ten minutes I was ready to go burn up the dance floor again. I checked myself in the mirror. My cotton boobs looked slightly lumpy and uneven. The right one was way bigger than the left. I should have known to carry extra stuffing in case of an emergency, but under the circumstances this was just going to have to work. I balanced out the cotton the best that I could, then smiled at my reflection before I went back to the dance floor. The dim light played to my advantage that night, like it always did, and I crossed my fingers nobody looked too closely.

Christy, who was breathless after dancing several full songs without me, asked between bites of air, "Where did you *go*?"

"My bra broke," I said in a loud whisper that got drowned out the minute the words left my lips.

"WHAT?"

A little louder now, "Umm, my BRA broke!"

"I CAN'T HEAR YOU!"

"MY BRA BROKE!!!" I screamed, just as the song hit a lull. *Ugh. Is this really happening to me?*

Christy burst with laughter that got higher and higher, bending over at one point to catch her breath and then reassuring me that she was glad I made it back. Well, at least *she* missed me. She gave me a quick once-over glance and nodded her head. "Nobody will even notice!"

Right. Nobody would notice. My flat chest wasn't exactly what people saw first.

We finished the stomp doing exactly what we intended to do—dancing. Our circle of friends moved until our feet were numb from so much jumping and our stomachs hurt from laughing so hard.

When I made it home, though, all I could think about was the evil three-way mirror at Katie's house. Forget the broken bra. Was what I saw how I really looked? Could it be that bad? I walked through Jeannie's room, which was quiet since she was on a date, and into the basement bathroom. The handheld mirror that I'd used to check my hair hours earlier sat balanced on the edge of the sink. Mocking me. I had the selfish urge to flip the mirror over and break it into a thousand broken slivers, just so it would know how I felt. *Stupid mirror. Stupid, stupid mirror. And stupid girl for looking in the stupid mirror.*

I picked the mirror up, and held it still in front of me for several seconds, daring myself to find the awful perspective again. It wasn't worth it. I put the mirror back in the same spot I found it—next to the blue sink that had a large crack right down the center. And deep within my heart, I complained.

This trial, it seemed, would never end. No matter how hard I tried, or how much faith I had in God's plan for me, my disfigured face would always be there, staring back at me from the mirror. Nobody could see how difficult it was for me to put one foot in front of the other day in and day out. I just wanted to be a normal teenager. Have a first kiss like Katie. Dance with a boy like Tracy Clead. Get asked on dates like Jeannie. Instead, I had to try harder than all of my friends just to get noticed. And even then, nobody would want to be with a girl that was born with a cleft.

Toots was fast asleep in the twin bed four feet from mine. I craved her peace. Her long brown hair parted straight down the middle to expose an elegant widow's peak that pointed to a sprinkling of freckles. Sleeping there, she looked so sweet. With her curved nose and full lips, she was beauty itself all tucked away safe and sound, deep in sleep.

Most nights we fell asleep together. Sometimes to help her drift away, I would tell her story after story — stories I kept in my head just for her. Two nights earlier, she had feared closing her eyes, telling me that she'd had a bad nightmare. She liked the story best of a young girl, just like her, who fell into the game of Candy Land, and the game came alive. The girl had to find her way out through the tunnels of licorice and pathways of hard candy. A slippery slide of taffy led her to a pit of bubblegum, and there she decided she would live happily ever after. Toots had me tell her that same story three times in a row in different variations before she finally felt safe enough to sleep.

Tonight I had made it home well past her bedtime, and she was quietly breathing in and out with her blanket gathered high above her shoulders in the crook of her chin. She hadn't needed my stories to fall asleep.

As I lay my head down on my pillow, I didn't feel soft cotton, but rather, a slip of paper. Without thinking, I stood up and went into Jeannie's empty room, where I found just enough light for reading. The last thing I wanted to do was wake up Toots. I took the note and held it against the light of the lamp, squinting to read the words. I fully expected to read a note filled with more instructions for when Jeannie wanted me to wake her up the next day.

The small note was created in crayon with my name in bold purple on the front, highlighted by four large colorful stars.

> *Dear Amy,*
>
> *I relly am glad you are my sister! I relly like you a lot. You are so pretty. You are kind too! You are a good sister! I like you. You'r hair is pretty too! You are the BEST SISTER in the WORLD,*
>
> *Love,*
>
> *Tami*

I refolded the note while my eyes filled up with private tears; her timing was inspired.

How did she know that tonight I needed to hear these simple sentences, right at this very moment? She thinks I am pretty. My little sister thinks I am pretty.

The hollow spot in my confidence was met with her sincere, sweet words, and nothing in the world could replace that gift.

CHAPTER FIVE

At eleven months old, I said my first word, "Mamma,"
followed closely by my second word, "Jeannie."

"AMY! Wake up!" Jeannie shouted from her
bedroom the following morning, a Saturday. Before I
could sit up, she was in my room.

"Wow! You look so pretty!" I said, hardly
believing she had gotten ready for the fashion show
without my hearing her.

"I put it in spiral rods!"

"Ohhhhhh, what are spiral rods?"

"Look, they are these new curlers that look
like hot dogs, and all you do is wrap your hair
around them, and when you take them off, your hair
is *amazing*!" She bent a rod right in half to show me
how flexible they were.

Her blonde hair, full and wavy, reminded me
of angel hair, as if she had just stepped out of a
fashion magazine. Right away I knew I needed to tell
Toots thank you. Her note rested next to my head,
under my pillow, all night long.

I found her upstairs eating a large bowl of
oatmeal. She was studying a heaping spoonful and
taking her time enjoying the bite by slowly letting the
spoon slide into her mouth. I wished so often that I
was more like her. Gram once said, "Toots is such a
thoughtful granddaughter." I always wanted Gram

to say that about me too, but really, nobody thought of others as much as my little sister did.

"I got your note last night," I said. "You did a really good job on the stars that you colored."

Toots looked up from her oatmeal and smiled back at me, not having a clue that the note had helped me through the night. I should've told her that it was her words, not the stars, that I loved the most. But she wouldn't understand what I was really feeling. Nobody could.

"Are you ready to go?" Jeannie asked, digging in her purse for the keys to the car.

"I'm ready. Wait. Let me get some money in case we have time to go to See's Candy."

Once in the car, Jeannie started to outline the plan for my role of modeling assistant: "The first thing I need you to help me with is taping up the bottom of the shoes."

"We have to what?"

"The stores in the mall only let the models wear the new shoes if we put tape across the bottoms. You know, so they don't look used. Check my purse and make sure I put in the roll of masking tape."

"It's here," I said pulling it out of her purse, into her peripheral vision.

"Next thing, after taping, will be going through all the outfits to get the accessories ready to go. I will only have minutes—*minutes*—to change once the fashion show starts, so everything needs to be in exact order."

"OK! I can do that."

At the final stoplight she leaned up out of her seat to re-apply her bright lipstick. She traced the arches of her top lip in two mechanical motions, then one single wave along her bottom lip. She could have done it with her eyes closed. I pressed my own lips together, rubbing the remainder of the Vaseline between the uneven edges. A flash of reality hit me — I'd never have lips like hers. Even with surgery.

In the dressing room I ripped tape and precisely wrapped it around the bottoms of the shoes, all the while thinking that this wasn't the glamorous role of "modeling assistant" that I thought it would be. Still, being around Jeannie and watching her work her magic with people was mesmerizing to me. She was like a giant magnet. She could get people to do things — and do them her way — all the while making them believe it was their idea from the beginning. Genius. Her hair, even after the two hours of prep work before the show, still looked big and full of body. She looked so effortlessly beautiful.

Before the show started the director filled me in on my role. "Now Amy, it's very important that you don't let the models get out of order," she insisted. "The music is timed for each outfit, so there is absolutely no room for lag. Make sure you keep the models coming in a steady stream, and if you have to — yell at them."

Me? Get people moving? Scream at strangers to get my way? I didn't have time to assess my approach; the show started and we were rolling within minutes. I made my way to the row of make-shift dressing rooms and prepared to encourage the timeliness of the first model.

"Kris, you're up first, and you kinda need to hurry," I said clearing my throat and trying to speak loud. Then onto the next few dressing rooms: "Two minutes, Lisa…Gretchen, you're up next."

I stopped at Jeannie's make-shift room.

"HURRY! Come *on*! MOVE!" I shouted.

"Coming. Crap. I lost an earring already. Quick! Help me find it!"

I flung open the curtain and put both palms to the floor. "It's right here," I said, grabbing it from behind her high heel. "Now GO! GO!"

She swiftly skirted past me to the stage, her hair catching the air of her movement and flying behind her in a ribbon of curls. My nerves calmed, and I felt a tiny sense of power. *Because of me, this show will go on*, I thought to myself.

I felt the beat of the music coming from the runway. The fast song, filled with a high tempo, woke up my legs. I started to dance right there on the back wing of the stage. *I* wanted to be up there walking the runway with the other girls. *I* was right for this job! *Who loves clothes more than I do? Who moves to music better than I do? Nobody!*

For a minute, I let my thoughts get the best of me, and I lost track of the next model. I just couldn't help it. All I could visualize was me under the lights on the runway in a pair of taped up high heels, wearing a bright yellow shirt with shoulder pads, purple leggings, and gold accessories. Those watching the fashion show would say to the person sitting next to them, "Wow, look at *that* girl. She is a true beauty." I would fling my big hair, then look over my left shoulder, my hands low on my hips, before turning and walking back down the runway in a near perfectly straight line. They wouldn't have time to notice my face, they would only see my confidence dusting the runway.

"Amy! We need the models!" the director yelled, clearly not aware that I was having a moment. "NOW!" Oh I hated, hated, *hated* getting in trouble.

"RUN! You're on next!" I screeched to a fresh-faced girl who was about my age. She frantically shoved her runway swollen feet into shoes a size too small. I waited right there for her, nearly tapping my toes with impatience.

Jeannie wrapped up the show wearing a fancy emerald green formal dress, and the applause echoed to the back of the stage, where I watched the final run through slivers in the backdrop fabric. She owned the stage. She was gorgeous.

For the next hour we re-hung all of the outfits she'd worn and took all the tape off the bottoms of the shoes, but not before she made one swoop with her hands at the edge of a metal chair in the make-shift dressing room and knocked off all eight of her fake fingernails at once. With two more swift pops, the thumbnails were off.

"Much better!" she said. "I hate fake fingernails!"

"Ahhh! I can't believe you just did that!" I gasped. "Weren't those so expensive?" I was baffled that Jeannie could just waste a set of good fingernails. I would've kept those things on until nature pulled them off. Without Jeannie seeing, I picked up a few used fingernails and tried to stick them onto my natural nails, but they were busted beyond belief.

"Hey, is Jeannie in there?" said a voice from just outside the changing curtain. I poked my head through the fabric long enough to see a guy with dark brown hair cut into an old-fashioned flat top which blended seamlessly into a mullet. He was curiously familiar. His eyes were flirty and clear, and his smile was bright and sexy. He was good-looking glory all wrapped up into one single man.

"Pssst! Jeannie! Some guy is out there, and he's asking for *you*. He is *so cute*! Like, the best looking guy I have ever seen! I am totally not even kidding you!"

"Shhh. Don't have a cow. Who is it?"

"I don't know! Who cares! He's so FINE!"

Jeannie stood up, fixed her outfit, checked herself in a small mirror that she had in her purse, applied a fresh coat of lipstick, and then stepped out from behind the curtain.

"Ron! I totally didn't know it was *you* out here! What are you doing at the mall?"

"I'm just here hanging out," he said, adding a smile that could melt snow. *Ahhh*, I thought. So *this* was Ronald Jamon Eastland. No wonder he looked familiar! I had spent many nights looking through Jeannie's sophomore yearbook analyzing his senior picture: dark hair, a classy red and white sweater, tan face, and ah…that smile. He was the one Jeannie was crazy about. Older by nearly two years and overflowing with classic handsomeness, he was the boy that she thought about more than all of the others combined. Jeannie jabbered on, telling him everything about the last several days with drama and enthusiasm. While she spoke she moved her hands up and down, engaging her whole body in the story. And while she talked, his eyes flickered, bouncing off her energy.

"How did you even get here?" she asked while I analyzed his tall frame from two steps away.

"I rode my bike down here, just to get some exercise."

"You rode your *bike* to the mall?" He smiled and nodded.

"That's crazy!" she said, and motioned toward me, "Have you met my little sister, Amy?"

"Nope. Hey there, I'm Ron," he said, wiping his hand on his jeans then sticking it out for me to shake. He glanced ever so briefly at my lip and nose, so small was the space of time that only I noticed. But he didn't wince or pull back. Just a glance. He didn't seem to care I looked different.

"Hi, yeah, I know who you are," I answered, then wished instantly I hadn't been so obvious. "I mean, yeah, I've seen you in Jeannie's yearbook."

He soon told us both good-bye and turned and walked away. We couldn't help but stare. The sight of his back pockets was far too good to let evaporate without noticing.

We rode home together—Jeannie and I—in the ocean blue Ford Escort, feeling a sense of freedom and fun. Jeannie was electrified and smiled wider than I had ever seen. We passed Ron riding his bike, and as we did, Jeannie honked. He looked at her as if to say, "Race me!" He beat us to the next light by a long shot, and then off he went until we could only see the speck that was his bike. He reminded me of Superman outrunning the train.

"I seriously cannot believe we saw Ron! RON! Did I look OK?"

"Jean, you look amazing!"

"But, look at all this heavy, gross stage makeup," she said passing her hand under her chin as if her face were on display.

"You look great!"

"What did we talk about, do you remember?"

"Just school, what he's doing now that he has graduated…oh, and how you missed him driving you home."

"Oh yeah! That's right! I do miss that. He would always say, 'you are the hottest sophomore,' and then, 'do you wanna ride home?' Of course, you know, I always did. I made all the senior girls jealous, 'cause he was flirting with me and not them. Oh, I can't believe that we saw Ron!" Jeannie was beaming.

"Hey, can we stop at Winchell's Doughnuts?" I asked, taking advantage of her good mood.

Jeannie didn't answer me. Instead she merged over a lane, made a left-hand turn into the driveway, and parked at the back of the shop before answering, "Yes!"

"I have always, *always* wanted to do that," I said to her after we had our doughnuts. "My whole life I have wanted to stop there, and today we did!" And with that, Jeannie cranked up the radio, and we rolled down the windows and headed for home, smiling and laughing with the wind blowing our hair wildly in our doughnut-crumb covered faces.

CHAPTER SIX

Kindness is the magnet that pulls a trial away from the constant aching and gives you wings to rise above.

Dad had read the Sunday paper, leaving it in a neat stack next to the wood burning stove before getting Toots to help him with his weekly household chore. "Let's 'cause on and get these dinner dishes cleaned up. I'll wash and you dry," Dad said, pulling her away from her art project. I sighed a bit of relief of having a week off helping Dad, grabbed the paper and placed it square on top of my legs—I was ready to relax. The bold headline screamed, "Hurricane Gilbert Gains Intensity," and I wondered how many more lives would be taken in his path.

I quickly set the bad news aside and skimmed the comics for "Blondie". Out of the middle of the section fell the thin weekend magazine, which I read faithfully each Sunday. I resituated myself in Dad's recliner, pulled my legs up into a crisscross, and comfortably placed my elbows on the sides of the chair. I turned the pages slowly, absorbing the faces of the movie stars. The makeup ads pulled me in, the models with their flawless smooth complexion and pouty lips, their hair pulled back tight in a ponytail so that all focus would be on their faces. I looked at their profiles: slopes and angles, curves and slants. After several moments and a few new ideas on how to apply eye shadow, I turned the page, and before I could register the next image, my fingers froze, my body tightened, and I sat—paralyzed. Staring back at me was the face of a young, disfigured Filipino boy, who had an open cleft lip and palate. I stumbled on my quick reaction of judgment. He was *so* ugly. His eyes, the color of wet mud, dug back at me with a mixture of sadness and begging—his lip shoved up inside his nose exposing the whole length of his twisted front teeth through the magazine ad. My gut hurt. The boy was just like me.

I glanced away from the paper and gave myself visual distance from his mutilated face. I felt the heaviness of embarrassment, guilt, and insecurity wash over me—and wondered where my compassion was hiding. "Hurry up, Tootsie, I am gaining on you," Dad said as he put another dish into the rinse water.

"Slow down, I'm drying as fast as I can!"

"You'd better keep up because I am a diesel powered dishwasher man."

I turned the magazine toward my body so Dad and Toots couldn't see what I was reading. The boys lip had tried to fuse together on its own making a near vertical gorge up through his nose. It looked awful and strange. I wanted to turn away from the paper and forget all about him and his misery, and pretend just like I did with myself —that nothing was wrong. Below his image the caption read, "This boy was found living in the slums of Manila in a garbage dump. He was born with a cleft lip and

54

palate and has been pushed out by his community. Cosmetic surgery is out of the question without your help." *Garbage dump?* "It only takes a few hundred dollars to give this boy, and others like him, the medical attention needed to fix his lip and palate. A new smile will keep him from being rejected, give him hope for attending school, for making friends, and having a normal life."

I rested my head on the back of the recliner and watched the fan spin around and around. Deep inside I felt a strange pull of unity between him and me. I knew his rejection. He knew mine. Yet, we didn't know one another. I wished that he could have the same doctors and care that I was surrounded with to ease his trial. Or that I had two hundred dollars to send to him. But most of all, I wished neither of us had to feel the pain of being born different.

"Who's ready to go to Grandma's house?" Dad hollered, wiping his hands dry, "If you're coming with us you'd better get all loaded up." I put the magazine down and covered it with the comics.

I found my shoes, laced them up, and felt the early signs of a migraine headache sweeping over me. The mirror from Friday night and now the Filipino boy had filled up my layer eleven, causing the dam to overflow. I dug my knuckles into my right temple in a slow circle to try and stop the pounding, but it was too late—the headache had found a home, almost as if it had been waiting to pounce and attack me.

"Hi Gram," I said with a quiet voice, passing her in the kitchen as she stirred a batch of caramel popcorn for us grandkids. The back door was the only way we ever entered Gram's house. Her small kitchen was a crisp combination of bright red carpet and spotless white appliances. "Amy?" She looked up from the bubbling sauce long enough to see the pain in my face that echoed my voice. "How are you feeling? Do you have a headache tonight?"

"Just a little one. I am fine, thanks Gram."

"Oh, honey. Go lay down on the couch and I will be there in a minute."

"Hey, Gramp," I said as I made my way to the long velvety peach couch, "how are ya?"

"A notch above shitty, A-Mousie," he said, patting my knee as I sat down. "How about you?"

"Eh. That makes two of us."

Gram came quickly with a cool pink washcloth which she doubled up then draped on my forehead after she instructed me to lie down. My head throbbed like bricks being thrown at the side of my head—I wanted to shut my eyes forever. The ache rippled through my body and took over my senses. *Maybe it will be easier if I don't go to school tomorrow. Just to escape for the day.* I pushed on the source of the pain with my whole hand, hard enough I thought surely I had smothered the source. But the headache pounded on so intensely that I could take my pulse by placing my index finger over my temple. I wanted to dig through my skin, reach into the throbbing, and rip it out of my head to stop the eternal aching.

"Is that better?" Gram asked, seemingly the only one who had noticed the pain I was in.

"A little. It just hurts worse than ever," I said, nearly crying for the fact that she cared.

Gram pulled the washcloth off my forehead, ran it through cold water again, and laid it back in place. And somehow, her kindness made the pain seemed bearable.

I wonder if anyone knows what I'm going through, I thought. *I hate this. I hate this pain. I hate where it comes from.*

The extended family slowly arrived, each coming into the formal living room, where Gramp carried on telling stories of the week while chewing on a plain thin toothpick, maneuvering it side to side between his gold rimmed teeth. I stayed still, trying to calm the pain. All around me normal was happening, but my world was a mess of confusion manifesting in the form of a migraine. Gram took the washcloth off my forehead, rinsed it with cold water again, and returned it to the same spot.

"Try and shut your eyes. You will feel better."

"OK, Gram, thank you."

I kept my eyes closed as I listened to Gramp tell his account of the week, his language filled with colorful adjectives and cursing. "Who wants a roast beef sandwich?" Gram asked, then took a count of the raised hands. "Jeannie, you come help me. Amy is resting her eyes." *Thank you, Gram. Thank you for loving me.*

When we were younger, Jeannie and I would call Gram on random Friday nights after she'd finished working at the IRS and ask if we could spend the night. Sometimes, Jeannie would boldly ask if we could have a Pepsi. "Just have a half a can," Gram would always say, followed by, "there's ice in the freezer." Jeannie would get out two glasses, fill them both with ice, and then split a can of Pepsi.

When bedtime rolled around Gram would pull out the hide-a-bed and lay out the red afghan at our toes just in case we got cold. Jeannie always preferred to sleep in the hide-a-bed, but not me. Sometimes, I slept on the floor in my Grandparents room, right next to the queen bed they shared. Gram, with her hair wrapped in light blue tissue paper, would sleep next to Gramp, snoring away. I wouldn't even dare breathe loudly. I wanted to be so, so, so good. In the morning I would hear Gram say to Gramp, "Be quiet. Amy is still sleeping." But really I was wide awake with my eyes closed, my face tucked deep into the covers. I would lay there until Jeannie woke me up for breakfast, which just so happened to be the same menu—orange juice, microwaved bacon, toast (always slightly burnt), eggs (always over easy), and Lucky Charms.

Gram would save Jeannie and me the chicken wishbone from earlier in the week to break during our special sleepovers. She left it to bake dry in the sun of the windowsill, then gave it to us to snap. Gram would say, "Make a wish, but you can't tell anyone, or it won't come true." I must have wished a hundred wishes standing there in her kitchen next to the window that overlooked the yard. And I didn't tell. Not one wish.

The washcloth, now tepid from my hot skin, molded to the shape of my head. My eyes, beating with constant pain, followed the shape of the formal living room and the wall-to-wall pristine carpet until they landed on Gram. There sitting in her chair, legs crossed, fingernails polished, and adorned in her favorite jewelry, she looked so pretty. She stopped listening to the conversation in the room and looked over at me with concern in her eyes.

I smiled my best smile. "My headache is all gone, Gram. Thank you so much for helping me."

"Oh, honey, I am so glad."

I saw the relief in Gram's posture, and once again she joined the conversation.

Yet, my headache throbbed even stronger.

CHAPTER SEVEN

White is not a color. It is a feeling that accompanies peace, hope, and beauty. White captures light and chases darkness.

Tracy Clead lived kitty-corner from Katie, in a rambler that had cactuses in the front yard, planted by her dad. Cactuses that had caught toilet-papering teenagers on more than one occasion. She and her sisters had developed large bosoms early on which we had given specific names: Big Mamma Mountain Tops, Big Chief Elephant Boobs, and Easy Rolling Peaks. Of course, Jeannie and I had nicknames for *our* bosoms, too: Little Squaw Flat Plains and Plateau.

Tracy Clead didn't wear a stitch of makeup (didn't need it!), loved to play sports, and got a perm faithfully every three months. She also loved me to the core. I was certain. By the second week of high school Tracy Clead was meeting me at my house to hitch a ride with Dad and me to school.

"What's in that?" she asked when Mom handed me my morning green drink.

"Oh! Blended greens!" Mom enthusiastically replied to Tracy Clead before I could get out my own explanation of disgusting green potion.

"Drink it down—it's good for you," said Mom.

"This is so gross!" I said before taking three gulps, stopping, then taking three more. "Gross! Gross! Gross!"

Tracy Clead coached, "Why don't you just drink it all at once, then it won't be so bad."

"Without stopping?"

"Ya, just drink it all without stopping. 'Cause when you stop, then you can taste it. I can drink a whole pop without stopping. Just concentrate and you can do it."

I slugged the drink back, took three gulps, and had to stop again. Tracy Clead was wrong. I couldn't drink it all at once, not the way she did anyway.
"I can't," I said, setting the half gone drink onto the counter, frustrated with my body. "I've never been able to do that." I took one more drink and left the rest in the glass. The surgery to close the hole in my soft palate happened when I was just a baby, the same time the giant opening in my hard palate was sewn shut, but it still didn't work like my friends. It didn't close off right when I tried to drink something.

"Scotacklica mouse or we are going to be late for school," Dad said, using his trademark word that meant 'let's go quick like a mouse.'

I met Katie at our lockers a little before school started. She smelled like Loves Baby Soft and hairspray. She was busy organizing her space just like she would her first apartment, adding carpet pieces, cut to a custom size by her dad, to the shelves.

"Hey, sexy woman! So my mom went to town this weekend and got me *two* new lip glosses," Katie said, handing me a fancy round container. "I thought you would really like this one. I don't need both."

"Wow! Thanks, Kates! Really?" I said, genuinely excited that she brought me a gift.

"Try it on right now, before we go to class. You'll love it."

"So wait, what do I do exactly? I mean, I don't ever really wear lip stuff."

Katie paused, then looked at me a bit dumbfounded. "You just take a little and put in on the end of your finger, like this, then spread it on your lips, and walla! That's it!" she said while demonstrating like a pro.

I turned my body toward her locker mirror so nobody watched me looking at my own face. The golden sheen went on so glossy and tasted delicious, like vanilla and strawberries. I smacked my lips together like I had seen the models do on TV. It sounded more like a bird hitting a window than the sexy sound it should've made. I couldn't tell if the shine exaggerated my lips or acted as a reflective camouflage.

Before I could gather my books for class, I saw Moose coming toward me out of the corner of my eye. Once the school year had started, he'd vaporized, and it was almost as if our summer of the Rebels had meant nothing to him. All I could think about as he approached was how much I had missed him and his crazy belly laugh. He greeted me in a friendly stride and started right into a conversation, but not before he glanced down with an odd expression at my shiny lips.

"Hey, Amy, do you want to buy my guitar?" he asked. "It's a really nice acoustic guitar with all of the beginner books, a case, and some picks, too."

I had to admit, I loved that guitar. Watching Moose play old Chris LeDoux songs on it in his basement during the summer, he sounded every bit like a country superstar himself. Not sure if he was serious, I questioned him: "Why are you selling it?" and further, "What's wrong with it?"

"Nothing, it's almost like new," he went on. "I need money for the Homecoming Dance. I really want to take Emily."

Oh. Emily. Maybe that was why he'd disappeared the last few months. He had a new girlfriend, and now he needed a way to finance taking her to the first big dance of the school year. I wanted to be Emily. Somebody's Emily.

"Yeah, well, I might be interested," I said. "But I'll need to talk to my mom first."

"OK, I'll hold it for you until I hear back from you," he said as he flashed me that famous Moose smile.

Playing the guitar sounded like a nice addition to my pool of talents, but what really excited me was Moose gave me a little attention right in front of everyone. *Ah, this is what it must feel like when good things happen out of the blue,* I thought to myself.

In class we made nominations for Homecoming Royalty. Soon after the roll was taken, nominations were being tossed out and written on the board. I started daydreaming about the fun chat I had just had with Moose. *Maybe it's time I learned to play a musical instrument. I'll bet if I bought his guitar he would teach me to play a few songs, and then he could get to see how fun I am one on one. Maybe I'll talk to Mom about buying the guitar!*

"Jeannie! We should nominate Jeannie!" shouted a guy from the back of the room.

Who? My sister? "Jeannie is my sister," I leaned over and whispered to the classmate sitting next to me.

"Jeannie is *your* sister?" she said, stopping short of saying more.

"My big sister!" I proudly stated. "Or I should say, my *older* sister." Within a few minutes the class had voted Jeannie on to the next round, and I had forgotten all about the guitar—for the moment, anyway.

During the break between classes, it was announced that Jeannie had made the top ten girls nominated for Homecoming Royalty. *HA! My sister! This is so cool!* I beamed as I headed to math, despite it being the most boring class on the entire planet.

Everyone talked about the Homecoming Dance the rest of the day, but Katie and I had an altogether different plan for how we wanted to spend that night—not dancing away in a gorgeous dress, or being proper with manners, or confused at the dinner menu, or laughing at jokes that were not funny. No, no, we had something epic in mind.

"I talked to my dad, and he's fine with the idea," Katie said as she twisted into her seat on the lunch bench. "We'll need to bring blankets, drinks, flashlights, and—let's see, what else, Amy?"

"What about pizza?" I said, remembering we had talked about that during the original draft of our plan. Pizza was my favorite part.

"Oh, pizza! My dad will take us to pick it up on our way there."

She smiled her devious grin that reminded me how much I loved my best friend. "Can you be to my house at six that Friday?"

"Oh, sure. Now, tell me again where we're going?" I asked, still confused by her adventurous plan.

"OK, you know where the freeway turns right before our exit? Well, there's a pedestrian walkway right there, and it crosses the freeway, and we're going to have our party up there! Suspended above all that traffic!"

"Uh, is this legal? 'Cause I don't want to get into trouble."

"I don't think my dad would be taking us and dropping us off if it wasn't OK," she said, then looked at me with big eyes. "Four hours of fun! My dad said he can come back and get us at ten o'clock." Her reassurance worked. I was in! Who needed boys anyway? Now if only we could convince Wendy and Christy to join us.

Christy arrived at our table a minute later with very shocking news that completely threw the conversation in a new direction: "I decided to shave the bottom half of my hair off last night," she said, looking so proud of her wild, rash, and very peculiar decision. "See, look!" She pulled her curly dark hair up so we could all see, and sure enough, it was shaved clean off in a straight horizontal line that ran from ear to ear. "So I was in the bathroom last night," she explained as we listened in astonishment, "and I just thought, that's it! I am so sick of doing my hair. It's too thick, and it takes way too long to dry."

"You just…cut it off? How?" asked Katie, taking the words out of my mouth.

"I just parted it sideways, then put the top part in a ponytail and shaved off the bottom part with an electric razor. It was pretty easy, and if feels *so* good. Here, feel it."

"What did your mom think?" I blurted out as I petted the back of her spiky head.

"She doesn't even know!"

"Wait a minute. Your mom has no idea? As in, you didn't tell her you were doing this?"

"No! And I am never telling her, either." Christy stated, then rotated so Katie could feel her head.

My mind started to buzz. *Why on earth would ANYONE want to do that to herself? Why? What will her mom think when she finds out? And how will she ever wear a ponytail again? Will she even have a chance at dating anyone now?* It looked so crazy, so rebellious, so unnatural, so...Christy! Her hair was one of her best features. Why she had just hacked it off, I couldn't understand, but—somehow—it didn't bother her what anyone else thought. Christy was a tomboy and tough as nails. She claimed that when she was done with high school she was going to become a truck driver. I didn't have a clue where she came up with her aspirations. I called her on it once, thinking she was making a joke, but as it turned out, spinning eighteen wheels was on her wish list of things to do after we graduated.

Even with the distraction of Christy's crazy news and our plans for Homecoming weekend, I was still stuck on what I saw in the mirror at Katie's house. In the days that followed the stomp, I had become more self-aware, trying to never turn my face to show my profile when I was with a group of people. The image of me in the mirror at Katie's house wouldn't go away. I saw it there, staring back at me when my life had a quiet moment, and I couldn't seem to shake it off. And there was Christy, totally perfect, and yet she changed the best part of herself. On purpose.

After school I found Jeannie's makeup bag undisturbed right where she'd left it that morning. I knew exactly what I wanted to do: erase my face. I searched through the bottles, eye shadows, and lipsticks until I found her liquid foundation. I applied it like thick paint, covering up my lips and accompanying scars until they blended in with the rest of my skin. My lips, masked in nude, faded seamlessly into the rest of my skin, and for a moment I captured relief. I stared at the mirror and imagined a new me: a small, sloped nose like Mom's; curvy lips; nice cheekbones; a dazzling Miss America smile. I dug in Jeannie's bag again and found a red lip liner. Like an artist, I sketched a new set of full symmetrical lips, much like the ones I practiced on my doodles during school. Then, very carefully, I filled them in with red lipstick. I smiled. *No, no, no! I look like a clown. A freaky-faced clown!* In frustration I grabbed a washcloth and scrubbed my face up and down with vertical aggression until it was clean. The scars stood out with shiny angry edges and my lips burned and tingled with irritation. My face stared back at me in the mirror. It looked so different from how I felt inside. I studied the image like an artist who looks at a painting that isn't quite right. With my finger, I pushed the end of my nose until it was straight, but then my lips crinkled. I released the pressure from my finger, and my nose and lips relaxed into a familiar crooked line. I traced my lips with my finger, putting my face so close to the mirror that I nearly touched it, breathing in the scent of soap still lingering on my skin, and concentrating on the nerve endings set alive by touch. I paused. Then wondered, *does anyone on Earth have eyes as blue as mine*? I stared at the iris, clear and bright, just like the day I was born. The tiny, colored lines looked layered, displaying a universe right there inside me, creating so much depth in such a small space. I felt certain I had a choice in heaven: to be born perfect or to be born different. I thought about what I must have said: "I am ready now. Send me and provide me with a life full of experiences from highs to lows. But on the bad days, please give me grace to shine brighter."

"Amy? Where are you?" Mom called from the kitchen, shaking my thoughts to a stop. Before I could get the lip liner and liquid foundation back into Jeannie's bag, Mom was standing in the bathroom doorway. She could see my clean scrubbed face and the washcloth, dirty with makeup.

"What are you doing in here?" she asked, puzzled. I flushed with embarrassment praying she wouldn't ask me why I had just washed my face.

"Umm, nothing really," I lied.

"The phone is for you. It's a boy," Mom said with a funny look in her eye. She held out the phone, the cord stretched tight, her hand covering the receiver.

"Really? Do you know who it is?" I asked, taking the phone and covering it again with my own hand, trying to be as cool as possible.

"No, he just asked for you," she said with a half-smile.

This had never, ever, ever happened to me. Not even once. My heart started to beat and my palms sweat. I picked up the phone, said "hello," and from the other end came the familiar voice of Moose.

"Yo, Amy, it's Moose. Did you talk to your mom yet, you know, about buying my guitar?" His voice sounded so hopeful and a tad on the desperate side.

"Oh, well, I will. I just haven't yet," I said, a bit disappointed that he had called for the one and only reason of trying to sell me something.

"OK. I have it here for you. Fifty bucks. That buys you everything," he said.

I promised to talk to Mom and let him know, but no way would I dare ask her for that kind of money. With the Homecoming Dance two weeks away, I was sure he would find someone with more money than me who wanted that old guitar.

As I hung up the phone, Dad burst through the back door wearing his blue coveralls.

"Every little kid and big kid, too," he called to my siblings and me. "It's time to haul wood!" I loved helping Dad with projects, and a project was just what I needed. With Jeannie out for the night on a date, I was the leader of the kids, and so I sounded the call for Todd, Toots, Justin, and Darin to meet outside. Down below the house, between the fence and the big maple tree, Dad backed up the old green

Ford truck, which was filled to the top with firewood.

We used our winter gloves, since there were not enough work gloves to go around, and started, one-by-one, to haul the dense, heavily barked wood up to the shed where it would sit until we needed it during cold winter nights. After about ten runs from the truck to the shed, Todd, my younger brother by sixteen months, had a great idea.

"What if we make a chain?"

"A human chain! That's brilliant!" I yelled to him, sparked on by his genius. Together we lined up the kids and started passing the firewood one piece at a time. It worked fantastically until the little kids lost interest. Then it was just Todd and me, making the trek from the truck to the shed while the sun was getting lower and lower, and our shadows longer and longer. Todd lasted another hour, but then went in complaining of a splinter in his index finger. I, on the other hand, loved seeing a project through, and even though my back was starting to ache and my hands were feeling raw, I wanted Dad to be proud of me. The fading light made the yellow and red fall colors come alive on the old maple tree. The air took on a cool edge, and—really—nobody would have even said anything negative if I'd gone back inside at that point. But my energy surged, and, all by myself, I unloaded the rest of the wood from the truck—first tossing it onto the grass that was fading to a fall green, then taking armload after armload up to the shed. My mind raced the whole time, and I thought about how much I loved working hard.

The wind started to blow, stirring up fallen leaves and whirling them around the trunk of the maple tree. *I wonder if a storm is coming*? I thought, noticing the added chill in the air. I threw the last log onto the pile and pulled the gloves off my hands, my fingers numb and cumbersome. I had an overwhelming feeling of satisfaction and pride as I opened the back door and went inside the warm house. Mom was at the stove, like always, stirring a large pot of chili, and she looked surprised that I was just coming in from the cold. Some say that spring represents the start of something new, but for me, it had always been the fall. The colors, the food, the cozy feel of the velvet night sky, the smell of pumpkin, and the way my cheeks burned with the cool air. *Maybe, just maybe, I will ask Mom about the guitar. And maybe, just maybe, she will say yes.*

"A-mouse, did you unload the rest of the wood by yourself?" Dad asked, interrupting my thoughts. He looked surprised when I said I had. His nod was all the affirmation I needed—I knew he was proud of me. The hard work of hauling wood made my arms ache and my legs want to lie still rather than stand. I went to bed early, feeling exhausted, satisfied, and oh so very happy.

The deep sleep quieted my body, and the unexpected snow that fell silently during the night calmed my mind. The snow journeyed from the sky in a whispered hush making a home on the colored autumn leaves.

When I woke, the snow lay motionless on the ground; so white, so new. I stopped at the top of the stairs that led into the kitchen and stared into the world of white, pausing without control. My heart instantly felt full of life. I felt as if someone had put the snow there just for me.

There had always been something about snow that took me back, way back, to when I was four years old. Beautiful snowflakes remain sketched in my memory from the day I first saw them. They danced down the double sliding glass doors, thick and light; a pale white sky masked the sunshine behind the storm. In my memory I was young, alive, protected, and also very curious. The snowflakes looked like white bees to me. At first there were two, then three, then more than I could count. They buzzed up to the window, then back into the wind, as if to say, "Hello, Amy Jo. Hello."

Swarming, happy, intelligent bees. The bees were my special gift from God. I loved how time stood still while I watched them float and spin from the sky to the ground. They were part of a simple confusion, and I could relate.

As soon as the sky started to open up with snow, I would assemble myself on the hard linoleum floor of the kitchen, near the glass doors, and curl my small toes over the heat vent. There, I would let my eyes follow one "bee" all the way from the highest corner of the window until it rested quietly on the soft forming snow. The process took concentration and care. If I let my eyes slip away for just a moment, I would lose sight of the bee I was following, and I would have to start all over.

Minutes turned into at least an hour, or about four cycles of the heat vent warming up, over which I loved to toast my toes to a nearly intolerable heat. My memory of what happened next is as clear as if it were yesterday. Dad bent down next to me. "What are you watching?" he asked, and I told him just the way I saw it: "I am watching the white bees." He laughed and corrected me, telling me they were actually just snowflakes. This annoyed me slightly, but I loved the attention. During each snowstorm from then on, I felt an obligation to make sure each bee made it to safety, and each time I watched, Dad teased, and each time he teased, I loved it even more. I would stay wrapped up there as long as I could, until the last bee landed.

My white bees have always been a part of me and seem to surround me on my darkest days, filling me with light and a surge of tangible hope. They were more than just snowflakes. They were blessings I chose to acknowledge and graces of God sent to protect, lift, help, and comfort me. My secret armor of white light. Some white bees were angels watching me from another dimension, showering my mind with glimpses of the future, guiding my purpose. Others were loyal friends and family cascading into my path to give me hope and confidence. My white bees were everywhere. On days when the snow fell heavy, my burden became light.

The sliding glass door through which I watched the snow fly to the ground was removed when Mom and Dad remodeled the house in 1981—a bittersweet day. In its place sat the doorway to a brand new addition. Out of sheer necessity, Mom had set about to change the footprint of our home to make additional space for our growing family. She spent many hours outside looking at the house, hand on hip, sketching things on her pad of paper and then walking around the property again. Then she would sketch more and more, oftentimes erasing and starting all over again.

The day Dad and his building buddy started the demolition by pulling the sliding glass door off the house, the other kids cheered. But not me. I curiously observed my refuge, all but the heat vent, tumble into a pile of rubble. I no longer had my special spot by the window, a safety that had held no pain. While I was there watching the snow fall, my legs tucked up close, I had felt no need to harshly compare myself to others — there had only been blessed peace, flooded in soft, graceful white bees.

CHAPTER EIGHT

Joy is a finding your vein of happiness and following where it leads.

Moose ran, half panting half laughing, up the sidewalk to meet up with Katie and me in the space between her house and his. I knew what he wanted, and I finally had an answer for him. With only a handful of days to go until Homecoming, I was his last-ditch effort to pay the way to the dance. I had finally gotten up the nerve to ask Mom what she thought about buying Moose's guitar.

"Oh, Amy, that's a great idea!" she said, not even seeming to *hear* that it would cost money.

"But, Mom, I said it's *fifty* bucks!" She just nodded and said that sounded fair.

"Really? So that's a yes?" I beamed but tried not to feel too excited. "It's possible the guitar isn't even available anymore. There were a lot of other people interested… Oh, and Mom, I will need lessons."

She agreed, and kept cooking dinner, adding spices to a large pot that looked like a vegetable swimming pool.

I tried to keep my cool as Moose approached Katie and me. I considered that he might have sold the guitar to another friend, or that he might have decided it was a bad idea to sell one of his favorite things. Despite my caution, I could feel myself grinning.

"My mom said it's OK!" I said to Moose, my smile stretching as long as the sidewalk we were standing on.

"She DID? Yes, Yes, *YES!*" he shouted, pumping his fist to the ground. Then he jumped twice in celebration before landing on both feet and croaking, "I'm takin' Emily to the dance" in his trademark low froggy voice. If nothing else, I had made him truly happy, and everyone liked to see Moose happy. He had a girl he really loved, and now he could make *her* happy. Oh, how would that feel, I wondered, to have someone give up something they treasured like Moose did his guitar, all for that kind of love.

We made plans to make the exchange the following day. When I arrived at Moose's house, he was polishing the front of the guitar, and—wow—she was magnificent.

"Hey, good lookin'!" he said as I walked into his large, open family room.

Me? What? I flushed red.

"I just put new strings on it, and now I'm going to get her all tuned up for you," he said, wiping off the last of the polish.

I couldn't seem to get past the "hey good lookin'" comment, so I just sat down on his couch, keeping my jacket on so I didn't look at all presumptuous.

"Now, I've put all the picks—and they are nice guitar picks—in this little pouch," he went on, "and here are all the music books that will teach you how to play on your own." He sat down at the piano and started plunking keys and twisting the tuners on the guitar to get the pitch just right.

I ran my hands along the couch upholstery, smoothing the fine fibers to all go in one direction. *This is so weird*, I thought. *I have never once been alone with a boy. Not once. What should I say? He just called me good looking. Did he mean that? Oh, I have no idea how to flirt. It was so different when it was the Rebels. But this one-on-one business, this is SCARY!*

"Well, you're all set," he said, clipping the case shut. "If you ever need me to show you how to play, just ask." I handed him the check for fifty dollars, he flashed that famous Moose smile, and I was on my way. *Why-oh-why can't I say the right words when I need to be cool? Why didn't I say more? He's the leader of the Rebels! He knows me! I should have tried flirting. At least something!*

I opened up the guitar case as soon as I made my way to our family room. Moose had polished the guitar, all right—using household dusting spray. That wasn't exactly what you were supposed to use, according to the very little I knew about taking care of musical instruments. I placed the guitar in my lap, just like I had seen Moose do, and the neck slipped right out from under my fingers. Another reason why dusting spray should not be used on a guitar.

With a better grip, I wrapped my palm around the underside of the guitar, crossed my legs, and laid the body on top of my thigh. My long fingernails tapped on the frets as the pads of my fingers tried to hold down two strings at once. *Yup. I am going to need lessons.*

I put the guitar back inside its red velvet home, then clipped all ten fingernails off and headed to the kitchen for dinner. The best part of the day, no question, had not been getting the guitar. Instead it had been the string of words Moose had said to me. Today, tomorrow, the next day, maybe forever, those words would keep me going.

The Homecoming Dance came and went. Jeannie wore a light blue dress with cream lace and did her hair in the spiral rods, complete with a pearl clip that pulled some of the curls away from her face. Her date was not tall or dark, but he was very handsome. I thought she should have won Homecoming Queen, no question, but it was not to be, and someone else took the crown home.

Our night of having our own dance celebration over the freeway on the walkway overpass ended with the cops saying, "You kids can't be here" — but not before we had a group of cute guys from another high school walk over the pass to see what we were doing. Katie flirted with them and offered them cans of soda. I paid attention to her sleek approach, memorizing her body language and the way she teased and laughed.

The days of fall were filled with football games, more stomps, and lots of brain bending math homework. The last Monday in November, though, was pure bliss. I passed Wendy on the way to my locker and yelled, "I have to hurry home today, so I can't walk with you!" She gave me an inquisitive glance and asked if everything was OK. "Oh, heck yes, better than OK! Today is one of the best days in the history of my family!" I ran as fast as I could and

pushed the doors going from the inside of the school
to the outside with more energy than one should
have after sitting through seven hours of classwork.
"Christmas is coming early this year!" I said to
myself between strides.

For years, Mom had driven a low, semi-
streamlined, chocolate brown station wagon with a
rumble seat. The wagon was equipped with a full
front seat that was big enough for four small children
and one driver, and a middle seat of exactly the same
length. Those seats had the shiniest vinyl covers
known to man, which had cracked under the intense
heat of the sun to show the yellow foam through the
fake stitches. During the years of "used and well-
used," the cloth ceiling started to give out and hang
low in our faces.

The one and only time Mom picked me up
from elementary school on a sunny day, I was
walking home with Moose and a few others friends.
They all begged for a ride home, and what could I
say? "Nobody get in! Our car is not safe! Fabric flies
in your face, and the floors are covered in biscuit
crumbs!" I ended up saying nothing. We all piled
into the car, and Moose couldn't believe that we
drove around with that fabric just flappin' away in
our faces. I didn't say one single word the entire ride
home that day. I just sank lower and lower in my
seat, hoping that he would soon forget all about the
ride in the "wagon."

When we got home I told Mom, "That was
the *most* embarrassing thing in the world!" She
looked at me as if she did not comprehend the
complete disaster she had just caused. "The car,
Mom! My friends were laughing at our car!" Mom

tried to fix the ceiling fabric after that by taking industrial thread and duct tape to it, but the effort was short lived. The stitches didn't hold up and the fabric came back down, until one day in a fit of frustration my dad reached behind the driver's seat and—with one motion—ripped the fabric clean out of the ceiling of the car. With one hand still on the wheel, mind you. All of us kids just sat there—stunned. But I must say it was a relief to be able to see out the windows again.

I raced home as fast as I could, thinking the days of the brown wagon would soon be a distant memory. "Faster, faster, faster!" I said out loud. My legs felt like feathers. I had a determined mission, and nothing could move my focus.

And then…there she was.

At the top of 100 East, I stopped and looked down towards my house. Parked in the driveway was the most brilliant, beautiful twelve-passenger van I had ever seen. The chrome on the front fender nearly blinded me as I ran toward home.

The van had a white stripe along the center and was blue on the top and bottom with a tiny pinstripe that ran alongside a center of dark blue. The Ford oval sparkled with newness. From the glossy coat to the shiny rims, the features were impeccable. With my backpack still on, I took a moment alone with the van. I climbed inside; the amount of room was breathtaking.

"So many seats to pick from!" I yelled to Dad, who had just stepped outside. "And they all have seatbelts!" I tossed my backpack to the driveway, and then, one by one, I sat in each of the twelve seats.

I tested the buckle, clicking it until it soundly shut, then bounced in the seat, and finally checked the view out of each window. My mind was so happy. This was the best day *ever* complete with the "new van" smell. I could picture all of the places we all would go in the van and all the fun we'd have. I vowed to try to sit in a different spot until I'd had a chance to experience a ride in all twelve places—or all eleven, until I could drive it for myself in just over three months.

My personal euphoria was broken quickly as the rest of the kids came home from school and marveled at the vehicle's splendor in their own way. "Oh! And the radio works!" I sung to the family. "There's also a tape deck! And smell that? THAT is a new car smell!" I couldn't wait to get my driver's license and drive it for myself.

Dad popped the hood and started to explain things that nobody understood. "Isn't this the BEST?" I hollered to Mom, who had now joined the small crowd. She seemed overly unenthused. Perhaps because the purchase was way out of our price range, and she was the keeper of the budget, and it *had* to balance each month. Jeannie glossed over the van with one sweeping look and then went back in the house. The rest of us hopped from one space to the next and even tried the captain's seats up front.

"Every kid, get in and get buckled up! We are takin' the van over to show Uncle Davie," Dad said as he climbed into the captain's chair. He adjusted the seat back, checked each of the three mirrors, and put the beast into reverse.

As we headed around the block I almost wanted to scream to my friends on 150 East, "Look at me now, guys! We have a van!"

Dad had planned to take the brown station wagon to her final resting spot in the acres of the backyard orchard at Gram and Gramp's house the next day, telling Mom he would get right on it, but instead the old wagon sat in the driveway until Thanksgiving Day.

CHAPTER NINE

Some pain we bury deep inside, hoping nobody will find the key to unlock it. And we pray that if they do, our strength will emerge to embrace it.

We arrived at Gram's house our usual twenty minutes late. Mom pulled into the driveway in the brand new van just as the cousins came rushing out to see our fresh wheels. I chose to sit in the middle seat of the front row for the ride over to Gram's. So far that was my favorite seat. Dad drove the wagon over, parking the ol' banger just below the barn, next to a few others in the car graveyard. When Dad met the family on the driveway a few minutes later he immediately popped the hood of the van. "My good gad-free," Gramp said when Dad showed off the guts of the engine.

I slid open the van door before landing with both feet on the driveway, "Hey, Gramp, did you see the inside? We have a radio *and* a tape deck! And twelve seats!"

"Look here at the pistons," Dad said leaning up and over into the insides of the van. "Watch them fire. See that? Now, keep your eye on the cylinder heads when I put my foot on the gas."

"Well, it sure as hell is nice," Gramp answered back from behind the hood.

The weather was cool and sunny—an absolutely stunning day for a feast.

I crossed the back door threshold and hopped up a step to the kitchen where Gram was checking on the turkey, the scent greeting me with a friendly puff as the door shut behind me. Ah, Thanksgiving, the best holiday of the fall season.

"Hi, Gram!"

"Happy Thanksgiving, gobble gobble! I woke up at 2 a.m. to put this turkey in the oven," Gram proudly stated, as she did each Thanksgiving. She inserted the meat thermometer, then turned to look at me. "Here, take these cups down and fill each with two ice cubes." Oh, did Gram ever know how to cook a turkey! And whip potatoes as smooth as silk, make gravy that would melt in your mouth, and bake rolls as fluffy as summer clouds. I looked forward to this meal all year long; in fact, I tried my best not to eat much the morning of Thanksgiving just so I could fit more in.

All the granddaughters had a job at Thanksgiving. Some put napkins on the table, others brought side dishes down. All the while Gram would state, "Be careful going down those stairs," and, "Hold it with both hands so you don't drop it!"

The meal finally began a little after one o'clock, after a prayer of thanks to God from Gramp for all we had been given. As soon as the "Amen" sounded, I could hardly contain my manners. I poured an enormous amount of gravy on the turkey, potatoes, stuffing, and then, not finding any patience, I took my first delicious bite. Gram hopped from the kid table to the adult table throughout the meal, making sure there was enough food to go around, including rolls hot out of the oven. The meal always lasted as long as our stomachs could stand. Then we all settled in for story time. I loved listening to my aunts, uncles, Dad, and Gramp tell stories of the week and of the past. Gram didn't join in on the stories, and instead piled the dirty plates high, using one plate to catch all the scraps.

When the tables were put down, the dishes washed, and the pie served up, it was time for the tradition of old family movies. I found a comfortable spot on the floor, the red shag carpet hugging my blue jeans. Dad got out the old 8mm camera and set up movie reels that dated back to "the good ol' days". The cousins all bunched up near the front of the projector and made shadow animals in the large square of light while Dad worked to get the film in straight. As the movie rolled, all the adults chimed in with stories about the family members on the screen, some who came before my time. I sat next to the bookcase near the back of the room, soaking it all in and enjoying being around my family. What could be better?

The movie ended before long, and the lights were turned back on. I glanced around and found myself looking at the books in the case I was leaning against. War books, more war books, history books, more war books, and then, oh yes, Gramp's journals. He rarely missed a day of writing down the events of his life. I rolled my index finger along the journal backings one by one—1970, 1971, 1972, 1973... *Hey, the year I was born!* I wondered if Gramp had written about my birthday. How exciting that he kept such a good record, and so precisely organized. I skimmed the pages quickly, searching for March 11th. Gramp's neat cursive was impressive and legible. I stopped at March 9th, and read what he'd written for the day. He wrote about the weather, which seemed to be his opening line of choice for each day.

"Pretty nice day, but cold. The neighbor had thrown three dead lambs over into my orchard, so I threw them right back in his sheep pen. He'd better get the message, or I'll punch him in the nose."

Very nice. I was sure Gramp had been serious about that, too.

The next day, March 10th, he wrote about the weather again.

"Nice day, cool and cloudy. Got a call from Lynn, and he's taking Cheryl to the hospital. She's having pains, so guess we'll be grandparents again." *Hey! That's me! I am the reason why Mom is in labor! Ah, the next page is my birthday, my day in history!*

I turned the page over. In the top left corner a large number eleven indicated the day, and below it the word *Sunday* was listed. *I was born on a Sunday? That makes sense.* I loved that I had been born on God's day. My eyes slowly started to absorb the words on the paper, but I wasn't prepared. Of course, I should have known that his words would unintentionally cut me to the core. But I didn't know. The journal entry was so candid.

"Oh, what a shock and what a tragedy…" Gramp wrote, his cursive slightly shaky. My throat closed off, and my hands started to sweat. I prayed nobody watched me read or saw the emotion I instantly felt. *Grandpa thought I was a tragedy? Why would he say that? A tragedy? I was a tragedy.* The pain ripped up through my heart and got stuck in my lungs. My breathing became tight and painful.

"It just didn't seem that a thing like that could happen to our people." Gramp's script continued. *A thing like what? Like me? Oh, this was a very bad idea. Very bad. Please nobody notice me, nobody talk to me. Oh please, make me invisible.* I forced my tears down and kept reading.

"We went in to see her tonight, and she does look bad..." *So that is how everyone really felt. I must have looked awful.* The burn in my throat and eyes was unbearable. I reread the page, with tiny waves of shock zinging me with each line, then I stopped for several minutes to control my emotion, blinking fast to control any tears. When I had calmed myself down, I wanted to show Dad what I had just read—I needed him to tell me that wasn't how anyone had *really* felt. He would surely see my face and know that I was on the verge of crying. Certainly he would be sympathetic. I held the book out to Dad, holding my thumb on the page, my hand shaking. Not understanding what I needed, he took the journal and cleared his throat. He thought I wanted him to read it to the crowd! In his loud voice, he bellowed out the entire entry of March 11th, 1973 to my brothers and sisters, cousins, aunts, uncles, and my dear ol' Gramp.

Oh please stop, Dad. Please, please, please don't read any further. I didn't mean for you to read it to everyone! Please don't let the cousins hear the words of that day. It only gets worse the more you read... please stop.

The relatives sat quietly and listened; I wished for one of Gram's wishbones to make me disappear, like this day had never happened. His voice thundered on, and then came the line I was bracing myself for: "Oh, what a shock and a tragedy…" My tears could no longer be held back. I hurt from my bones to my heart, my eyes wringing like a soaked dishrag. My chest heaved. My cry amplified. I recognized the deep injury as it traveled through my vocal chords, dipping into the bottom of my pain, but nobody else did. The relatives stared at me with wide eyes, and yet, the words kept coming straight from Dad's lips.

"Dad, stop reading. Amy is really getting upset," Jeannie said, her eyes fixed on me. "Dad, please. That's enough." she insisted.

But on he went—in no way trying to hurt me, just trying to tell a good story. I didn't want my story told though, not like this. The pain gripped me and made me weak. My breathing turned erratic—pulsing my lungs as they absorbed the convulsing movement. I swallowed and gulped the air around me, trying to find an anchor for my eyes as the levee holding my lids burst. I only knew one way to escape: run. I covered my mouth with my hand and felt, beneath my fingers, wet skin soaked from tears that fell too fast. I ran up the thirteen stairs and into the shiny new van where nobody could see me release the remainder of my agony. All alone, I cried and cried until I felt my heart wouldn't understand what my mind had just read. *How could he think that of me? That I was a tragedy? How could Dad not see that I was pleading for him to stop reading? Why did I even show him the entry? Why would my Grandpa write that about me? My dear Gramp that I love so very much.*

The van was quiet and safe. I wanted to go home and hide in my room, under my blanket, away from my family, those I loved the most. Minutes passed. The salt water streaked my face and dried in lines that ran from the corners of my eyes to the end of my chin. At last my heart slowed down. I felt ruined and utterly defective. The unwanted spotlight had burned a fire right into my ugly face. I could take the stares from strangers or the laughs from kids my age who didn't know the real me, but family—how could Gramp have felt that about me? I replayed the word *tragedy* over in my mind. I was a tragedy. I slid my fingertips under my eyes, a film of black mascara skimmed the top layer of skin. I wiped it on my jeans and wished I had never picked up that journal. And then, all at once, there was Gramp. He pushed through the back door, with his own tears running down his lightly whiskered cheeks. He fumbled, trying to open the van door, and then, when he could look right into my eyes, he lay a trembling hand on my knee and said, "Oh, Amy, honey, I am so, so sorry." His words got stuck, and his tears drowned the sentence. I tried to tell him it was OK, but my voice wouldn't work. For many long moments strung together he patted my knee as he tried to get past the emotion long enough to tell me how much he loved me.

And finally, he did.

My eyes burst, and I let the tears fall freely while my chest heaved in and out—partly because of what I had just read, but more so, because I heard Gramp say raw, untrained words of utter kindness and love. The sun was starting to set and the golden light tried to seep through the tinted van windows.

Small, warm sunspots landed on my face and on Gramp's hands.

Two weeks later, on a Sunday, I went back down to Gram and Gramp's basement. I slipped away while the cousins were watching a television show and everyone else was visiting in the living room. I found the journal, a half an inch out from the rest of the books, as if it said to me, "Try again."

I thumbed through the old pages until I once again found March 11. This time, I was prepared, and it was just Gramp's words and me.

"Both Fern and I cried, but don't suppose that does much good," he said about and Gram and him. "We sure feel bad, but all you can do is make the best of it." The next day, he skipped writing about the weather and wrote about me again: "The baby is still on our minds, but we feel better about it. She is such a sweet, innocent little thing. I know she'll have lots of love and care." *He called me sweet.* He could see, then, that I was alive and had a personality and *will* to survive.

On March 13 he wrote about the weather, like he did on all the days before I was born. "Snow this morning for a change, coming down lightly." My white bees. With me all this time. Even from the very beginning.

The next day, March 14, the snow fell heavy: "Another snow storm. I can't remember a winter draggin' on like this. The sun came out in the afternoon, and it was quite nice," Gramp had written in black ink. "I think everything will be OK with Amy Jo." And that was the first day he had used my name.

The next day, the fifteenth, at just under five days old, I had my first surgery. Dr. Tanner, a well-known general surgeon, performed the operation. Aunts, uncles, Gram, and Gramp arrived at the hospital at 7:00 a.m., then waited several anxious hours until they took me into surgery to repair my upper lip. The surgery on my tiny face started fine, but when the hands of the clock lined up to the noon hour, I stopped breathing due to complications with the anesthesia. The doctors worked to keep my lungs full, but my body didn't want to wake, slumbering well below the normal depth in a trace of unhealthy comfort. One hour, two hours, three hours passed.

But the bees were with me.

They paused from the storm and watched and waited from above. Swarming high, ready for their chance to come and meet me. The bees echoed the grace of angels, both in heaven and on earth, as they armed me with the strength to keep going. And at last—I took a breath again all on my own. I am certain I chose to stay.

Those first few days, Mom had little time to recover from my delivery. She instead learned how to take care of me, her broken baby, to the best of her ability. Dad was right there with her, absorbing the methods for feeding me, listening to the doctor report back on the numerous tests that had been administered, and always caring for me. Mom and Dad, pulled together by the gravity of trial, were intent on giving me every opportunity to grow and be healthy and beautiful.

Within a week I was able to go home with Mom, Dad, and big sister Jeannie. And when I did, the snow fell so thick and fast and with such determination and power that the electricity all through town was taken out for days on end. The newspaper headline read, "Storm Buries Northern Utah, Schools Closed, Traffic Snarled." The storm had affected more than our immediate area: "A record-smashing snowstorm virtually paralyzed Ogden, Weber County, and most of Northern Utah today," the newspaper article had read, "knocking out electrical power and phone services, closing schools, and isolating many communities. More than 50 utility poles snapped and 35 others broke.

Some called it a blizzard, saying they hadn't seen such a storm in all their years. Snow started falling in the morning, and by afternoon it had piled to depths of more than two feet. We went to Gram and Gramp's house that night, where the adults ate a bucket of chicken in the dark with the light and heat from the fireplace surrounding me in my new aqua blue baby blanket. I am sure I listened to the hum of conversation there in the peaceful warmth with my family.

Later, at home with Mom, Dad, and Jeannie, we entered into a dark house with no electricity that soon was filled with light from an old kerosene lamp. All night long Dad would wake with Mom every two hours, he to light the lamp and she to feed me with a tiny dropper. It was the only way to get nourishment into my complicated mouth. My parents felt unity in those hours of working together, giving me life over and over again. Even on the edge of winter changing to spring, the snow fell day after day, almost as if the bees wanted to stay to protect and carry me along.

And they did.

CHAPTER TEN

At nine months old, I learned to climb out of my crib, trying again and again until I succeeded, astonishing my mom with my will and determination.

"Jerry Baker said his daughter was born with a cleft, too," Dad told Mom one afternoon when I was just four months old. "He said they went to Primary Children's Hospital, and a Dr. Broadbent worked on her lip. But I don't know. I think Dr. Tanner did fine on Amy. Maybe we shouldn't worry about it. Seems like she's been through enough."

"She's a strong little baby," Mom answered while she looked down at me, my hand clutched around her finger. The scar from my lip surgery with Dr. Tanner had healed with a rough raised edge. Dr. Tanner must have been like a seamstress who was running late. He'd quickly stitched me up, only fixing the right side of my lip, pulling it tight into an upside-down *v* without concern for the appearance of the scar. The other side of my lip had been left untouched. Of course, everyone had thought that it looked one hundred percent better than the "before". Maybe I had looked better, but I didn't look right.

Jerry worked with Dad, and he kept bothering him with his information about Dr. Broadbent, even stopping him in the hallway between classes saying, "You really must call Dr. Broadbent, even if just to get a second opinion. He's a highly skilled surgeon, and you won't be disappointed." Dad would listen, but what he really wanted was for him to quit offering free advice. As the weeks went on, Mom studied my lips and pictured my future, wondering if there was more they should be doing—she knew that they needed to try again. For me.

"I think we should call that Dr. Broadbent like Jerry suggested," Mom said to Dad over supper one night a few months after Dad had first mentioned his name. Dad nodded in agreement. This was hard for him, he didn't want to offend Dr. Tanner or criticize his work. He had been there for the family numerous times, operating on Gramp and Dad, too—but he was *not* a plastic surgeon. Dad felt moved to try this new doctor and get Jerry off his back once and for all. And so, with a hint of reluctance and an ounce of hope, they called Dr. T. Ray Broadbent and made an appointment.

"Yes, I can help your little baby girl," he said with pure kindness the first time we all met, "but I will need to start over. I will correct both sides of her lip as well as move the incision on her right side so her lip isn't pulled up so tight. But I must warn you— this is just the first step." Mom bounced me in her lap as she listened to him explain the different combinations of cleft lip and palate, from cases involving just a tiny notch in the lip to the most severe circumstances, like mine, adding that the conditions can occur simultaneously or in combination. Mom nodded, then bent down and kissed the top of my head. He said that because I was born with a complete bilateral cleft lip and palate the two gaps in my upper lip extended through my jaw and hard and soft palate. The defect, he explained, originated from a lack of fusion from the lips to the oral and nasal cavities. A fusion, he continued, which should have occurred somewhere between the sixth and eighth week of pregnancy. He mentioned velopharyngeal inadequacy, and said I would have hypernasal voice resonance, a condition he would work to correct as I got older. Mom and Dad listened carefully as he discussed the many other surgeries that were ahead. As he finished up, he looked right into my baby blue eyes and smiled, saying he would take good care of me—as if he could sense I knew what was ahead. When he left the room Mom and Dad looked at one another, feeling blessed that they had been led to him.

Three months later we were at the hospital waiting for Dr. Broadbent to start my lip repair surgery. Mom ran her fingers through my baby fine hair as the nurse found a vein for the IV. Dad made certain to tell the anesthesiologist about my reaction to Anectine. Gram and Gramp and my aunts and uncles were there too, in the waiting room. Like a fine craftsman, Dr. Broadbent un-did the work of Dr. Tanner, carefully cutting into my upper lip to open the scar. He worked meticulously, focusing on the detail and shape of my lip, fixing both sides with his precise stitches and artful skill. When Mom laid fresh eyes on me after he was done repairing my lip, even with all my bandages and arm cuffs on, she cried tears of gratitude for the difference it had made. She thanked Dr. Broadbent and God. Dad called Jerry right away and offered his *own* sincere thanks. I stayed there in the hospital under close observation for six days, and finally Mom, Dad, and Jeannie came and took me home.

Once my bandages came off Mom took me and two-year-old Jeannie everywhere with her— up to the peach orchard, to church, into town for shopping, and visiting relatives. Gram couldn't believe Mom didn't cover my face when we went out and about. Instead, Mom showed me off, not giving a second thought to the reactions of those we encountered. I don't remember those first months of my life, but somehow the fibers of my soul recorded all the times Mom proudly put my face to the sunlight instead of hiding me under a blanket.

Eleven months later we once again traveled to see Dr. Broadbent, this time so he could close the wide open hole in my hard and soft palate, a hole that was completely separated from the bone and muscle. "I wanted to wait until Amy Jo was eighteen months old to do this surgery," he said to Mom and Dad upon our arrival, "the timing is critical. There are two outcomes we want to see when the surgery is complete. The first is improved speech; the second is minimized growth disturbances." He explained that achieving good results with the palate repair were much more difficult than achieving a good result in the lip repair. "The hard palate plays an essential role, along with the tongue, in making sounds associated with T, J, and D. He propped my mouth open just slightly to show Mom and Dad where he intended on making an oral incision along either side of the cleft edge. He pointed to the area on the palate where the tissue flaps would then be stretched to the middle and secured with layers of stitches. Mom listened, keeping me warm in a blanket, talking softly to me to ease my hunger pains from not having my morning bottle. Dr. Broadbent explained that my cleft was a difficult case, one that would require exactness to make certain that the palatine arteries were preserved during the surgery. Dad asked how my pain would be managed when the surgery was over, his sensitive voice edging close to tears. The staff said I would be well taken care of. Mom gave me one last squeeze before the nurse laid me down inside the baby gurney and wheeled me away.

Dr. Broadbent worked on my cleft repair for several hours, talking through the procedure with the other doctors as he repaired the hole that extended up directly to my nasal cavity, and back through my uvula. Hours later I woke, my tiny mind a mix of disoriented haze and unfamiliar feelings. My tongue searched for the gap, my landmark, and instead found a rough bed of stitches. I am sure Mom picked me up, rocked me, and told me stories in my ear while I went in and out of sleep. Soon the nurse took me from her, insisting Mom go home, rest, and take care of my new baby brother, Todd. She said when you come back in a few days your baby will be good as new, and once the stitches are out you can feed her anything you want. Mom nodded, feeling exhausted, and left me to recover in the hospital while she went home to manage the growing household. And I missed her. Ached for her familiar voice. Cried in pain as I suffered through the unknown, not knowing yet what it meant to be brave and strong. The nurses gravitated toward me and became my new comfort. The scents of the hospital replaced the earthy aroma of Mom. When Mom and

Dad came to get me three days later, the nurses danced around me saying they wanted to keep me at the hospital forever.

Months later, Mom was banging pots and pans getting dinner ready, and there I sat on the floor, undisturbed by her racket. My speech hadn't improved as much as Dr. Broadbent said it would. The whole concept that something might be wrong with my ears hadn't crossed her mind until that very moment. So she clanked the pans together even harder, making the air ring with the tangy sound of metal on metal. Still, I played quietly next to her, not offering her any sort of satisfaction for all of the noise. She knelt down next to me. "Amy? Can you hear me?" I kept playing, indicating that her voice was not being absorbed into my ears. As soon as she could, Mom got me an appointment with an audiologist and learned that I had fluid in my ears that had been there for some time. The doctor summarized for Mom that children born with clefts are at a higher risk of developing middle ear problems, "We aren't certain why, but research points to a poor functioning Eustachian tube. Cleft patients like Amy Jo will have ear infections often. Luckily, we caught this one before it caused permanent hearing damage." He continued, "When she swallows, yawns, or sneezes her middle ear isn't aerating—a vacuum is created, and her middle ear filled with fluid. Antibiotics will help." When the infection cleared up I could hear. I baby jabbered to Mom and Dad and laughed at silly Jeannie.

I remember with clear distinction, as if it happened yesterday, the day I realized my lips were different. The vivid colors and scent of the day are all right there cemented in my mind. I wasn't old enough to go to school, but I was already a communicator—if only in my mind. Mom's lips were beautiful in how they moved and worked together as they opened and shut when she smiled and laughed. She had a friend over visiting, and they were busy by the sink cleaning up the dishes while the other children were playing down the hall. I looked up at Mom and her friend and saw how the cupid's bow and dip just under the nose played off one another, like artwork. Mom's lips, full and happy, were fascinating. I continued to watch and listen, and watch more. I reached up to touch my own lips, and, to my surprise, I wasn't able to feel on my own face the familiar valley I had just seen on Mom. I walked to her bedroom, in a fog of confusion, to her enormous round mirror and studied my own face— quite possibly for the first time. I tried to find my cupid's bow. I ran my fingers across my lips, over and over, back and forth. Almost as if I continued tracing I would eventually uncover the treasure I was looking for. Time froze, and it was just me and that vast mirror. And I knew.

For a brief twisted span of seconds, I thought I was wrong. I must be wrong! Everyone I knew had a cupid's bow—a beautiful sweeping cupid's bow. *I must have one, too*, I reasoned. *Where is it? Why isn't it here? I can't find it! This can't be! It has to be here somewhere. I must be the only one who knows, I need to tell Mom! Right now!* I nearly ran down the hall, tugged urgently on her floral shirt, interrupting her conversation, and asked in my tumbled language, "Why doesn't mine look like yours?" She looked down at me, confused with my speech, then nodded her head in agreement to a question she didn't hear right and went right on visiting. All day long I put my finger above my lips, searching and searching for the answer to the burning question I had on the edge of my mind. But, I didn't find an answer that day, and soon the questions faded into the background.

When Jeannie grew old enough to catch the bus halfway down 100 East, I couldn't wait to follow her. I missed her all day long. The hours stretched on forever, and I wondered what she was doing and whether she was having fun without me. At home with Mom I helped her with all her projects: doing the dishes, folding the clothes, and cleaning the house. "I'm a good helper, huh, Mom?" I would ask her as we dried and put the plates into piles.

"Yes, you are my helper, my teacher, my shadow, my perplexity, my ever inscrutable, always loving little Amy," she would answer back. When the school day ended I listened for the push of the air brakes on the bus followed by the sound of Jeannie running up the street and into the house. She would fling the door open, her hair a tangled mess, then swing her backpack to the floor and race into the kitchen. I would run after her and listen to her fast words as she spilled stories about the adventures of her day. Recess! Snack break! Reading! Friends! When I turned five, I too wanted her same experiences. But my path was my own. Starting with more surgeries.

CHAPTER ELEVEN

I knew, even at the young age of five, that the future was a marathon of surgeries, procedures, and therapy.

I didn't know what an operation was, but Mom explained what would happen to me the best she could the summer she and Dad took me to the hospital for another procedure. I wanted to go back home, I didn't like all the attention, and I didn't like wearing hospital clothes. We waited in a room divided by a dark, fabric curtain where they both talked to a doctor about the medicine he would be putting into my body. Soon I was being wheeled away in a large crib, far away from Mom and Dad. I tried to memorize the twists and turns of the hallway so I could find them, or they could find me, but the route was too confusing from my perspective.

"How old are you?" asked the nurse as she leaned down to tape the IV to my small arm.

I looked straight ahead and held up five fingers on my opposite hand, spreading them apart as far as I could.

"Five! Wow! You are getting so big!"

I nodded my head. The surgical cap covering my hair scratched against the stiff cotton sheet, but I didn't speak a word.

The IV was positioned mid-way up my right forearm, and my arm throbbed where the nurse had placed the strip of white sticky tape. I was scared to move, even the slightest bit.

The ceiling towered high above me, and every wall that fell from it was painted stark white. The cold metal crib that I lay in made me feel like such a baby. I turned my head all the way to the left and looked through the metal rungs into the room adjacent to me. I saw a room filled with bright white lights.

"I'm going to have you wait right here until Dr. Broadbent is ready for you. Then we'll take you in for surgery," the nurse said as she wheeled me into the hallway waiting area.

I nodded my head again, trying my best to comprehend the unfamiliar surroundings. I stretched my ears and listened as closely as I could to the voices coming from the room.

"Dr. Broadbent is going to be doing the palate-lengthening operation on her today," said a voice coming from the big, bright room.

"He's been seeing this patient ever since she was six months old," said another voice. "Her case is one of the most severe bilateral cleft lip and palates we've seen at this hospital. She still has many surgeries ahead to make her face look normal. They'll probably follow her into adulthood."

"Did you know Dr. Broadbent is one of the best plastic surgeons in the world for cleft-palate repair?"

"He was top of his class at Duke University. He's very talented."

Then a door swung open, and I heard the whoosh from the pushed air followed by deliberate motion and the sound of a clipboard hitting a hard surface.

"Hello, students. I'm Dr. Broadbent. It's a pleasure to be teaching you today. I'll be showing you a technique for improving the speech of this patient, called a pharyngoplasty." His voice was familiar, but I didn't know why. My mind raced to catch the answer. "The operation will be done by attaching a flap of soft tissue from her throat wall to the back of her soft palate."

"How will this improve her speech?" asked a younger man.

"Well, if the palate and throat don't touch, air leaks into the nose and produces nasal speech," he clarified. "Are there any more questions before we begin?"

Were they talking about me? Where is Mom? Why isn't she here yet?

"OK, it looks like Dr. Broadbent is ready for you now," the familiar nurse said, her rainbow hair tucked up neatly into her own surgical cap, the elastic edges gripping her smooth forehead. She unlocked the wheels, put both palms on the side of the crib, and pushed.

I sunk as deep as I could into the mattress, my face pointed up, feeling scared and so very alone. The wheels creaked when she made the turn from the hallway into the big, bright room.

She stopped in the center, locked the crib in place, and in an instant she was gone. As the minutes passed that day I was certain I was in the wrong place. Not one single person said hello to me, almost as if I didn't exist. Yet, I could hear them buzzing around me in a productive fashion. I thought if I didn't move, they would go about their business and forget about me, and then Mom and Dad would come looking for me and take me home—and I wanted to go home more than anything.

"Hello, Amy Jo," Dr. Broadbent said, leaning over the crib from behind my line of sight. His eyes were kind and good. I knew him, and my body relaxed—if only just slightly. "We're going to move you to the operating table where your surgery will take place," he said, and then before I could re-arrange my thoughts, there were two people on either side of me. "On the count of three, we'll need you to become as light as a feather, OK?"

Eight hands lifted me from the crib to the table in a swift display of teamwork. My cotton gown tangled around the tubes, and my nurse quickly set to work repositioning them, snapping the cord onto the IV tower and taping it into place. Then, her focus came back to me. She attached a sticky circle that had a wire coming out of it just above my heart and put some sort of a cover on my pointer finger, which instantly throbbed. All the while she was fielding requests for surgery preparation. In the background I heard the sound of metal instruments bouncing on metal trays, moving to the beat of soft footsteps. Dr. Broadbent's voice was calm and low somewhere behind and to the left of me as he talked to others in the room. I couldn't hear anything, no matter how hard I tried to stitch together his words.

The students came by and looked down at my face, glancing so briefly they didn't catch the fear in my eyes.

"Can you count to one hundred?" Dr. Broadbent asked through the white surgical mask over his mouth.

I shook my head.

"How about to fifty?"

I shook my head again.

"Well, I want you to start counting as high as you can, OK?"

I nodded and wished I knew how to count higher; they all wanted me to count to one hundred! And I didn't know how. The vein in my right arm was suddenly filled with a cold sensation; it felt gripping and fierce as it followed the length of my arm all the way up and across my shoulder. I shook with a sudden chill.

"One, two, three…" I started, trying to stay focused on what number came next.

"Good job, Amy Jo. Keep counting," Dr. Broadbent encouraged, his eyes steady on mine.

My mind felt so heavy, so tired — so very, very tired. I wanted to show him how high I could count, but I could hardly remember the order. "four…five………………sev…en…………….." The room became fuzzy, and my focus skewed as I tried with all my might to keep my eyes open, but my lids pressed heavy on my lashes. "……….e…i…g…h…t…," and then I could no longer hold on. I looked up at Dr. Broadbent and saw a flash of white before I disappeared into a deep, wonderful sleep.

While I slept, he worked. And I felt no pain.

The surgery that day ended so fast in my mind, like I hadn't even slept. When I emerged from my medicated slumber, there was Dr. Broadbent again, his eyes winking back at me while the white surgical mask relaxed around his neck. His kindness enveloped me like a security blanket, smothering the pressing fear and anxiety I had felt hours earlier when he'd asked me to count for him. *Ask me to count again*, I thought, *this time I won't mess up and you can see how smart I am*! "You were a brave little girl in there, Amy Jo. We fixed your lip up a little more, and worked on the inside of your mouth. You will feel better in a few days."

Soon, Mom and Dad were standing above me. Dad's hands wrapped around the edge of the metal crib as he watched me try to keep my eyes open. *How did you find me, Dad? Who told you where I was, Mom? I am so glad you found me. So glad. Please stay. Don't leave me again. I was so scared without you. Stay with me. Stay.* Mom slept next to me on a hospital cot for a handful of nights while I recovered, but when I was healed and ready to go home, it was Dad who came to get me in the old green truck. The morning sun that day hit the top of the parking garage and bounced in a happy song up to wheel rims and off again in a lovely reflection. Dad bought a cold fudgesicle and unwrapped it as we approached the truck. "Here, A-mouse, this is for you," he said between confident strides. I grabbed hold of the ice-cream stick and tried to take a bite, but my lips were numb and my mouth didn't work right. I gave it straight back to him without explaining myself. After I scooted in the driver's side and moved over to the passenger's seat, I held the fudgesicle so Dad could get behind the wheel, passed it back to him, and it vanished in his mouth in two bites. We rode home together with the long gear shift between us and the road runner sticker smiling back at me on the side mirror. Happiness swept over me, despite everything, I loved my life.

"When she's older, we'll need to do quite an extensive cranial facial surgery to correct her jawline and transplant bone into areas of her face that appear flat," Dr. Broadbent told Mom during a follow-up visit. "She will also need to have work done on her nose to open up her nasal passage for better breathing. We will do our best to cosmetically repair her nose as well with a rhinoplasty. More surgeries will be needed to refine the shape of her upper lip, but all of that will come later, no need to worry about those surgeries yet." He winked at me every so often as he talked to Mom, acknowledging my presence.

I listened as they talked about my face, taking in silent breaths through my mouth, my legs hanging inches above the floor, while wondering when "older" would happen to me. That same year my brother Justin, five years younger than me, was born. Mom and Dad brought him home from the hospital and all of us kids gathered around him in awe, touching his bright cheeks and petting his bald head. Dad insisted that if we looked deep enough into his baby eyes we could see heaven— the wondrous place he had come from days earlier. I tried and tried to see heaven, staring at him so long my eyes coated over with dry patches, but all I ever saw was my own reflection bouncing back from his dark pupil encased in the color of sky.

Finally, it was my turn to go to school. Mom dressed me in a deep pink corduroy dress, with a matching shirt, and curled my fine auburn hair into ringlets that skimmed my jawline. "There now, don't you look like a star," she said, holding my shoulders in her hands and looking me square in the eye. I felt a surge of independence as I walked through the back gate. I *was* a star!

"When we get on the bus you can sit by the window, OK?" Jeannie said as we waited together at the bus stop. "If the bus gets into a wreck, here's what you do," Jeannie taught me as she reached her crossed arms out into the air. "Put your head between your arms and hands on the seat in front of you."

"A wreck?"

"Yeah, but I haven't been in a bus wreck yet. We just do these drills sometimes. Our bus driver's name is Woody."

"Woody?"

"Yup, Woody."

"He has big hair."

"It's called an afro."

"An afro?"

"Mm hum, that's what you call big fluffy round hair."

Jeannie put her arm around me as she guided me to our seats on the bus. She let me sit next to the window.

Tracy Clead got on the bus next eating a toasted egg sandwich folded in half, acting as if school was just another casual event in her day.

The yellow bus traveled along the rows of houses, over the bumpy street, past the acres of fruit trees, and up the small hill to the school. I looked out the window as I tried to count all the passing cars, feeling the rush of adventure take over my senses.

Jeannie walked me to my classroom and a new world waited for me over the threshold. An exciting world Jeannie had told me all about. She led me to my teacher who took me by the hand and showed me the cubby with my name on it, told me where to put my towel for nap time, and placed my box of crackers next to the back sink. My teacher was so nice, her hand warm, and her eyes kind. But there was something else in that classroom that I hadn't expected. Something Jeannie hadn't told me about. Right away I could see the kids looking at my face, blinking a few times, then turning away from me as if I didn't belong. My excitement for the first day of school soon turned into anxiety. I felt farther away from Mom than I ever had, a stranger in my own body. I didn't think anything was *that* wrong with me, but even at five-years-old I knew what it meant to be ignored, and my self-concept adjusted to match the stares. I said as little as possible as I absorbed my new surroundings. And all of a sudden I didn't want to be noticed. I didn't feel like a star anymore.

The teacher gathered us in. "Children, please find a circle to sit on. Now, who here can read this word?" she asked, pointing to a large open book leaning against an easel. I tried to make myself invisible by keeping my head down. A few hands shot up in the air. I didn't know the first thing about reading. In fact, I had a hard time even talking. Each time I tried to say something, the consonants came out like blended up noise. In my mind, what I said was clear—clear like the big sky in fall. The sentences felt poetic and came together in syllable rhythm, tapping into my emotion and intelligence before I actually spoke. Then, talking fast, I would spill out what I was trying to say, but when the words went from my brain to my lips it was a sea of confusion. So I listened, wondered, and observed, talking just to those in my family who had learned to interpret my language. Gram used to say, "Amy is so shy." But I wasn't shy, not even on my quietest days. By early winter the teacher was asking the students to read along with her, if they could, in unison. The black bold symbols didn't make any sense to me. I couldn't understand how the other kids could look at the book and follow along.

At school they assigned me to a speech therapist that would stand in the doorway and call me out of class. The other students would stop what they were working on and watch me leave. The faster I tried to leave the more noise I made. I didn't want to know what they were thinking. After school our family would travel to a university forty miles away once a week for my speech therapy lessons. While the rest of the family would go and do a fun activity, I would learn how to make my T's and S's. My teachers would tell me, "Amy, you are our best student. You are doing great! And so pretty, too!" They gave me total and complete attention and leaned in to hear my every attempt at proper sounds. The building where I met with the teachers had a large, open area, broken up by cubicles, which were lit only with natural sunlight. I would sit on a metal chair just my size, swinging my legs back and forth, trying my best to be so good and say the words how they asked me, focusing on my enunciation. But I never seemed to get it right.

When I was dropped off at speech, the rest of the family went to play along the river. I ached to be a part of the fun. Todd lost a shoe in the water during one visit. It just floated away down the river. The shoe was all the rest of the family could talk about. "Oh, how sad that the shoe just drifted away, and nobody could catch it! Oh, now what will we do with the other shoe? Now Todd will have to wear his *old* shoes!" If I hadn't been in speech therapy, I would have jumped in and saved that shoe, wading out into the rushing stream until I had it safe in my hand. My siblings would have cheered for "Amy the Hero" while I waved the dripping shoe high above my head in victory. For a moment I wouldn't have been "Amy that had to go to speech therapy."

At home, Mom would work tirelessly on pronunciation with me, but saw little progress. One night after dinner, Jeannie started to make a fantastic hurricane sound in her mouth, "Hoooochkkttttt!"

I sat next to her, staying clear of the spray exiting her mouth, watching her dampen the table.

"I'm spitting," she said glancing my way. "It's easy, just make this sound, hooockkkktttt! Curl your tongue back, pretend there is a spoon sitting on it, and then flip it at the very end at the top of your mouth—that's how I do it anyway."

I tried it, doing exactly what she taught me. After several attempts I was spitting, just like Jeannie. Jeannie's went farther than mine. I kept at it, trying my best. I couldn't get the distance, but I had the technique down.

"Amy!" Mom shouted, rushing toward me with wide eyes, wiping her wet hands on a dishcloth. "Do it again!"

"*Again*?"

"Yes!"

I looked at Jeannie in confusion.

"Do it! Show her how I taught you to spit!"

"OK, watch out, I don't want to get any on you, Mom."

"Again!" shouted Mom, "again!"

"Hooockkkkkttt!"

"Again!"

"Hoooooooocccckkkkktttttttt!"

"Hey, Mom, watch me spit, too! Mine goes far!" Jeannie offered.

"One more time, Amy! Do it again!"

"Hoooochkkktt!"

"Amy! Amy! You did it! You just said the 'T' sound! All on your own! You're doing it!"

Jeannie caught on smiling from ear to ear, "Amy! Say cat!"

"Cat."

"Say hot!"

"Hot."

"Say flat!"

"Flat."

"Say Todd!"

"Todd!"

My family exploded into applause and celebration—spitting had led to speaking. Mom clapped in amazement, then put her hands over her cheeks and laughed and laughed, shaking her head in marvel. My victory that day was hers, too. Small as it was.

CHAPTER TWELVE

Courage is born from battling your barriers. Win or lose.

When Jeannie was seven-years-old she saved Katie's little brother from drowning. She jumped into the deep holding pond, clothes and all, and swam out after him telling him to hang on even while his head was bobbing up and down in distress. I couldn't believe my eyes. Jeannie was rescuing him. She hadn't even thought about her clothes getting wet or how she would have the strength to haul him on her back while swimming at the same time. When she pulled him to the edge of the water he was gasping for air— his skin translucent and pale. All of us kids stood around in wonder and awe of valiant Jeannie. That was the day she became the neighborhood hero. Her bravery was her instinct. I knew that she would save me one day, too, if I ever needed her.

By the time I entered first grade I still didn't know how to read, I wanted more than anything to follow along with the other kids, but instead I moved my mouth open and shut in silence. Mom assured me most students learned in second grade and that I wasn't the only one who couldn't quite read, but I had my doubts. Most all of the other kids had caught on and were reading small sentences without any help. When the teacher sat next to them, her finger below the words, she would give off a joyful sound when they read without prompting. I tried to figure it out, yet it was every bit a mystery to me as the stars that shone in the sky. It was just one more challenge I didn't want to talk about, one more thing that set me apart from the other kids.

I sat in the back row in the classroom, two desks away from the teacher. Behind me, hanging from the ceiling, was a gallery of large paper tooth cutouts, one for each student, with our names written at the top. My teacher explained when a student lost a tooth they gained a sticker. The first few months of school several of the students got star stickers to put on their tooth. Mine stayed empty. The tooth cutouts adorned in stickers mocked me, almost as if they knew my facial deformity would also effect the growth of my permanent teeth. I thought about sneaking the package of stickers off of the teacher's desk, stealing a large red and silver one, and posting them on my paper tooth when nobody was looking. My permanent teeth did eventually start to come in, but they were a disaster—a true, blown-up, crazy disaster. The two front teeth weren't centered, but instead took up space on the right side of my mouth. Other teeth tried to fit in the best that they could, but the spacing was all wrong, leaving a gap a half an inch wide in my smile. It was as if someone had tossed a pile of dice into my mouth and where they landed was where they grew.

One Monday morning all of the students met in one large classroom for an educational video lesson. The lady on the video taught us all about cartilage. "Cartilage is springy! Now take your finger

and push your nose all the way down, until it's flat."
This is easy I thought. *My nose is already flat.* I kept my
finger on the end of my nose like the other kids, but
when the lady in the video said, "OK, release your
finger! Your nose will bounce right back into place!"
mine just stayed the same. I looked sideways toward
the other kids, envious, wondering what it must feel
like to have a bouncy nose. Luckily, we got to bend
our ears next, I bent my ear in half just to prove I was
as normal as the other kids. It sprung right back into
place when I let go, like the lady said it would, and I
nodded along with all the others.

After school I would run to my room, change
into my play clothes, and meet Katie in her backyard.
We made winding trails through the tall weeds and
grass in the empty lot next to her house, playing hide
and seek and laying next to the warm dirt until dusk
had settled and it was time to go home. Sometimes
Katie would ask if I could stay for dinner, and her
mom would pull out the red "I am Special Today"
plate for me to use. A plate reserved for the highest
honor and the most superior of guests. They would
serve me first, pass out compliments, and give me
the biggest helping of dessert when dinner was all
cleared up. My chest would burn with gratitude. At
Katie's house I felt truly special.

"In a few minutes we are all going to the gym
for an afternoon of fun," my teacher said one Friday
at school. "Everyone will participate, no exceptions."
We lined up in alphabetical order and walked to the
gym where we waited for instruction. "Now, listen
up, class. Each of you will be given a balloon; your
job is to blow it up, then run as fast as you can to the
other end of the gym and sit on it until it pops. You

will be divided into a relay team with kids from the other classes, so you will each be a link in the success of your team." I shivered with anxiety. Blowing up a balloon was physically impossible. I had attempted to blow one up on my own at home once. The air had traveled from my lungs, out my nose, and in a hundred other directions, but it didn't go into the balloon. It was simply impossible for me to create a vacuum in my mouth to complete the task. I took the balloon as instructed and stretched it out like the other kids, then put my lips around the ring and tried with all my might to get the balloon to fill with air, causing a sharp and painful headache to jet to the space between my eyes.

"Teacher? I can't do it." I quietly said after several attempts.

"Everyone participates. That's the rule. Nobody else is getting any help. Keep stretching it and try again. Hurry, please."

After the other kids had their own tight, shiny balloon in hand, I got the attention of one tall brunette teacher from the other class. She had brought a balloon-filling contraption, and it looked helpful. I *needed* it! But instead of helping me right away, she made me try again and again to blow up that stupid balloon on my own while she watched me. I stretched it and stretched it until I was positive it would work. Everyone was waiting for me. They watched me. Standing there with their hands folded, staring at my fat lips trying to blow up a skinny balloon. My heart nearly beat out of my chest in humiliation. I wanted so badly for their eyes to be looking somewhere else, *anywhere* else! I puffed, and the air stung my palate, then I tried again and blew so hard I thought my face would burst – still no air made it into the balloon. In an impatient motion she finally let me use her fancy balloon pump, and once it was blown up, she handed it back to me to tie off. At least *that* I could do.

I hoped the kids would forget my disaster of trying to fit in. But, I was wrong. My failure to blow up a balloon created a distinction between me and the normal kids. There was one boy, meaner than all the rest, who sought me out, making sure I knew each day that I didn't belong. He was the boy who blew his balloon up and then smashed it flat with one giant thump. He was the boy determined to make my life a living hell. He was my bully.

"HEY, FAT LIP!" he would yell to me during recess. He loved the way his voice cut into me. I tried my best to ignore him and push aside the cruel words that marked me as defective. He would follow me around on the playground spitting words at me so painful that it felt like my face was being dragged across the asphalt. My insides would twist with raw humiliation. At recess he would push up one side of his lip and laugh and point at me, kicking dust up as he walked across the sandlot toward me, shouting again, "I *said*, HEY FAT LIP! I am talking to you!" My heart would pound as I desperately looked for a place to play without him bothering me. The teasing was relentless, and his hollow laugh would echo in my ears long after the sting of his words was gone. He gathered other boys into his pack, and together they worked to make my life miserable by taking away my small amount of confidence with their foul power. I wanted the teachers to come out and tell him to stop it, but I was left alone to face the bully and his friends.

My only safety was to hide. I would race down the length of the playing field, camouflaging myself by staying close to the fence. Then, reaching the bottom, I would sit next to the abandoned playground set, holding my knees tight to my chest—digging the sand out that had made its way into the lip of my shoes. When the bell to come in would ring, I would hop on my invisible horse and gallop up the edge of the field, my heart pounding like thunder, as I slipped into the line moving toward the classroom. I did this same routine until the bully and his pack discovered my path, then once again my face was vulnerable as I sought new refuge from the teasing.

By second grade, the funding for the buses was cut and so all of us neighborhood kids banded together and made the daily trek to school. Most days Mom would walk with us, at least half way. I didn't tell her about the bully.

I would wear my brown, knit face mask with only holes for seeing and breathing. Todd, Toots, Jeannie, and I would all walk to school, bundled up in the cold with our masks on. While I had my brown mask on, I felt free for a few minutes, and I would look around at my sisters and brother and think, *I look just the same as they do now.* When we would arrive at the school and I would pull the mask off, my hair was a wild, frizzy mess, but I didn't care—for a short time, I'd had freedom from my lip. If the weather was clear we would all ride our bikes. When the final school bell rang at 3:15 in the afternoon, I would grab my blue and white coat with red stripes and move my feet as fast as they could go to my bike. If I was fast, I could avoid the teasing. I would put my hand over my mouth and run.

It didn't always work, and then the prickly words would cut me so deep, my heart would beat in my throat. I would leave those words on the playground, those words that I shoved into layer eleven, and ride my bike home. The faster I rode the better I felt, the wind catching in my snarled hair and whipping it against my back.

The hurt would linger when I got home, the words replaying in my head. I would try to make myself invisible by hiding in the basement, under the stairs next to the hundreds of bottles of dusty fruit, and listen to Mom one floor above, pacing back and forth making dinner. The pain followed me on the playground and followed me home. I would run my fingers along my lip, and push my tongue along the scar at the roof of my mouth. This, I knew, was my silent journey. The sounds of Mom cooking dinner were comforting, but I couldn't pull myself away. I would wait under the stairs, all alone, until someone noticed I was gone.

"Where's Amy?" Mom would ask. The kids would all say they hadn't seen me since we got home from school. Soon, I would feel good enough to reappear, and I was always glad I had been missed.

"How is school going, A-mouse?" Dad asked me one afternoon as we traveled the canyon to speech therapy. I told him about the organized games we played with the teachers supervision, and left out the part where I hid during recess.

"Fine. Katie and I play four-square sometimes. It can be hard 'cause if you get a foul ball you are out, so I have been working on my underhand move. None of the boys like me though. They don't like the way my face looks," I answered dryly, rubbing my temples with my finger to ease my headache. I didn't want to tell him or Mom any details, I didn't want to talk about any of it. Not about the bully, or the horrible things he said to me, or how I worked for hours after school to forget him. Mom took me to an otolaryngologist that year who recommended, after many middle ear infections, that I have ear tubes put in. The doctor used fancy words to describe to Mom more of my medical problems. "Kids with clefts have a malformation in the upper airway, which in turn leads to the middle ear continually filling with fluid. Your daughter has had multiple ear infections in a short period of time, and if things continue this way she will have hearing loss." The doctor told Mom that the tubes would help to alleviate the fluid and would stay in place for six months to a year, and then fall out on their own. I knew all about that. Tracy Clead's sister, Kelly, had tubes. One had fallen out and Tracy said it was as big as a pencil eraser covered in ear wax.

My bully was persistent and continued to haunt me with teasing during recess. "Your lips look like they came from a rabbit!" he would laugh at me. "Do us all a favor! Put a bag over your face!" I thought about it, too, that it would be better if I had a bag over my face. One day I had a great idea, to hide in the large playground conduits, where nobody could find me. I listened to the other kids playing

outside the conduit making moats and castles in the
sand. The spot was my private shelter. I would roll
my back into the curve of the tube, bend my knees,
put my feet up on the other side, and close my eyes,
feeling comfortably invisible. I was surprised that
nobody discovered or noticed me sitting in there, day
after day—even though some of the kids made a
game of jumping over it or sitting on top. I wanted to
play and make friends, but what I wanted most was
peace from my face and relief from my pounding
headaches.

My peaceful hiding spot didn't last long. One
day, the bully found me. He startled me awake to
reality, in a horrible game of hide and seek, as he
discovered my refuge. He crouched down low,
stretching his arms up to the top of the cement rim,
digging his chewed off fingernails into the top edge.
He set about at once to destroy me. "Hey, you guys!
Fat Lip is in here! Told you we would find her!" My
foot slipped on the concrete surface in my haste to
free myself from the bullying before escaping out the
other end, running as fast as I could, zipping my
jacket all the way to the bottom of my nose. I could
hear them chasing after me. Yelling at me. Tearing
me apart. Burning me shut with horrible names.
Inside I screamed to myself, *I am beautiful! I am
beautiful! I am beautiful!* Never again did I return to
that spot, my home on the playground.

Our teacher came to us with a playground
issue. "Tattling has gotten out of control. You
students are old enough now you don't need to be
running to the playground supervisor and telling her
every little thing that is going wrong." I was glad
that I hadn't had the courage to tattle on the bully.

Then *I* would be the one getting into trouble. "Just learn how to figure things out on your own. If you are bleeding or need a bandage, then come find one of us. But stop the tattling!" I resolved to never tell the teacher or the playground supervisor about what I was dealing with. I wanted someone important to *see* the hell he was inflicting on me as he blocked my happiness, ruining my days upon days. I wanted to be rescued. So, I told the bravest person I knew. I told Jeannie.

She insisted, "Wait by your classroom door for me after school, and I'll come and get you." I would stand there with my backpack strapped crisscross on my back, looking down the long hallway until I saw her coming toward me, and relief would burn down to my toes.

Jeannie watched for the bully during recess, marking his path with her focused scrutiny as he made his way from four-square to tetherball. And then it happened, just like I had told her. From her spot on the playground she saw him chasing after me, pushing his lip up and laughing his empty laugh. When I stepped to the right, he would mirror my action, blocking me with his big frame, making sure I couldn't pass until I heard him loud and clear. That night Jeannie devised a plan to stop him once and for all. The next morning she filed her nails to a point for better scratching and wore her Sunday shoes to school because they kicked harder. Throughout the morning she waited for the right opportunity for retaliation. She got her chance after lunch while we were all outside on break. She took off running straight for him, not even thinking about the fact that he was bigger and stronger—just took off, storming him, grabbing his collar and shoving him up against the brick exterior wall of the school. With her right hand she hooked a shot at his face smashing in his nose until he was a bloody mess. It was just like she'd seen in the movies, when the good guy gets the bad guy. She came after him each day after that, too, screaming at him during lunch recess, chasing him, kicking him, and yelling at him to "stay away from my sister!" All the while, the recess supervisor looked the other way, knowing this girl was right. Jeannie didn't flinch as she stood up to the bully. She made it her job to protect me. She was my bully fighting angel.

One anonymous boy in my classroom delivered a message to me in secret, and in his own way, silently stood up to the bully.

"Mom! Mom! Mom!" I yelled nearly tripping over myself coming into the front door that Valentine's Day. "Mom! A boy gave me a giant valentine! Look, Mom, a big heart filled with chocolates!" My excitement overflowed as I dumped my backpack out and held the gift high in victory. "See, the handwriting is a boy's! Nobody else got one like this, just me," I beamed.

"Oh, Amy. Who could it have been? I am thrilled for you! This is a real treasure. What a wonderful thing to have happen on Valentine's Day! Go show Dad!"

At dinner that night, my smile and soul shined on bright, and when the dishes were cleaned up I shared my chocolates (just one each) with my brothers and sisters. The rest of the family celebrated along with me, the lively burning in my tummy spinning like a tornado, filling me with complete happiness. *Who did this for me? Who?* I thought tossing and turning in my bed that night. I only knew that whoever was brave enough to give me a Valentine must have wanted to counteract the bully and his harsh treatment.

At the end of third grade the teacher announced we would be making "Warm Fuzzy Books", or books of compliments and nice things, spotlighting one student at a time.

When it was my turn, I was sure there would be mean things said about me. I was positive. After school I took the small book to my bedroom and shut the door. The cover was made from soft pink fur. I ran my fingers across it, petting it into one direction, not certain I wanted to chance reading the contents on the pages. But each student, even the bully, had written at least one nice thing about me. Most students said I was polite and that I was good because I didn't cheat. Many said I had nice hair (which was a total lie because I only washed it on Saturday nights per Mom's instruction). A few even said I dressed nicely. But one boy—one boy unknowingly summed it up, writing what I needed to hear most when he quite accurately stated, "I like you because you have lots of courage."

I did have courage.

I read his page so many times the paper turned soft as tissue.

CHAPTER THIRTEEN

The wind moves the waves that direct the ship above the ocean floor—but when a storm throws waves high into the darkened sky, the ship is tossed about in the open sea and must wait for the captain to gain control once again.

Winter the following year was record breaking. Businesses caved in under the weight of the snow, and people were forced to shovel off the rooftops of their own homes. Dad would holler from our roof to our neighbor's roof, "Hey, Bob, how's the snow up there?" Bob would yell back, "It's heavy and wet; I need to get it off before the roof caves in. I wish the snow would give us a break." Mom built us a thrilling tubing slide that started at our roofline, curved around the deck, and ended in the backyard next to the maple trees. One day as we were driving down 100 East Dad said, "I'm tired of all this snow. It's getting old. We haven't had a fetchin' break in weeks. Look at it—just look! It's piled four feet high—it won't melt for months." No matter what Dad said, I didn't care if it took all year to melt. I loved having snow on everything and anything.

Eventually the snow *did* melt. At school the playground seemed to come alive with the jitters of spring. A new crop of mean boys emerged, a year younger, and feistier than the others. They were like a pack of horseflies, biting me and stinging me with their words that landed on my back until I shook them off. I was lucky enough to have a best friend who stood by me. I always told Katie she was my gift from God. I meant it, too. She could've been best friends with any girl in our class. But she chose me. When all the other girls were passing out friendship safety pins with tiny colored beads, Katie gave one to me and told me it represented her best friend pledge. I was so proud of the symbol of our friendship and immediately pinned it on my tennis shoe, hoping the other kids would notice. Katie was fearless, like Jeannie, and would run after the mean boys when they started to make fun of me. I secretly loved having her defend me with such feistiness. She would swing her backpack hitting them with all her force. "That is just not nice! You just don't say those things to someone! She can't help it! She is my best friend! Leave her alone!" When Katie returned to me she would calmly say, "Do you want to play tetherball?" I would nod and walk with her, holding a headache tight within the bounds of my beating mind. Katie would grab the ball high in her left hand and smack it with her right hand sending the ball and the rope orbiting around the rod at a fast speed.

"Wow, good hit."

"Your turn," she would say, passing me the ball. I would hold it the same way, and hit it with the palm of my hand and watch it barely make it around once.

"Good job. You'll get it, we just need to keep practicing." The pack of mean boys kept their distance from me when Katie was near. They knew, just like me, that she was powerful.

Two days before the fourth grade let out for summer, I went to the local orthodontist, who went by "Dr. B", for the first time. I was so excited! Lots of other nine-year-olds had already gotten their braces on, including Katie. "OK, let's take a look," Dr. B said as he propped my mouth open wide that first visit. He poked around inside it for a while, until I wasn't sure I would be able to close my jaw again.

"What do you think?" Mom asked after realizing he wasn't going to offer up any information readily.

"Her two front teeth are not anywhere near where they should be, which is why she has this large gap here on the left side of her mouth. She is also missing her incisors. I expected that with her bilateral cleft. What's also interesting is that the other teeth are all different sizes, see here?" He lifted my lip up as high as he could so Mom could get a better look, and I felt the cold air drying out the underside. I knew what he meant. I had been brushing those strange teeth faithfully for years and flossing up into the even more messed-up gum line, which was crisscrossed in uneven scar tissue and gaps. "Often with a cleft palate teeth just come in where they can. She really doesn't have any supporting bone—that's one of the biggest problems. What we need to do is find a way to expand her palate and try to move the teeth into a better position," he said moving my head from side to side. "But look here, on the bottom they are all there just like they should be, and even straight." Dr. B stopped, then scratched his head. It was clear he wasn't sure where to start. "I have to admit, this is a fairly complicated case. Can you get me the number for her plastic surgeon? I'd like to coordinate care with him. I'm sure after she has her cranial facial surgery when she is a teenager that much of this will be corrected. Oh, and her dentist, too. I need his number. Give the information to the secretary on your way out." The only thing Dr. B could do in the meantime was what he knew worked on the other kids. So he cemented my brackets on the back molars and prepared me for braces. It wasn't fun at all; in fact it was a terrible, horrible, rotten, awful day.

After a few months he had us come back to his office. He had been to an orthodontia conference and met with other professionals who had treated cleft patients. Armed with new information he tried a special brace, one that stayed glued in my mouth. "This is a type of modified maxillary expander. It will widen Amy's palate and give us more room to work," Dr. B explained. Each week I would take a tiny key that fit into the top of the brace and crank it three times to painfully expand my palate. My teeth, well, they didn't seem to move. Not one bit. Eventually he took the special brace out, which smelled like a garbage dump by then, and tried something else. I would sit in his chair, month after month, challenging patience.

Before long, the nights started to cool off and the chill of winter closed in on autumn. On those cold nights Mom would build a fire in the wood burning stove, turn the lights down, and read to us from books about faraway lands and mythical creatures. We would pull our pillows up to our bedroom doorways and lay a blanket out. She would put her back up against the hallway wall and thumb through the book while spraying the scent of old pages down the hall until she found the spot where she had left off the night before. And there she would read us story after story while we quietly listened. When Mom read to us during the evenings, our house was peaceful and content—the opposite of how it was during the day when the house echoed with sibling contention. I always liked the peace better, but during the last few years of elementary school all of the pain that I had buried inside started to erupt when I walked through the front door of our home after school each day. Once Jeannie left for junior high, the bully found the hole in my confidence, and just like the cleft I wore on my face, he ripped the gap open and reminded me I would never look normal. I wanted to be tough and figure it out on my own. Eventually the turmoil inside me found its way out. I knew that my temper was getting out of control.

On January 1 of that year, I made a set of New Year's resolutions, and I was determined to keep them:

1- Keep my temper down
2- Be nicer to my family
3- Write in my journal

The first few days started out great, but it wasn't long before I had broken my number one and two resolutions. One night my brothers' bickering got on my nerves, and I exploded, my temper flaring fierce and red hot. I screamed at Mom with all my might, "I can't take it anymore!" I opened up the drawer of crayons and threw them all over the kitchen. They hit like hail, digging smatterings of wax into the linoleum. Channeling my fury made me feel better in the moment. "Everyone makes me so mad! I am *so* sick of the noise. Those two are always fighting!" I felt out of control and explosive. I grabbed a stack of white paper and threw it at the table. I *had* to do something; the monster inside me was too loud.

"Amy, when you get this way you turn ugly," Mom said with her eyebrows pushed together and her voice stern.

I already am ugly! So what?! I thought spitefully. She could tell I had no intention of calming down.

"Count to ten and try and settle down, or just go to bed for the night. We don't need this behavior."

"Counting does NOT work!" I screamed, "I've tried it! I don't WANT to settle down! I hate this! I don't even want to be in this house anymore! Just shut up! I don't even *like* you, Mom!" I started grabbing silverware from the table and hurling it to the floor. "You don't even care about me! You've *never* cared about me! All you ever worry about is everyone else—I hate it here! I HATE it!" I slammed the door leading to the basement so hard that it vibrated. Right in my path was Darin, who was just four years old. I felt like he was always breaking things or messing up my stuff, so his presence only fueled my temper. "Get OUT of my way! NOW!" I screamed at him, then shoved him aside with my fists tight.

I stumbled into my room, my chest tight and painful. When I was alone, I couldn't ignore what I already knew was true: *You're going to regret how you're acting right now. Just stop, and be nice. You don't have to be this way. This isn't you! Darin didn't do anything wrong. Don't take your frustration out on him.* I would collapse on my bed, feeling spent and beaten, inhaling and exhaling fast and deliberate. As I tried to fall asleep, the regret of my actions soaked into me, weighing me down. *Who am I? Why did I say such horrible words to Mom and why was I so mean to Darin? I don't like who I am, and I want to change. I must change! I don't know how, though. I have no idea what to do. I need to get rid of this awful feeling.* Mom had been there for me, *always*, and this was how I'd repaid her—by being a horrible daughter and saying things that weren't true. *Please, God,* I prayed that night, *I need Mom to know how sorry I am. I don't even know how to tell her. I can't, I just can't. There is no way I would even be able to get the words out. I hate my temper. I just want to be me, but sometimes when the boys at school are mean, I don't know how to deal with life—and I know that it's not right. I just need Mom to know how sorry I am. I'm hurting so bad, but I'll keep trying. I promise. Please—if you are listening, will you find a way to take my words to her heart? Tell her I love her. More than anything.*

My room was dark that night, with only the filtered light from the streetlamp penetrating through my sheer curtains. I heard footsteps coming into my room, but I didn't understand. Over an hour had passed, and the house should have been quiet with sleep.

Mom? Is that you? Why are you here? Just…pretend you are asleep, I told myself. *She won't know the difference.*

Mom sat on the end of my bed, not speaking a word, just sat there. Then she took her hands and placed them on my feet—I could feel the heat from her palms melt into the tops of my toes through my blanket; I kept still, with my lower lip turned under as I choked back tears. That night I knew God had found her and taken my words to her heart, and I knew, too, that I had found *Him*. It was a miracle. God had delivered my message, and Mom had forgiven me.

After that night I tried the best I could not to lose my temper and to keep calm, but it didn't work. At school I was brave, but at home, I was angry. I felt it was my right to release my frustration physically and verbally on my siblings, just like the bully at school did to me. Someone once told me, "Sticks and stones may break your bones, but words will never hurt you." That person didn't have a pack of bullies. I hated the rage, and the rage fed on the hate. I was stuck. I fought even harder with my five siblings, carving scars in their faces by scratching them with my fingernails until they were sobbing and crying for Mom. And each time, I felt better for a second and then worse for hours.

A month later Mom had a solution. She wanted to take me to a neurologist to see if there was something wrong with my brain. "I made an appointment to get Amy tested," Mom said to Dad as I listened in on their conversation one night. "Her temper is out of control, she is angry all the time at home." I thought there must be something wrong with me, too. *There must be*! After our appointment the Doctor ordered a round of tests that involved keeping me up for a full twenty-four hours so that he could check my brain. Mom used ice cubes on my bare feet to keep me from drifting into sleep as I lay

in Dad's recliner with the door open and no blanket
on, so I wouldn't get comfortable. Morning finally
came, and I was beyond exhausted.

I worried that the Doctor would sit Mom and
Dad down after the test and say, "You know, Amy is
hiding how she feels deep inside this secret layer
eleven. I opened up her brain and saw the confusion
inside. She's a mess in there, and she's coping with
far more than any ten–year-old should ever have to.
It's probably causing her rage and her headaches,
too." I was so grateful that after all the testing, he
couldn't actually find anything wrong with me and
told my parents I was going through a stage. I was
more determined than ever to let go of the demons
that kept dragging me down.

The next day I spent all afternoon cleaning
Justin and Darin's room, complete with putting the
bedding on their bunk beds, and leaving them each a
small note. When Darin needed my attention a few
weeks later I invented a game called "funnies" that
involved a piggy-back ride all around the house. I
loved the feeling of his small hands on my shoulders
and his light laugh on my back. I thought I had
conquered my temper.

Mom and I made our yearly trip to visit Dr.
Broadbent during the last few months of school.
"Amy, have you ever put a puzzle together and
found one piece was missing?" he asked.

"Mmm hum."

"Sometimes that piece is the most important
to make the puzzle a picture," he continued. "When a
baby is born with a cleft lip and palate, it's the same
as having an incomplete puzzle."

"OK."

"But, instead of looking for your missing piece, we need to create a new one out of what we have." I focused on his analogy, enjoying that he was talking to me and not Mom. "The surgeries we have done so far have started to improve the way you look. We've closed your lip, your palate, and have done operations to help you talk better. I know you would like to finish with all of this, wouldn't you?"

"Yes," I nodded.

"Well, the good news is you are growing, and that's exactly what we need to have happen during these years," he paused, then looked at my chart. "Let's see, how old are you, Amy Jo?"

"Ten."

"All right, when you are a teenager, somewhere between thirteen and fifteen, we will do the cranial facial surgery on you. Now, this is a big operation and will take quite a bit of time to prepare for and recover from. Afterward, though, you will see remarkable changes in your face— the waiting will be worth it, and the puzzle piece? Nobody will even know it was missing."

I smiled and peeked to the future. *When I have that surgery, all my problems will go away*, I thought.

Dr. B continued his orthodontia treatment plan for me. He would joke with the other patients my age as they sat in adjacent chairs to me, waiting for his time, "Who d'you think will win the Super Bowl?" and "Yes, I did indeed singe all my eyebrow hair off. I did it pouring out a hot pot of potatoes— don't try that at home, kids. I'm telling you, it is not a fun experience." He would become serious as he wheeled up close to my chair, leaning my head back,

and looking inside my confused mouth. I wanted
him to joke with me like he did the other kids. The
braces cut into my cheeks, leaving deep grooves
where the wires would catch.

Near the end of fifth grade something magical
happened—I became an artist. The kids grouped
around my desk each day to see what I was drawing,
and they would sincerely tell me how good I was.
One boy who sat next to me looked at what I was
drawing once, while the pencil was still in my hand,
and asked, "Did you do that?" I just answered with a
half nod, kept my head down, and kept drawing. For
a kid, my skills were just a hair above average, but
that bit gave my personality a boost, and I started to
find my voice. It was small as a whisper, but still, I
liked the way it sounded. A lady in our
neighborhood, Mrs. Millard, who was a *real* artist,
had seen a note card with my cursive signature on it.
"Amy, I can tell you have talent. Won't you please let
me teach you how to paint?" She wasn't about to
take "no" for an answer, even though she assumed I
was shy. Inside I felt alive! She could see I had
possibilities! I began walking to her house for free
lessons once a month on painting, drawing, and
color, while she filled up my confidence with a new
beginning. I had a talent! I was good at something!
Each time we did an art project in class I became the
center of attention, as if my troubles dissolved away
when I held a pencil or a paint brush.

On March 11 of the following year, I turned
eleven years old. Mom and Dad were gone on a trip
to Washington DC, so I got to stay with Tracy Clead.
The night of my birthday Tracy Clead's whole family
made me feel special. Her mom made my favorite

dessert—strawberry shortcake—we played a game with noodles to see who could spell "Happy Birthday, Amy" the most times, and for the final event we broke a piñata, spraying candy all over the floor. "This is your special birthday, Amy," Tracy Clead said that night after we were done with the festivities. "You turned eleven on the eleventh. I'm glad you spent this birthday with us." Eleven was my secret number, and I had a feeling Tracy Clead knew all about how important it was to me.

Before long I joined Jeannie at junior high, the dreaded in-between school. Jeannie had already been there for two years, and during that space of time we had somehow grown apart. She seemed so distant. In the evenings she would sit in her room on her bed and read romance books with pictures on the cover of men with big muscles and women with long flowing hair. "You have to be a teenager to read these books," she would coolly say to me when I asked what she was reading. She wouldn't even glance up from the book, only stopping to dog-ear her last page, turn off her lamp, and go to bed. I felt helpless without her. *Why is she shutting me out? I need her to tell me about romance! I need her more than ever!*

I was determined to get Jeannie to be my friend again. At school I followed her into the bathroom that was rumored to be just for the elite ninth graders. "What are *you* doing in here?" Jeannie asked. "You're only in seventh grade. You can't use *this* bathroom." I was sure she was kidding. Besides, I was already halfway into stall number three and couldn't hold it. I could hear Jeannie at the sinks, laughing with a few of her friends while she put on a fresh coat of pearl pink lipstick. When I exited the stall, she practically yelled, "YOU FORGOT TO FLUSH!" I didn't. I mean, I never *ever* forgot to flush. Ever. I tried to tell her she was wrong, but she just walked out the door, with three other ninth-grade girls in tow. I suddenly realized she'd just wanted to embarrass me. From then on I used the bathroom for seventh and eighth graders, but at home I kept trying to share my life with her.

"Jeannie, did you ever have Mr. Foy for Math?" I asked one night while Mom was cleaning up the dishes and Dad was reading the paper. It was an uncommonly quiet night.

"Hmm?"

"You know, Mr. Foy? He has so many chins I could learn my multiplication on them!"

"Mmm hmm."

That was funny! I thought with frustration. *Laugh!* I decided to try again. "I met a new girl in math. Her name is Stacie. She already has a boyfriend. She buys him treats and stuff. So now I've met two new friends this year because on the first day of school, a girl named Heather stopped me in the hall and asked me if I wanted to be her friend. We have three classes together, and we've been friends all year now."

"Huhmmm."

"But math is so hard for me. Was it hard for you?"

"What?"

"I was just asking you if you had a hard time in Mr. Foy's math class when you were in seventh grade. Did you?"

"I don't really remember."

"Anyway, today someone stole my black math folder right out of my locker! I heard them laughing when I went to open my locker, but I didn't know what was really going on. Tracy Clead took me with her to lunch and told me afterward that I could keep all my stuff in her locker from now on, but I don't know her combination. That's top secret."

"Mmm hmm."

"Tracy Clead and I worked in the lunchroom together today, too, did you know that I am working there? And then Mom pays me since my lunch is free."

"Yeah."

"So, anyway, we worked together today and I got to wear a hair net and gloves and help the lunch ladies bring trays of food out to be served. I like serving lunch because sometimes we get extra rolls."

"What?"

"Umm, I just said that today Tracy Clead and I served lunch together, like we always do."

"Oh. Mmm hmm."

"I'm thinking I might run for office in eighth grade. I'm starting to make a lot of friends, and I think I could win! But I'm only going to run for the office that the girls vote for, Girls Association. I counted the other day, and I have fourteen friends."

"Cool."

Is she listening to me? "I think I'm going to start making posters and stuff."

"Huh?"

Nope. I guess not.

Suddenly the evening wasn't so quiet. "Jeannie!" Dad hollered, smacking the newspaper against the kitchen table and ripping it right down the center. "You'd better stop what you're doing and listen to your sister!"

"What? I *am* listening! I'm just busy!"

"She's trying to talk to you, and you're ignoring her!"

That night I fought back the thought that Jeannie might not ever want to be my friend again. I wanted to tell her that about the mean kids at lunchtime, the ones who threw food at the back of my head, and when I would turn around they would laugh at me. I wanted to tell her that, despite it all, I was being brave just like she had taught me and making more friends than I thought I ever could. I'd hoped that she really had been busy, like she'd said she was all the other times I'd tried to talk to her, and that she would soon come back to me the way she used to be—as my big sister.

"Here, I made this for you," Jeannie said to me days after our one-way conversation. She handed me a homemade paper mache jewelry box with a big *A* on top made of mounds of the newspaper batter. "I'm really sorry I haven't been a good sister lately."

"Wow. Thanks, Jeannie! I love it!" The box was just big enough to hold a few necklaces or rings.

"It's still wet, 'cause I just made it, but when it's all dry you can paint it if you want." She had worked hard on it, and I knew that with the gift came her full apology. "Also, I think you should run for office," she continued. "You would do a really good job."

Each day I checked to see if the box was dry, keeping it safe on top of a piece of wax paper in my room. I made sure to tell Jeannie often how much I liked it. She had spent time making something special just for me, and just the thought of it made me realize that she *did* care. But one day her actions woke my anger. My temper got the best of me again, and I snapped. I took the box, still slightly wet in the middle, and went right up to her face, breaking it in two so she could see how much I wanted to hurt her. It worked. She ran right to her room and started to cry, and I couldn't believe that I had caused tears without even thumping her. After I realized the consequence of what I'd done, I tried my best to fix the box, but the glue fought to stick. I apologized to Jeannie over and over again the next day, but nothing I said could take away how I had made her feel. She hurt for a long time over that, and I did, too. I was tired of letting my temper win—my ugly, no good, punching, kicking, screaming, stinking, poisonous temper. I made a pact with myself that night to not just *try* but to *do*. I kept the box, broken pieces and all, high up on my display shelf where it became a constant reminder of my actions. When the box dried, the words on the newspaper became legible, and I thought the words were better to look at than any paint I could apply. So I kept it just the way Jeannie made it.

I lost the election later that year by three tiny votes, and it was Jeannie who went in and petitioned with all her might to the Vice Principal for a re-count. Pleading with him to be fair and let the students' votes count who were participating in the girls P.E.

classes and had been missed. He just shook his head and said, "Sorry, we have already declared the winner." Jeannie came by my locker that day after her attempt to get a re-count and told me with certainty, "Amy, even if it is just you and I that know that truth, I know you are the real winner."

CHAPTER FOURTEEN

Insecurity often comes on the heels of victory when we least expect it, and then stays longer than we anticipate.

"I have done it!" I shouted to anyone who would listen. "I have really done it this time!" There, standing in the kitchen at age fifteen, I had finally made the perfect chocolate chip cookie. Mom didn't bake cookies or dessert in any fashion, so I had to learn the hard way through trial and error. She did, however, buy the ingredients for me, including white sugar.

The secret for the perfect cookie eluded me for years, but when I finally got it right, it seemed so *simple*. For melty chips, I needed to use semi-sweet chocolate chips *and* milk chocolate chips. And for a fuller cookie, I added more flour until the cookie had the right texture for baking. And butter! Butter! All these years I'd been using margarine. What was margarine, anyway? And nobody told me that the myth of room temperature butter was just that—a *myth*. Cold butter was so much better for a fluffy cookie.

Satisfied with myself, I confidently waited for the rave reviews to start pouring in from my brothers. I grabbed a plate and loaded up a stack of five cookies—each nearly exactly the same size, thanks to my genius idea of using a teaspoon scoop instead of a spoon to get the batter onto the sheet. I poured a tall glass of milk and then sat down to enjoy my dessert. But, before I could, Katie was at the back door. *Ah, good, someone who will really appreciate my baking skills.* Not this time, though. Katie was busy scheming, and she looked right past the cookies.

"So I have an idea for your first official date." Katie announced.

"Whoa, Kates, that's months away."

"I've thought it all through, and I am going to ask Nate to take you on your first date."

"Nate? As in the family friend of yours that lives an hour away?"

"Yes, and you can't say no 'cause I'm already planning it. We're going on a double date!" She went on to give me the details: "We'll drive down there and meet our dates at Nate's house, then figure out what to do."

"Does he even want to go with me?"

"Of course, yeah!"

"Wait, I thought *you* liked him! Don't you?"

"He is more like a brother or a cousin to me," she clarified. "Anyway, he has a friend that he is setting me up with. Amy Jo, we are going to have the best time. Don't be nervous!"

It sounded fun—well, kind of. I was glad it was a long time away. I needed to prepare. *Will he pay? Will he get my door? Will he think I look pretty despite…everything?*

Before heading back home, Katie grabbed an outfit from my closet. The set-up we had for trading clothes was a *much* better deal for me than it was for her. Before she left, I loaded a zip lock bag full of cookies for Katie to share with her family. It felt good to—for once—return the favor of sugar and clothes both in the same night.

Katie and I had a secret code for when she walked back to her house. I waited for her on the back deck, and when she made it safely to her own deck, she would flash her porch light. In return, I flashed mine. On, off, on, off. Oh sure, we could've just shouted, "I'm OK!", but having a secret code was way cooler. She clicked the light back and forth, and I flashed mine back before I ducked back inside the house, leaving the cool air outside.

I snagged a few more cookies and headed down to my room. Three strides away from my door the red phone, tucked away on the wall of the laundry room, rang. *Probably just Katie,* I thought.

"Hello?" I answered, expecting to hear her friendly voice on the other end.

"Is Amy there?" a guy said. His was a voice I didn't recognize.

"Uh, yeah, this is Amy," I said as my heart started to beat a little faster, the mysterious reveal just seconds away. *Who could it be? Wow! I like boys calling me!*

"Oh, good. I just wanted to call and tell you that you are SO UGLY!" Click.

Umm. What just happened? Was that a prank call? Who would do that to me? My adrenaline turned from hope to humiliation.

Not saying anything to anyone, I went to bed. The dark gray feeling lay like a cloud above my head. My thoughts faded into a world that I kept intimately close, so very close. My old nemesis, teasing, was back. Tears fell fast and silent down my cheeks. Only the cat was aware of my pain. She found me, like she always did, and hopped up on the bed in one graceful bound. There she lay, next to me, until I fell asleep.

The next night the call came again.

The same words.

The same voice.

I thought about telling someone, but Mom was already right in the middle of a family phone emergency. One of the kids had tripled the phone bill, which had just arrived in the mail, by calling a suspicious number multiple times. Of course nobody would admit to the crime, but someone had to have called that number. Mom finally decided that if nobody would come forward saying they in fact made the pay-per-minute phone calls, she would call the number herself. She tapped her foot while she waited for the caller on the other end to pick up, all the while staring down three guilty kids.

"Hello, this is the Santa hotline! Wait on the line for the next available elf for you to tell your Christmas wish list to!" Mom hung up the phone then lined up the three youngest kids for her eye interrogation. It didn't take long before Toots, Justin, and Darin each admitted to having called the hotline, hoping to increase their loot odds from Santa. So no, I couldn't exactly unload my newly resurfaced insecurities on Mom. She had her work cut out for her as she tried to figure out how to get the phone bill paid with the limited household budget.

I lay on my bed once again, falling back, letting my legs hang off the end, and felt my face

burn red with the crush of humiliation. I looked at
the ceiling, covered in tiles with thousands of holes,
remembering the night I thought I could count each
one. I tried to make myself forget about the prank
calls. Life felt so unfair. *Why is this happening to me? I
don't even know who this person is. Why would he want
to hurt me?* I closed my eyes, thinking if only I had
been able to have the plastic surgery on my face
during the summer as originally planned, I wouldn't
be feeling this way, and the teasing would've ended.
Things would be *perfect*. I'd had such high hopes for
starting my sophomore year with a new face—put
together by a brilliant plastic surgeon with intelligent
fingers. I had known, ever since kindergarten, that
this surgery was on the horizon.

The trouble had started when Mom and I
went to Salt Lake for the surgical consultation
appointment while I was still in ninth grade, but the
day was bittersweet. I was thrown head first into a
situation I didn't know was coming. When we
entered the examination room, there was a new
doctor there with Dr. Broadbent.

"I want to introduce you to Dr. David S.
Thomas," he said, looking right at Mom once he had
greeted us in his typical kind fashion. "I have
decided to hang up my surgical cap and retire. Dr.
Thomas is taking over Amy's case, and I have full
confidence that he will give her all the care she
needs. He is an able, skilled, and highly trained
doctor in the field of reconstructive surgery."

Dr. Thomas moved forward and shook
Mom's hand, then looked at me and smiled.

Wait? Who? What did you just say? You're leaving me? No! Why now? Don't you know that this is the biggest yet of all the surgeries? Why can't you just hold off on retirement just a few more years? Please stay! For me!

There, sitting on the examination table, which was covered in thin fragile tissue, I found myself so confused. Part of it was just being scared of the surgery, the big one, and part of it was I felt betrayed by Dr. Broadbent. He looked on, three steps away from Dr. Thomas, with his arms folded, but his eyes were focused on me.

For years he had been the one to operate on my face, time after time, finding a way to improve my senses, my image, my breathing, and my life. Yet there was Dr. Thomas, standing so tall next to him. He was handsome and had the same kind light that had warmed me up to Dr. Broadbent all those years ago. I was so confused. I didn't want to have to think about a new Doctor. It was hard enough thinking about the surgery.

Dr. Thomas started right in, detailing his plan for my surgery: "Because Amy was born with a bilateral cleft she doesn't have enough bone to support her nose or her top lip, and if you look at her cheeks, they are quite flat, which indicates to us that she will need additional bone in those areas. We will graft bone from her hip or head and place it into those areas that need more support." Then looking at me, he said, "If we take the bone from your skull, we'll have to shave part of your hair off your head, so that is something you will want to consider." I tried to imagine myself with a giant bald spot next to my ear, then dismissed the thought as quickly as it arrived. *This is really happening.*

"For some children born with severe clefts, like Amy, the upper jaw doesn't develop properly. What ends up happening is the lower jaw grows forward and the bite becomes grossly uneven," Dr. Thomas said, while looking at my profile and pointing to the jutting out of my lower jaw. "During the cranial facial surgery we will complete the correction by cutting the upper jaw and moving it forward, then securing the jaw and bone graft with plates and screws."

Dr. Broadbent listened and nodded his head, while Dr. Thomas continued with the surgical plan, "We will also be doing a sliding genioplasty, which essentially means we will cut out the horse shoe shape under her chin and slide it forward. All of the incisions will be under her skin. For the genioplasty we will go under her lower jaw"

"What will her recovery be like?" Mom asked, her brow pushed into a deep furrow.

"Long, and unfortunately, quite unpleasant. We will keep her in the hospital for five to seven days, and her jaw will be wired shut for six weeks."

I gulped hard. My eyes started to gloss over and my chin fought to hold back the welling emotion. *Six weeks?* I nervously spoke when I got the chance, my voice cracking as I tried to get my question out, "I don't know where I want you to take the bone from for the graft; when do I have to decide?"

"You can tell me when we take you into the operating room. No need to make the decision now," Dr. Thomas reassured me, adding a small smile.

When he was done talking, Dr. Broadbent took three strides toward me and then bent down so he was at eye level. Just like when I was small. He put his hand on my knee and paused before speaking.

"I know you are scared, and this is all very hard for you to go through. But I want you to know that I trust Dr. Thomas. He will take good care of you. Do you know he is one of the best surgeons for cranial facial surgery?"

I shook my head no, taking in a quick breath that sounded more like I was ready to cry.

"Amy Jo, you are such a beautiful girl. You always have been. You have been a special patient to me for many years." I tried to make eye contact with him, to draw in his last bits of help and comfort, but the realization was too intense. I bent over and covered the hot tears streaming from my eyes, trying to hide from the feeling that I kept protected. There was so much pressure to forge blindly ahead, and he was right, I was scared. I couldn't understand why he would abandon me at my greatest hour of need. And the surgery was far more complicated than I had imagined. *Screws? Metal plates? Bone graft? A shaved head?*

"Let's go for ice cream," Mom said, surprising me as we left the appointment. "I think there is a place here I used to go to when I was a kid." Within a few minutes she had spotted the old fashioned shop with the '50s décor, facing north toward home. She talked and I listened while we ate our two flavors of ice cream, and I settled into thinking again about the future. Soon we were laughing—mostly about how handsome we both thought Dr. Thomas was. But deep down I questioned if I would ever really be able to trust him to work on my face. For many days after that first meeting I thought about what Dr. Broadbent told me, and finally, I was ready for the surgery—the one that I had waited over a decade for. My mind raced in a million different places each night as I lay in bed thinking, and thinking some more about how I would look. I could hardly stand the wait! It seemed summertime wouldn't ever break through spring.

Then, just as things seemed to line up, the deck of cards fell. Mom and Dad pulled me from the chaos of the kitchen and into the quiet living room one night just a few weeks after our meeting with Dr. Thomas to tell me the devastating news.

"Amy, we need to wait a year on your surgery," was all I heard.

"What? What...what do you mean *wait*?"

Mom and Dad exchanged a connected glance.

"Dr. Thomas called today, and he feels it would be best to wait one more year."

"Another whole year? No! No!"

My airway tightened in shock and confusion as I tried with all my might to stop the tears from coming. The fierce emotion was soon beyond my control. I begged Mom. I pleaded with Dad, nearly screaming, "Please, *please* let me have the surgery! I need it. I need it! I can't wait another year! I don't want to start high school this way! Please!" I hardly recognized myself as I increased the intensity of my appeal, "You don't understand! I am ready! Please! Mom? Dad!? I am ready!"

"Amy, oh, Amy… I am sorry," Mom replied, Dad standing next to her.

"Dr. Thomas really is insistent that we wait another year," Dad said.

"Tell him no! I need the surgery now! You don't understand. I can't keep going like this! Please!"

"There's nothing we can do, Amy, you're not done growing. Your bones have to be ready in order for the surgery to be a success."

My voice caved in, nearly inaudible. "I don't care if I am done growing, Mom, please. I have never complained about *this*. I have tried so hard to be good. Please won't you fight for me and get me the surgery? I need it so bad." The tears fell faster than I could wipe them away. I was desperate to have her side with me, cave in, and understand what I needed.

"I know this is tough on you, Amy. But we need to do what the doctor is recommending. Dad and I have talked about it and we feel strongly about waiting."

"You already talked about it!? Without me? So it has already been decided?" My temper spiked and my hands started to sweat. Mom nodded.

I buried my head and covered my ears to hide the tears and muffle the noise of their response. That day I felt let down and all alone. My parents, of all people, should have been the ones pushing for the surgery. I couldn't understand—not any of the thousand times I tried to—why they didn't fight harder for me. *For me* who had taken on the tormenting of the bully. *For me* who endured hours of endless speech therapy. *For me* who wondered if I would ever go on a date. *For me* who was counting on the surgery to change my life. *For me* who held all the hurt inside. For me.

For a split second I told myself I never wanted this trial, and I never asked for it, but just saying those words in my mind hurt me in a thousand other ways. When I finally calmed down the next day and could think clearly, I asked Mom, "Tell me again why I have to wait?"

"Well, like Dr. Thomas said when we went to visit him, this surgery is dependent on your facial bones being fully developed. He has valid concerns that you are still growing," she repeated much like the Doctor must have told her. *Does he even know what he's talking about?* I wondered. *I'll bet Dr. Broadbent wouldn't have made me wait if he was still my surgeon.*

"If we do the surgery now," Mom explained, "we will likely have to redo it, and we don't want to do that to you."

My heart was broken, and I was unsure if I could last another entire year of stares and criticism. But there was no changing the answer. I wasn't finished growing. Neither Mom nor Dad nor Dr. Thomas could change that.

A few days after Mom delivered the bad news about the delay in the surgery, she pulled me aside once again. She knew what a tough thing it was for me to not be able to go through with the surgery like we had planned. Kneeling down next to me, she looked me in the eyes. "I got you something— something very special," she said, handing me a white, square box. In the background the other kids were running around the kitchen, making noise and causing commotion, just begging for her attention. She stayed focused and watched me open the box that was sealed with a fancy sticker, clearly from a jeweler.

"What's this for? Did you get one for Jeannie and Toots, too?"

"No. No, this is just for you. Nobody else in the family is getting one."

When I opened the top of the box and folded back the tissue paper, I saw the most beautiful silver butterfly jewelry box, big enough that I would need both hands to hold it. My eyes filled with tears, but this time, I didn't let them fall. I bravely held them there, balanced as carefully as I could, while I took the butterfly out of the box and examined all the fine detail quietly to myself. I couldn't even muster a "thank you" I was so touched, but Mom knew that I loved it. I thought, *All my life I will keep this, and all my life I will be reminded of the beauty of the butterfly and this exact moment when I met the crossroads of utter disappointment and soaring love.* I took the jewelry box right down to my room where I carefully read all about how to take care of it so the silver wouldn't tarnish. I took a clean, white cloth and dusted the opaque glass case and the silver butterfly, just like the brochure instructed. My room sparkled with the new addition. For well over an hour I stayed in my room and marveled at the gift, thinking all the while, *Mom does* know *me. She does know my struggles, and she does indeed love me so very much.*

The prank call that had happened just minutes earlier became a distant memory as I thought through the events that happened seven months ago. I knew the surgery would come, and the teasing would have to eventually end, but for now I needed to remember to enjoy all the countless things about my life that were unique to just me. And the great things were so easy to find when I stopped thinking and started looking.

I quietly stopped, until I found my inner light. Generations of women in my family had gone before me, and like angels, they watched over me from another dimension. Tonight, I felt them cheering me on, telling me it would get better. *You can do this, Amy. You can do this.*

CHAPTER FIFTEEN

A camera captures time and sentiment and never lies. The best photos are ones that show the true spirit of life in full color and don't hide any flaws.

"What time is your date coming?" I asked Jeannie, who was putting on her mascara in a long sweeping motion just inches from the mirror.

"In about a half hour," she answered. She held her lips steady in the shape of an oval as she spoke. "Can you take my picture before I go?"

"Sure. I'll go get my camera. Meet you upstairs."

"Let's go take some pictures out front by Dad's green truck," I suggested, while leaning down from the top landing as she made her way up the stairs to the kitchen.

"Good idea. Make sure you get the light behind me on my hair."

How would it be to just smile, and not have a care in the world? I wondered as I watched her. *I really should be jealous of her, but I'm not.*

The photo shoots with Jeannie were so different from how I felt when class pictures rolled around; I'd always made sure to do a closed-mouth smile, pursing my lips together, which would inevitably make my cheeks look puffy. For fourth grade school pictures, I worked so hard to get the best smile out of my face that I forgot to look straight into the camera, and both my eyeballs wandered to the top of my head. When they were developed and delivered to our classroom, the teacher turned mine upside down as he laid the packet on my desk, not making a comment as he walked by. I knew the pictures must have been horrible, so I waited until the packet was hidden away in my backpack before I peeked inside. My instinct was right, I looked like I'd been hit over the head with the ugly crowbar. I didn't give those pictures out to anyone, not even Gram.

But with Jeannie as the photographer taking pictures of me in our yard before her date came, I relaxed, and we had so much fun. I even smiled my natural smile. She was right there, coaching me, telling me how amazing I looked. "You should take one with your monkey. You'll always want to remember you had a stuffed animal that you loved."

"Oh! Good idea! What pose should I do?"

"Let's go inside and you can sit on a chair with him," she said as we walked back to the house together. "That's it, now put your knee up and rest your elbow on it. Oh, cute!" I pulled a smile that felt a little cheesy, but I didn't care, and Jeannie snapped the photograph.

By the time Jeannie left on her date, we had taken nearly half a roll of film. I could hardly wait until we finished it off and could take it in to get developed.

I sauntered into Mom's room and stood in front of her large mirror, practicing my smile. There in the reflection, over my shoulder, was her cedar chest. It seemed to be a permanent fixture in the corner of the master bedroom with blankets heaped on top in a neglected sort of fashion. I hadn't paid much attention to the chest in the past, but boredom drove my curiosity, and I wondered about the contents inside.

I propped open the lid of the chest and leaned my head inside, breathing in the superior, rich scent. Mom's father had made the cedar chest for her as a gift, taking great care in creating a patchwork of warm woods that came together in a star design. My hands passed over worn albums with rigid spines, an antique picture viewer, bits of old wedding dress fabric, and a brand new baby book—but then my eyes focused on a box of slides near the bottom corner. Dad had taken pictures for years with his Nikon camera, developing them to slides instead of photos and keeping them in the cabinet above the fridge. To see a box of slides in Mom's cedar chest seemed strangely out of place. I was too curious not to look inside. I pressed my thumb on the plastic edge and popped the box open, then shook it just right so all of the slides lined up to one side. I carefully took the first slide between my thumb and pointer finger, making sure not to touch the film, and held it up to the light. In the small frame I saw a disfigured newborn baby. I pressed my eyebrows together as I pulled the slide closer, spinning my legs around to capture the light coming in from outside. *Is that...me?* I took the slide down from the light and looked at the date stamped along the edge: March 1973. *It is me. These...these must have been taken the day I was born. Before the surgeries.* I shuffled through the slides, one after another, frantic to gain knowledge of those early moments. I looked at them closely, deeply, as if I could transform myself back to the beginning. To the first cry of life, my lungs filling, my heart pounding, my arms reaching. The slides clearly showed my upper lip divided into three unequal parts, all loosely hanging in a jagged zigzag just below my nose. Mom hadn't ever told me how bad it was. There was a strange dark hole where there should have been a sweet pink baby mouth below a tiny button nose. I put my fingers to my face and traced the scars left by two giant bilateral canyons which sliced through my lips, gum line, and the roof of my mouth through the back of my throat. I looked closer at the slide. The deep openings started from my disfigured wide nose, pushing it up until it was hardly a nose at all.

I sifted through more slides, eager to connect with the baby who didn't seem to notice anything was wrong. One showed me in an incubator with a small sensor over my heart and tubes taped to the inside of my nose. Others were close-ups of my face. The slides spun a response in me that even I couldn't have predicted. I loved them. They were *proof* I had come from something hard, and I had survived! I was born without fear, bearing bravery with each breath, destined for great things. Great things that would come from within me and *not* from the perfection I didn't have. My heart started to grow with fantastic reaction, my mind piecing together the miracle of my birth and the "me" that might not have been if life had been easier. I had found a treasure in these slides of my birth. As I continued looking through them there was one slide that found *me*. I stood, pushed it up against the light in the window, and there I saw Mom holding me close, looking down at my sweet, naïve face and loving me. Chills caught my skin and raced down the length of my body. I always knew that Mom loved me just the way I was, but seeing it—*really* seeing it—I felt the truth rush through me, waking me up. Mom had often told me about the day of my birth in her sweet recollection: "The first thing I did when the doctor handed you to me was run my fingers through your dark tuft of hair and kiss your soft cheeks. You snuggled into my arms and lay next to me, warm and content, and fell asleep." She had told me, too, a message of pure love that was imprinted deep within me: "From the minute you were born, I knew you were something special, and not for one second did I feel sorry for you or me. You were a blessing." I must have recognized her voice and her peaceful, calming tone that first day of life. Tiny me, all wrapped up in her undiscerning arms. I am sure I looked a mess, an impossible, un-fixable mess. Yet, somehow, there she was, loving me down into my soul and needing me every bit as much as I needed her.

I took the slide of her and me and two others from the stack of favorites and put them in my hand, closing my fingers softly around the edges. With my free hand I put the items back into Mom's cedar chest just like I had found, hoping that she wouldn't notice I had been snooping. I passed her in the kitchen cooking supper but didn't stop to say one word. I walked downstairs to my room and hid the slides in secret with my finest treasures.

When Jeannie and I finally took the film of our impromptu photo sessions in to get it developed a few weeks later, the pictures of her were just like I thought they would be. There wasn't one bad shot, except that my shaky hands had made some of them a bit blurry. When I sorted through to the pictures of me, I stopped, surprised. I looked so *pretty*, radiant, and vibrant—just like Jeannie had told me. My lips were fat and crooked, my nose flat to one side, my smile a mess. But I saw something in those photos I realized I'd known was there all along—the beauty was coming from the inside.

CHAPTER SIXTEEN

From their lofty vantage point above the world, the mountains quietly see it all. The poetry of ridges, peaks, and valleys call to those who live below.

"Do you want to go night skiing this weekend?" Katie asked, shaking the light snow off her winter coat before hanging it in her locker.

"Night, as in its *dark* outside? How will we see where we're going?"

"They light up the slopes with these gigantic lights, and it's soooo fun. I like it better than daytime skiing because you don't get the sun in your eyes. We could ask Wendy and Christy if they want to go, too."

"You know, I want to learn to ski better, but what should I wear? I don't have anything for skiing."

"You can borrow some of my stuff if you want."

"I'll need to, 'cause I don't have any ski pants."

"Just come over tonight, I will find you something," she said, always willing to help me fill the gap between what I *had* and what I *needed*.

The following weekend the girls of the Rebels went over the hill to the ski resort up in the valley with Katie behind the wheel of her family van. She wore her tight, hot-pink, shiny lycra pants that were not meant for skiing at all but looked *incredible*, like how Wonder Woman without the brass bra might look if *she* were a night skier. Katie's family went skiing all the time, and when they did she would keep her pass and hang it on the zipper of her jacket as a souvenir. She let me borrow a pair of ski pants from her house, just like she promised she would, which I paired awkwardly with my regular winter coat. The pants hung on my skinny legs like a grocery bag. I wished I had lycra pants, too. And a jacket that jingled with ski passes.

I was *below* a beginner level, and Katie, Christy, and Wendy were well above my novice status—way above. Somehow the ski resort was the one place that I feared snow and loved it all at the same time. The girls each encouraged me to improve, with Katie saying, "You're getting so good at this you're making me sick!" I knew she was exaggerating. I hadn't once seen her heaved over because I was blowing her mind with my skills, but her pure enthusiasm for me to stretch outside my comfort zone was the mark of a true best friend.

"Guys, remember, I really can't ski very good," I re-announced as we exited the ski rental shop.

"I'll ski the bunny hill with you for a while, if you want," Christy offered, cheerful and sincere. "It's a good run to learn on. Usually there are a lot of kids over there, but since it's night skiing there won't be too many."

"Wendy and I are hitting the face. Meet us back at the lodge in a few hours?" asked Katie, snapping into her polished ski boots.

Christy patiently skied with me over to the bunny lift, stopping and starting at my pace.

"Look at the snowfall. It's coming down so fast," she said to me as we soared high above the runs on the lift. I spoke only when necessary while we were riding the lift so I could properly exit and stay on top of my skis. I'd had a few rough exits on our previous trip to the mountain, including one in which the lift seat had hit me square on the behind and sent me skidding down the slope backwards. My mortification was complete when I heard the cute guy running the lift laugh while saying, "Skier down, please stop the lift," on his radio. Nobody had warned me that you actually had to start moving the minute your skis touched snow. So I concentrated instead of talked. Once successfully off the lift and with my skis in line, I cautiously maneuvered the trail, making sure to avoid all danger. Christy met me at the bottom of the hill, making it down in a flash of a minute, and together we would ride the lift again and repeat the fun.

"I think I am getting the hang of it, Christy," I said after over an hour of cautious skiing.

"I saw you coming down that last run, you were really going fast! Keep it up and you will be skiing the face in no time."

"Oh, I don't know about that, the face of the mountain goes straight down."

"All right, Amy, show me what you got," Christy hollered as she glided off the lift. "This is going to be your best run! See you at the bottom!"

I'm actually getting the hang of this, I thought to myself. *I wonder if I'll be able to go down the face one day, like the other girls. Gosh, I'm going so fast now! Wow! The snow is taking me to a crazy speed! Look at me, skiers of the mountain! Look at me! I am so cool right now!* Swoop, swoop, swoop, went my skis, cutting into the snow. My mind was wandering. I felt free! So alive! Swoosh, swoosh, swoosh. To the left, to the right. *Nothing can stop me now! I am keeping up with the fastest small children! Look at me go!*

Then, just as I was about to hit ultimate euphoria—CRASH! Screeek! Cliinnkkkgkk! I hadn't even *seen* Christy, who had been somewhere to my side, until we'd met head on, tangling in each other skis. One of mine popped off and took an independent ride down the mountain.

"Are you OK?" I asked her, horrified that we had crashed on the *bunny hill* just below the main lift.

"I don't know…I don't know…"

"Oh no, shoot, so you are *not* OK?…Umm…do you want me to help?" I was pleading inwardly that she'd refuse. *Please say no. Please just jump up and say you're fine! Oh, I am so embarrassed. I don't want anyone to see us. Please get up.*

"I think I'm hurt," she finally said between groans. "Can you go find someone to get me down the mountain?"

"Um, yeah, sure. Where do I go?"

"Go to the lodge. Hurry, I think I hurt my ankle."

Luckily for me, I had only gone a few steps in my clunky boots before the ski patrol arrived, swooping in on their red and black sled. "So do you mind telling us what happened here?" asked the officer. I found his handsome good looks intimidating, and that didn't help as I tried to think of an intelligent, acceptable response.

"Well, I just . . . actually *we* just...crashed. I didn't see her."

"Is this your first time skiing?" he asked Christy, while bending down to assess her injury.

"No."

"I'm the one that probably crashed into her," I said. "I'm still a new skier, and I was making a turn, and then there she was, and neither of us had time to move."

"Mmm hmm," he responded, while assessing my ski outfit with one glance. "Well, you need to watch where you're going. Have you heard of the term 'blind spot'?"

"Um, no."

"Hey, look! Someone crashed on the *bunny* hill!" a guy called from the lift above us, laughing with his friends who shared his chair.

I held up my lone ski. "Yup, that would be us!"

"Your friend is hurt, likely a sprained ankle. We're going to need to take her back down to the lodge on the snowmobile."

"Oh, OK. Christy, I am so sorry. This is all my fault."

"No, it's fine. I'll see you down at the lodge. Just tell the girls what happened. We should head home."

My nose ached a bit from the crash but not as bad as my conscience. *How could I be so selfish?* I asked myself. *Why was I so worried about what other people thought and not about my friend who was hurt?* Christy hadn't once judged me or treated me different because of how I looked. She was consistent. She didn't flinch when I needed her to ski with me on the bunny hill all night, but the minute the embarrassment was turned and it was *her* who needed the help, I shriveled up. I stood next to the fresh snow mobile tracks without Christy, watching the machine carrying her down the mountain as it disappeared into a gray dot. It was an eerie feeling walking down the mountain in the dark, trying to find a solid path to follow so that I didn't fall into deep snow. *I am never going to do that again,* I thought. My cheeks burned from the wind and from the shame. I wished I could take back my actions.

Day after day winter continued to be fierce with a storm bringing in hurricane-force winds that knocked out power all over the county. As I lay in my bed the night of the windstorm, I could hear the two maple trees moaning in agony as their branches worked to hang on to their rooted trunks. Toots was scared that the trees would blow over and crash into our bedroom, and truthfully, so was I.

The next day we learned that the bitter cold winds had mangled several power poles, uprooted trees, damaged roofs, blown over brick walls, and was to blame for numerous car accidents. The snow was piled into tall waves like something out of a dream, pushed there from the massive power of the wind.

"I am the king of this mountain!" Todd hollered to me from atop a snow drift as we both assessed the situation. I followed him across 150 East

166

over to Tracy Clead's house, watching my footprints make only a light imprint on the firm snow before the evidence of our presence blew away. Against her fence, which lay parallel to a large field, the snow was shaped in an enormous upsurge. Tracy Clead and her siblings soon joined us, and together we clawed to the top of the snow mountain. The rest of the neighborhood was a quiet hush with only the sound of our voices and the heavy wind pushing through, breaking the silence.

Christmas Day was altogether different—calm and peaceful with several inches of pure, new snow blanketing the ground. All day long the flakes came down, not stopping until every last branch was draped in white. Gram gave each of us granddaughters a pearl ring, and it was undoubtedly my favorite Christmas gift. When she gave me mine I couldn't get over how smooth and round the pearl was, and all from a single grain of sand. My Auntie Julie, a refined and classy woman, made the comment that her favorite pearls were deformed. My heart sank; I hated that word. Just the sound of it conjured up insecurity that immediately made me think of my own deformity stamped upon my face for all to see. I asked her what she possibly could've meant, and she answered: "Most oysters carry pearls that have formed just how they are supposed to. But they all look so alike. A deformed one tries to grow the right way, but can't. I think it has the most beautiful shade and shape. They're harder to find, and in my opinion, the most beautiful. Auntie Debbie has one. You should ask her if you can see it." A *deformed* pearl. I couldn't imagine why anyone would want what she described.

When we drove home late that afternoon, I could see Old Ben looking down at me, streaked in grey and white, with shadows hidden in the deep canyons. I spun my new ring around on my finger and thought that surely one day I would climb to the top ridge of the mountain so that I could look down at the valley below with the perspective of the angels.

CHAPTER SEVENTEEN

Talking about the weather only proves interesting if the weather itself is interesting to talk about.

"I just *hate* when it's plain old cold, cold, *cold,*" Wendy said on our way home from school. "I want it to snow or do *something, anything!*"

"Me too. I wish a blizzard would hit," I said, thinking that the forecast had said something about a storm approaching. I rubbed my hands together fiercely and wiggled my toes to keep them from freezing. I held my hands in a fist to keep my pearl ring from sliding off my cold, shrunken fingers. The outfit I wore to school wasn't exactly winter wear, including my too-small shoes that left the tops of my feet bare to the sharp cold. But I was sticking to my goal of not wearing the same outfit twice in a month, so sacrifices had to be made. Plus, spring was supposed to be next month, and I was optimistic. February was *always* cold and boring. The only good thing about the month was Valentine's Day candy. As soon as Wendy left me to walk down her street, I ran the rest of the way home as fast as I could. With each step my shoes cracked from the cold and the bottoms of my feet felt the rough pressure of the gravel pound through the thin barrier. *Why does it feel like this distance home is so much farther in the cold?* As I broke through the front door, I knew Mom would be there, maybe making a fire in the wood-burning stove or starting dinner.

"But, Mom, I don't have a showcase talent. That's the problem," I heard Jeanie say as I hung up my backpack and kicked off my shoes to stand barefoot on the brick platform next to the wood-burning stove. I stood dangerously close to the stove, absorbing the heat into my bones, moving only when the burn was too intense to stand it any longer.

"Now, tell me again, what's this pageant all about?"

"My school counselor thought it would be a good way for me to earn scholarship money for college. It sounds like fun! I mean, I am not actually taking it very seriously."

"Oh, Jeannie, pageants aren't the typical stage productions I am comfortable being involved in."

"What do you mean, Mom? You are great at being a drama coach," she said, pulling her hair up and into a ponytail. "Just think of all the plays you have directed. It's basically the same type of thing. Plus, it will be something fun for us to do together."

"Well then, what about doing a theatrical reading for your talent?"

"A *reading*?"

"You could do something from Shakespeare and add in your piano playing and tumbling," Mom suggested, gaining comfortable ground at the idea of Jeannie's pageant turning into a drama routine. *All together? I thought. As one talent? Weird. Mom has seriously weird ideas. Don't listen to her, Jeannie! Run while you can! Just sing or do something normal! This is a pageant! A PAGEANT!* After a few minutes Jeannie was considering Mom's strange notion, nodding along as Mom offered suggestions. *Really? Snap out of it, Jeannie! Save yourself!* Mom was clearly preparing her for a drama skit, not for a pageant. In fact, the word "gown" wasn't even mentioned! I found myself curious about the whole affair, so there I stood, rotating my body around the warm blaze, until it was time to sound the bell for supper.

"They estimate this will be the largest storm of the winter," Dad read from the paper at the dinner table. "But the weatherman likes to be wrong. I bet we don't even get a flippin' inch." He dribbled a bit of dinner down his dark coveralls, then scooped it off his clothes with the edge of his mess kit style fork and ate it.

Right, I concurred silently. *We haven't had a big storm since the week of Christmas. Why would one come now?*

"Whose turn is it to do the dishes?" Mom asked, pushing her chair out from the dinner table.

"Mine," I answered. "Hey, Dad, how about you help me tonight since I helped you on Sunday."

"Can't. I gotta go get those brakes done on Mr. Seeley's car."

"Oh sure, leave me all the work," I said, moving the dirty dishes to the sink.

"I'll help," Toots said. "You wash, and I'll dry. Next time you can help me."

When I woke the next morning, the ground was covered in a light dusting of white. *Huh, some storm.* I suppose the weatherman had been right about one thing: it *had* snowed. I grabbed my breakfast of a bran muffin and green drink and swung my backpack up and around my shoulders before heading out the door. Dad was already outside with his white shirtsleeves rolled up, scraping the crystallized snowflakes off of the windshield. From inside the cab I could better see the miniature hexagons that sparkled into the air when they were freed from the glass. Dad climbed into the driver's seat, started the engine to a meaty roar, rubbed his hands together, and dug the gear shift into reverse.

"Amy, you should do one thing a day that you don't like to do," he said as we started down the road to the high school. "That's how you build character." The heater flared hot, pushing warm, musky air into the cab. During the ride I tried to think what that *one* thing a day might be for me. Nothing stood out. Dad parked the truck, and together we walked up the stairs to the high school, taking two steps at a time. By afternoon, the sun had come out, and all of the snow had disappeared into thin air. Poof. Just like that. And nobody knew if there would be more before spring.

"Amy!" Katie shouted to me when I got to my locker. "I talked to Nate last night!"

"Nate?"

"Your first-date-Nate," she laughed, "You know, the guy I am setting you up with? So, we are all ready to go for your first official date a month from now. He is setting me up with his best friend. They were thinking bowling at 49th Street Galleria. What do you think?"

"I think I'm nervous."

"He is so nice! Way fine, too. You will have so much fun with him."

"As long as you are there we'll have fun. But really, Kates, I'm kinda scared."

"You can bowl, right?"

"Well, yeah, I mean, sometimes I get gutters, but Tracy Clead and I used to ride the bus to the bowling alley every week, so I should be OK."

"Listen, I am not letting you be nervous. You are going to have an amazing first date with a handsome boy. Plus, I will be there. We'll have a blast!"

My heart split into two emotions: gratitude for a best friend who knew I would probably never get asked on a first date without her help, and nerves associated with being on a date with a boy who didn't exactly choose me. *I wonder if Katie told him about my face? Did she warn him?*

When school was out I decided to ask Dad to give me a ride instead of walking home with Wendy like usual, but when I got to his office he had a student in there, talking his ear off. She was rambling on about her life, the boy that she liked, and all of her drama. Dad seemed interested enough—well he was trained to look interested, anyway, with his counseling background—but I could tell he was ready to go home. Maybe I would be his excuse. I stepped into the office "A-mouse!" he said, sounding altogether too excited to see me.

"Hey, Dad, can I get a ride home?"

"'Course, you sure can," he answered. The girl shot me an annoyed look over her shoulder.

"So like I was saying…I'm not sure if he even *likes* me! His friends tell me he does, but he never once has spoken a word to me. Not a single word! So I have no idea if he wants to date me or just be friends. I just don't know what to do."

"Uh huh," Dad said as he packed up his briefcase, sending signals that it was time for her to go.

Then she turned the conversation abruptly to me: "Do you ever get bugged that you were born with a birth defect?"

Wait…what? I don't even know you! I took two steps back from her, collected my thoughts, and lied, "I never really think about it."

"I bet you wonder what it would be like to have normal lips and nose though."

"Sometimes, but it isn't a big deal." *I have only known you for seven seconds! Now please, stop asking me questions.*

"Well hopefully one day, maybe in heaven, you will have a normal looking face. Think how pretty you could be."

"Oh. Yeah. Well, really, I like the way I look, I think I look pretty right now," I shrugged while moving toward the classroom window so she couldn't see my face.

"But you know what I mean, right?"

"Mmm-hum."

"Have you had a bunch of plastic surgery and stuff?"

"Yeah."

"Are you done? Like, you know, with getting your face all fixed?"

"No, I still have some more," I said balancing my backpack on my shoulder as I thought about the big surgery looming in my future.

"When?"

"Oh, I'm not sure yet. Hopefully this summer."

"Cool. I hope it helps. I think I would wish for a different face, you are so brave about it all and stuff."

"Well, this is the one God gave me, and I like it. I really don't get bugged with how I look."

Dad, somewhere in the background, was nervous. I could tell. He was fidgeting and trying to act as if he couldn't hear the conversation. The girl was trying to be nice in her nosy kind of way, moving to sit up on a desk, swinging her crossed legs like she owned the place, but it just rubbed me all wrong. How dare she invade my space and pound me with the questions I didn't even ask myself.

"Let's scotacklica, A-mouse," Dad said while motioning with his free hand that the classroom needed to be empty before he left. She hopped off the desk and flipped her hair as she passed us.

"I'll come back tomorrow and tell you more about that guy that might like me. I am still so stressed on what I should do. Like, seriously, dating is so confusing sometimes!"

After school Dad and I rode to the nearby sandwich shop for a snack. He talked about the weather, and I nodded along. "Get whatever you want," he said when he pulled up to the drive-in window, so I did — a turkey sandwich and three chocolate chip cookies. They weren't nearly as good as my famous cookies, but they were warm and just what I needed to finish off the school day. Dad took the long way home, crossing a set of railroad tracks that ran perpendicular to a large field. As the tires hit the tracks I simultaneously lifted both feet, closed my eyes, touched a screw high above my head in the cab, and made a wish. Just like I did each time we crossed those tracks. I wished for the surgery. And wished people would stop looking at what I couldn't change.

That girl had pointed out my flaws—just bluntly pointed them out and put me on the spot. Using her perfect pouty lips to tell me all about how she noticed I wasn't like her. What did she expect me to say? I couldn't understand why she wanted to dig into my pain. I bit into my cookie. *This adversity will only make me stronger and give me character*, I reasoned. *Character. Yes, character! Huh.* Now I could see what Dad had been saying during our morning ride to school. I did have character. Lots of it.

While we slept in our warm beds, the real storm came in, and in the morning we woke to a blinding display of white. Every tree, branch, and roof was heavy with a bright layer of hushed snow. The streets, unplowed and filled, measured nearly a foot of clean snow.

Dad left early for a meeting, so it was up to me to find a way to get to school. With Jeannie carrying out her new routine of leaving later than me, Katie said she would drive us to school in style, but when I got to her house it was a different story.

"I don't want you driving in that snow," her dad said as he put on his coat.

"I can do it! Just let me take the van. Come on, Dad!"

"The plows haven't come and you don't have any experience in heavy snow."

"I've been driving for over a month! I know what I am doing!"

"Not today, Katie. If you want a ride, I'll take you in the truck," he went on. "Now please get your backpack and load up."

"Why don't you trust me? I said I can do it!"

"I'm driving you and that is the end of the discussion, young lady."

Katie huffed toward me and I couldn't help but laugh a little. She was so determined!

"For the record, I think you could have driven in the snow," I whispered.

We piled into her dad's truck, an old yellow Ford with what looked like fairly decent tires, and got ready to pull up the street of 150 East. Oh, the snow was just fantastic! The back end of the truck fishtailed up the street, then nearly turned all the way around.

"Whoa! Cool!" I said, holding on to the edge of the glove box so I didn't smash into Katie.

"Darn it, darn it, darn it!" Katie's dad spouted out, as he tried to gain control of the truck, his fists wrapped high and tight on the steering wheel. I wasn't nervous, I was excited! The truck skidded sideways down the street pushing the front tires into the hidden curb and gutter before coming to a stop. Butterflies rushed my tummy, just like a rollercoaster. Katie flipped on the radio, but a loud voice was interrupting the music: "We have cancelled school for a snow day for all schools within the region. The Salt Lake airport is reporting snow levels of more than eleven inches."

"Did he say what I think he just said?"

"Shhhh, let's listen for our school."

"That's it! Our school is on the list, Amy Jo!"

Ah! Wishes DO come true! I leapt out of the truck, hollered my goodbye to Katie, and ran across the street and through her yard, splashing fresh snow up my legs and onto my face. Unlatching the fence, I dashed back into the warm house covered up to my knees in frosty white.

"School is cancelled!" I yelled to anyone still home.

"What? It *is*?" Jeannie asked, her voice animated, the last word going up an octave. "Great! I can work on my talent now." Jeannie and Mom had stayed up all night collaborating on the theatrical reading/piano playing/tumbling talent cluster disaster. I still thought it was weird. So weird. Mom had introduced the idea of a donkey being part of the reading. Better yet, *she* would be the voice of the donkey. She had been recording herself doing an "eee yaaw eee yaaw" donkey sound over and over until she got it just right. She tried it at various levels of volume and tone. It was disturbing. No mother should ever, ever sound like that. Each time Mom tried again she would clear her throat, record her donkey voice, listen to it, then shake her head and try it all over again. She was *consumed* with the donkey noise! *What's her benchmark?* I wondered. *Does she know she still sounds human?* Together Jeannie and Mom had decided Jeannie would be playing the part of Titania, the queen of the fairies, one of Shakespeare's lovely characters. Titania falls in love with a lower class laborer, who, in fact, has the head of a donkey. In this case, one that happened to sound like Mom when behind the furry head came, "Eeee yaaaw!" All of this was entertaining and as far away from pageantry talent as one could get. I tried not to think about Mom and Jeannie and their embarrassing donkey-talking escapade. Pageants were supposed to be classy!

The snow plows eventually made it up our street and piled up the snow into a mountain of white caterpillars. The snow called for me to get outside. "Hey, Todd," I shouted down the hallway, "do you want to go out and play in the snow? Like we used to when we were kids?" Before I could finish my sentence he was running past me toward the box that stored our snow boots. Out we went into the deep white and played, conjuring the magic of feeling small again, catching snowflakes on our tongues and making snow angels. Then we made intricate tunnels, hollowed out a large snow cave, and created a playground of obstacles to jump over and into.

"Let's make the biggest snowman ever engineered!" Todd said to me with his brain ticking away.

"How big do you think we can get it?"

"Let's start with the base, and when it's done we'll see how much snow we can lift on top of it." We rolled and pushed and lifted. In the end, the largest snowman ever born in our backyard stood eight feet tall and faced the house in a grand gesture of height.

"Let's go get a carrot for his nose!" I said, totally thrilled.

Todd ran into the house and came out just as fast. He had even managed to grab two raisins for eyes. I found two scrappy sticks for arms, and together we sat there in the snow and marveled at our creation.

"Do you think anyone has ever made such a big snowman?" I asked.

"Probably not."

"Thanks for coming outside with me today, Todd. Remember when we were little and used to go sledding together over on the big hill? Just you and me? And then we would come home when we were too cold to stand it any longer and spend the rest of the day listening to "Peter and the Wolf" on your old blue record player?"

"Yeah, I do." He smiled and then paused, catching his thought and forming it in mid-air: "You know what, Amy? Your face doesn't look different to me anymore. You're just my sister, and that's all I ever see."

I stopped and looked right at him. "Really? Why did you just say that?"

"It's true. I never see what's wrong with your lip or face."

"Sometimes I think it's all people notice."

"Well, most of the time I forget you even have any problems. You are just Amy to me."

I smiled and lay my head back against the snowpack. The world seemed to fall still, and our play quieted. I looked way up into the sky, as far as my sight could reach, and all I saw were the flakes falling onto my blushed cheeks. I closed my eyes and let the falling white bees cover my face, melting as soon as they landed.

The following month, I turned sixteen. The Rebels surprised me by changing the marquee at the local carhop to read, "HAPPY SWEET SIXTEEN, AMY! LOVE, THE REBELS" All lit up, the sign was epic. It was finally my time.

CHAPTER EIGHTEEN

"Why do diamonds remind me of you?
Well, you know, diamonds aren't perfect
They have flaws, too.
But despite their cracks and occasional faults
People still prize them so highly, they're locked up in
vaults.
They want them in rings, on scepters, on crowns.
Just like you, Amy, they want them around.
So just keep on sparkling and know that it's true.
Your big sister, Jeannie, sees a diamond in you."
---A poem from Jeannie

"What do you think about this one?" Mom asked as she held up a dress with an odd-length hemline.

"No, no. No way."

"How about this one?"

"Nope, too churchy."

"This one?"

"Too much like a grandma dress."

"Wait a minute, what about this one?" Mom said as she held up a long white cotton dress with flowing fabric off the shoulder that mimicked butterfly wings, a tie around the middle, and layers of ruffles that went from the waist line to the bottom hem.

"Well, I don't hate it," I said. "Hmm... I actually might kind of like it."

"It does fit within my budget," Mom said, holding the price tag in her fingers and taking off her glasses so she could get a closer look. It would have been easier for Jeannie to borrow an elaborate dress from one of her friends—cheaper, too—but Mom wanted to give Jeannie the gift of a new dress, just for her, for the night of the pageant.

Jeannie was too busy to come with us to look for the dress with the pageant, now days away. So Mom took me, the fashion consultant, and we went downtown to the shops to look for the dress. We tried the mall first, but nothing seemed right, so Mom suggested we go to Clifton's. Oh yes, Clifton's. I had seen this shop many times, but did it carry high fashion? Not even close. Clifton's was a store that catered to older ladies who wanted practical dresses that covered their knees—and sometimes ankles. Dresses made of at least a fifty percent polyester blend, dry clean only, with big pearl buttons. Still, the store had a selection of nice formal attire hidden near the back along the last wall, above the creaky floor.

"Well, it is white and simple," I said, nodding along with Mom.

We kept trying to picture if Jeannie would like it and how she would look in it and if it would even fit right. Back and forth and back and forth we went. But clearly, there was no other dress in sight that matched what we needed *and* Mom's slim pocketbook.

"Oh, I think Jeannie will look nice in it," Mom finally said, settling on an answer. "Let's get it!"

"Well, then OK!"

We approached the glass counter for payment, and the polished old lady with tight gray curls in her hair and a slim tailored suit carefully hung the dress in a bag for transportation home. The process seemed to take forever. Her service was meticulous. I stared blankly into the glass counter below, and there a sparkle unexpectedly caught my eye. "Oh, wow," I said aloud. "That ring is so pretty!"

There, six inches below the glass, lay rows of rings. One caught my eye. It was a ring with energy and good luck. I could just feel it! The ring had been waiting for me. How else could it be explained that nobody had purchased it?

I pointed to it and asked, "Can you tell me about this ring?"

"Oh, that is a nice crystal ring with several stones," the sales lady said, clearly impressed with my good taste.

It must be so expensive, but I would love to buy that for Jeannie as a good luck ring. "How much is it?"

"Fifteen dollars." Hah! I *had* fifteen dollars! I even had it with me. I didn't have much more than twenty dollars to my name, but I knew I had to buy that ring for Jeannie.

"Can I try it on?"

"Certainly."

"Oh, Amy, it's so pretty!" Mom said. "It goes nice with your pearl ring, too."

"No, it's not for me, Mom. I want to buy it for Jeannie to go with her pageant dress," I said, glancing her direction. She paused for a second and then smiled.

"Yes, Jeannie will make the dress sparkle, and the ring will make her hand sparkle," Mom said.

The sales lady wrapped the ring in a small velvet box, taking the same great care as she had with the dress.

"I think we did just right. We picked a winner," Mom said while laying the dress carefully on the back bench in the van.

"I think so, too, Mom. It's simple and pretty. Jeannie will look great in it."

At last we were on our way home to show Jeannie our wares, a successful shopping trip in the books. I nearly burst with excitement carrying the tiny box in my hands on the ride home. I opened the case over and over again, checking to make sure it was still was as beautiful as when I bought it, all but five minutes ago.

"What's *this*?" Jeannie exclaimed upon examining the dress. She didn't squeal with delight or want to rush to try it on. "No. No. No. You are going to have to take it back. I need a *pageant* dress, Mom! This is a churchy dress. I'm not wearing this thing."

"Go try it on, you'll see it looks fine," Mom coaxed, her voice a little hurt.

"It's not going to work! No way. I can tell you that. I will have to borrow a white dress from a friend, if I can even find one. Where did you even get this?"

"Please, just go try it on," Mom tried again.

"We got it at Clifton's, a shop for ladies' apparel," I said, no longer sure I should hold the title as the family fashion consultant.

"The dress seriously looks like it has wings. It's embarrassing."

"I am sure once you put it on you will see how pretty the dress is," Mom said, her hand on Jeannie's back, pleading with her to go change.

A few minutes later Jeannie appeared with the dress on. Mom didn't hold back, "Oh, my, yes. That's just right, Jeannie. Don't you see the potential now?"

"There is nothing about this dress that I like, Mom. It needs to be more flashy and fitted. Besides, it's *cotton*. Pageant dresses aren't made of cotton."

"Look at how the ruffles move when you walk. Go ahead, spin around."

"Mom, come on, they are *cotton* ruffles. You aren't helping."

Mom placed her hands on her hips, exhaling a deep sigh, "Look, I wanted to buy you the dress for the pageant, A borrowed one just won't do." Then, taking in an equally deep breath, "We don't have the money to buy a fancy dress, Jeannie. I would love you to wear this dress that I picked out for you and that you look absolutely beautiful in. Please."

Jeannie stared for a moment into Mom's eyes, listening to her plea, glancing down to run her hands along the fabric. Her shoulders caved in ever so slightly when Mom was done talking, "OK, Mom. I will wear it. For you."

I quietly stepped downstairs to my room, thinking what a foolish thing I had done in buying a ring to go with the dress. I spent nearly all my money on a piece of jewelry that wouldn't be worn. There was no way I could give it to her now. What if she didn't like it just like she didn't like the dress? I couldn't bear to be hurt like that over something so small. I put the ring safely inside my butterfly jewelry case. I wondered for a minute if I should keep the ring for myself. I could put it on and fool people into believing that I was engaged. A funny thought. I didn't know that I would ever get married. *Will I? Will someone ever see the real me?* If I did get lucky enough to find someone who loved me that much, I hoped the ring would be cut clean, sending off light in a million different rays. For now, I didn't let my mind go to that place that other girls dreamed so easily of—rings, kissing, a big fancy dress, and of course the groom.

The blind date with Nate that Katie set me up on turned out better than I thought it would. He was polite and at one point even told me I was good at bowling. He paid for the activity and dinner, too, just like Katie had said he would. My first date was behind me. Success! I had arrived as a dating teenager.

A few nights after I had purchased the ring, Katie came to get me in her family's van that she had permission from her dad to drive. Her van was big, like ours, but only held nine passengers. I climbed into the copilot seat, which was upholstered in red to match the outside paint job, strapped on my seatbelt, and got ready for a good time.

"Roll down the windows!" she said as soon as we were out of my driveway.

"Wait, what? It's *freezing* outside!"

"I know, I know. I'm going to turn the heater on. Full blast!"

"Haha! No way! Are we allowed to do this?" I asked, putting my fingers around the temperature gauge.

"YES! Do it!"

Katie was so much fun. Her mad logic was genius!

"Hey! I am warm *and* cool!"

"See! Now, where should we go?"

"Let's go roam the streets and honk at people!"

"Oh yeah, girl!" she replied while hitting the play button on the tape deck. "We need some music to rock this van!"

I never asked about Nate, my blind date, or if he'd had fun—or if he liked me. I sort of knew all along it was a one-time deal. When we pulled up 150 East to take the van home to Katie's house for the night, there was Moose, walking right up the middle of the sidewalk.

"Hey, Moose!" Katie shouted. My goodness did we ever feel cool in that van of Katie's.

"Excuse me, sir?" I asked, leaning out of the window, the warm air from the heater smacking me in the face. "Do you have any Grey Poupon?"

"Hardee har har," Moose said, adding a belly laugh at the end of his joke.

"Katie, time to come inside," her dad called from the front porch, just as we had started to make a new plan. She dropped me off in the middle of her driveway, and then pulled the van into the garage, only adjusting twice. So smooth.

Soon, it was just Moose and me. I still had no game. I had no idea what to say or how to say it.

"Let's go get some fries," he said. "Or do you have to go home, too?"

"No, yeah, I mean, that sounds good," I said, adding, "I don't think my parents will care at all."

I didn't exactly have a curfew. Mom ruled the house on trust. Moose and I walked three houses down and got into his car—my first unofficial *real* date. We pulled up to the drive-in window and he looked at me and said, "You can't tell anyone that this was a date, OK?"

"Sure, that's fine," I said. Of course I was going to tell people! Katie for sure and maybe Wendy. *No, scratch telling Wendy. She might be jealous.* Oh, and I had to tell Mom!

"Give us one order of big fries," Moose said to the girl through the window. And then he handed her some cash. "Have you ever been to the haunted boiler room?" he asked, turning to me.

"Haunted? Like the one at on the east side of town by the old inner city high school?"

"Yeah, that's the one. Have you been?"

"No. Nope. Never," I answered shaking my head back and forth.

"OK, that's it, I am taking you to see it right now."

"NOW!?"

"Yup, and you have no choice cause I am your ride home," he laughed.

"Is it really haunted? Come on, you've gotta tell me everything before we get there!"

"So the legend goes back fifty years or more. There was this janitor, and his whole job was to keep the boiler going. He would shovel coal into it all during the day to keep the school warm."

"Go on," I said, grabbing a fry and taking a small bite.

"Well, one night he was told he had to work from midnight 'til morning—it just so happened to be a full moon that night," Moose said, turning east to continue to the haunted school. "He was putting coal into the boiler around one in the morning, and the boiler started to make this crazy sound—but he kept loading it with coal. 'Cause that was his job and he didn't want to get in trouble."

"Mmmm hum."

"He kept at it, and the boiler started to get angry and shake, like she was gonna blow. The whole room started to fill with smoke so bad, he couldn't breathe." Moose looked straight at me, his eyes big. "The janitor started to panic and turned to run out the door to the outside, but someone had locked him in. He pounded and pounded on the door trying to get anyone to hear him, but nobody helped."

"He couldn't get out?"

"There was only one way in and one way out: a big steel door. A small window at the top of the door was his only hope. In a last ditch effort he put both palms on the window and shoved as hard as he could, but the window was made of industrial strength glass and didn't budge. He pushed his face up against the window, screaming for help, and not a single person heard him."

"That's awful…"

"No. I'm not done. The next part is awful. The boiler blew up, throwing hot coal and fumes into the room—and the janitor burned to death. They found him the next day, melted so bad, it was hard to recognize him. This will gross you out, but someone said they could see his palm prints burned into the window. Since that day, on each full moon, the ghost of the janitor comes to visit the boiler room. If you knock three times he will answer."

"That's just creepy."

"Hold on, is it a full moon tonight?"

"Moose!"

"Ha! Just kiddin', it's not. But if it were…"

We pulled into the dark parking lot of the school, and Moose led us down the crumbled concrete stairs to the door of the boiler room.

"Wow. The door is big. And looks heavy, too."

"My theory is someone locked him in on purpose, and that's why whenever anyone comes down these stairs at night he haunts them. You know, to get them back for letting him burn to death."

"That is so morbid. So now what do we do? Just stand here?"

"You stay here, knock three times, and I will go up top and listen."

"What? NO! I don't dare! Stay here!"

"Chill out. You will be fine, there is no full moon, so he won't talk to you tonight anyways."

I wiped my hands along the sides of my jeans and got ready to knock. "Moose?" I hollered up the stairs. "Are you sure this is safe? Are we going to get into trouble? Moose?!"

"Just knock, I am up here listening."

I pulled my fingers into a fist then knocked as hard as I could—three raps in a row.

I waited then heard a faint voice coming from the boiler room. "Gooooo awaaaay. Gooooo awwaaaaay." I bolted up the stairs, catching my footing so I didn't trip. "Moose! Moose! I heard it! I heard him! I heard the man! Moose! Where are you?! I heard the ghost!"

"You did??" he asked, running from around the corner.

"YES! I did! It sounded like a real person! Well, kind of anyway."

Moose started to laugh and hold his stomach.

"Ha ha ha! You are so gullible!"

"Was that *you*? UGH! You totally freaked me out! But wait, I thought I heard something coming through the *door*! That couldn't have been you!"

"I know, ha! I have this down to a science. I just yell through this grate and it sounds like it's coming through the boiler room door," he laughed, pointing behind us.

"OH! You are in the biggest trouble with me now!" I said, punching his arm. "I swear I thought the ghost was after me!"

The whole way home we shared fries and laughed, and he drove way faster than he should have. I didn't want the night to end. When our favorite song came on the radio, Moose turned it up so loud my ears started ringing. I threw my head back singing at the top of my lungs: *Don't need nothing but a good time! How can I resist? Ain't looking for nothing but a good time, and it don't get better than thisssss...here's to ya!"* When the guitar solo came on, Moose took both hands off the wheel and did an impression of a heavy metal superstar, banging his head back and forth at each stoplight. Then he shoved a handful of fries in his mouth and laughed harder than I had ever heard.

And the thought occurred to me that maybe my luck was changing.

He dropped me off at home and gave me that Moose smile that I loved. A rush of energy stayed with me all night long. Inside, my body was laughing and full of tiny butterflies. I knew that Moose didn't have any true interest in me and probably wouldn't, but none of that reality mattered. Just fries. Big fries. And all kinds of possibilities.

Jeannie left the following Monday to spend a week in the big city getting ready for the pageant, and consequently, my blind date with Nate and the half-date with Moose faded into the background. Nobody asked me about either. Well, except Mom.

The pageant was held on a Saturday night in a hall as grand as a palace with red carpet that bounced when you walked on it and the most impressive of all the chandeliers I had ever seen high above our heads. During the pageant I sat next to Mom, who had an aisle seat. Down the row from me were Dad, Gram, Gramp, Auntie Julie, Jeannie's best friend, and even the principal, Mr. Heninger, from our high school. We were out of our league here, I could tell. Pageants were not the sort of thing anyone in our family ever did. The other pageant moms were dressed to the nines, mirroring what their daughters would likely be wearing in equally fashionable attire during the pageant. I could hear their excited chatter high above all regular conversation. Click, click, click went their shoes. Yak, yak, yak went their mouths. Oh, were they ever taking this seriously.

Mom sat next to me, in one of her nicest Sunday dresses, a pair of sensible shoes on her feet, and her hands clasped comfortably in her lap. Her hands were working hands with years of labor in every fold. She didn't pay to have her nails done, but rather, kept them clean and clipped. When I was a child I would look at Mom's hands and memorize the deep and faint lines until I was sure that I knew them as well as I knew my own, thinking that if I were ever captured by a spy and told to identify her hands out of thousands in order to be released, I could do just that. In church she would take a piece of paper and a pen and trace my hand. Then, she would decorate each finger with a funny face. Each week her hands would knead dough until it was shiny, smooth, and springy. She would fashion the dough into a dozen loaves, then bake them just in time for us to come home from school. I loved her hands.

"Mom, did you give Jeannie the ring?" I asked leaning in. I'd decided to give her my gift right before the pageant.

"Oh, yes! I did give it to her, and she just loved it."

"Really? She liked it?"

Mom looked at me and nodded.

Down went the lights. The crowd hushed. Up went the music, and in an instant all the contestants were spilling onto the stage for the opening number. But my eyes were only looking for one. All of the

dresses were white, shiny, and new, like true ball
gowns. The sparkles from the dresses caught the
spotlights and shone to the back of the audience. I
searched the stage for Jeannie, and at last I found her.
Her plain, white cotton dress looked so bland next to
all the other girls' dresses. Yet, it moved like air, and
she filled it with masses of confidence. When she
twirled her dress, it flew up all around her ankles,
and it looked every bit as beautiful on her as if she
had been wearing a costly ball gown. Her hand
moved toward the audience, and oh, how I strained
to see the ring. *Please! Let her have loved the ring enough
to wear it tonight!* I couldn't get a good look at her
hand. She was moving too fast. *Did she decide not to
wear it?* Then the lights caught the crystal and the
ring sent light all the way to our row. *There it is!* I got
chills from my head to my toes. She loved the ring as
much as I did, and maybe she knew it held luck, too.
I knew that the ring was special, but more so, I knew
Jeannie was.

When the dress was not what she wanted, she
wore it anyway as a gesture to Mom. During dress
rehearsal two days earlier, the director told her she
would have to do an eight-count dance solo during
the physical fitness routine, and Jeannie said, "I can't
dance," to which the director replied, "What *can* you
do?", implying that pageant girls should know how
to dance and *not* necessarily talk to donkeys. The
night of the dress rehearsal, Jeannie took her eight-
second solo, and with a bit of "I'll show you," did a
backhand spring followed by jump splits and won
the physical fitness category. *Hah! Take that!* We all
knew she would win the interview—there was no
question on that.

The whole night seemed surreal as Mom and I sat next to each other and the MC counted down the overall winning contestants from fifth place. When she got ready to say the name of the winner, I knew she would say Jeannie's name. And she did. Zoom went the spotlight, up went the lights, and our little row of fans went crazy. CRAZY! Except Mom. She just sat there, stunned! Then her hands went up to her ears with her fingers spread out like elk antlers before clapping together around her nose and lips.

Against the odds of singing to a donkey and wearing a plain cotton dress, Jeannie walked away the winner—my sister, the pageant queen.

CHAPTER NINETEEN

*True happiness emerges when you just throw your arms
into the sky and live to enjoy the moment without worry of
what others may think.*

"Jeannie, the phone is for you—again," I
said, while stretching the cord through the kitchen. It
seemed that ever since the night of the pageant two
months earlier Jeannie had been receiving non-stop
phone calls filled with congratulations and accolades.

The national pageant, hosted in Mobile,
Alabama, would be held in the summer, but this was
supposed to be my summer. *My* time. I had waited,
then waited some more, and waited again, and
finally my summer of the big surgery had arrived. I
had to have the surgery. But somewhere in all that
waiting, Jeannie had been winning, and I was scared
that I wouldn't get to have my surgery. Summer
lasted only so long! I needed time to recover! How
could I possibly both have the surgery and support
my sister? *Maybe it is OK*, I thought. *I mean, I like who
I am, and I am getting used to how I look. It isn't that bad!
Hardly anybody says anything anymore, not even the
bully. I am in the PRIME of my life.* Now, the year I
hadn't wanted to start was the one I didn't want to
end. My sophomore year was almost over.

My next appointment to see Dr. Thomas was scheduled for the following day. He wanted to see if the bone structure in my face had developed enough to move forward with the surgery. That evening, though, my mind focused only on dancing, and I put all doubt of whether I had become physically ready for the surgery out of my head. Our youth group had been invited to go to an activity thirty miles away, and I needed the dancing to clear my head before the next day's appointment.

The dance hall was covered in shredded newspaper, had a disco ball hanging from the top beam, and music—*dancing* music—blared from the speakers on the stage. *WOW! Look at this!* I marveled. *This group went to so much work! I love this night!* As soon as we walked in, I could feel my feet moving, and why wait? I ran and slid on the newspapers, moving to the other side of the room with a shrill of laughter coming over me, catching me off guard. I liked the new me, the one that said, "Why hold back?" I knew if others believed I was OK with who I was, then they would be as well. For too long I had hidden behind the shadows of my scars, my beautiful scars, but tonight I was going to wear them like a queen wears her crown. They were my most prized accessories. I was going to shine from the inside out! That was my secret—to be exactly me: a caring, happy, fun girl who loved to dance, bravely tried flirting, and who hopelessly made wishes.

"Wow, there aren't many people here," I said to Wendy. "I'm so glad 'cause now we'll have more room to dance."

"I only count sixteen people, but eleven are guys," Wendy said. "That should at least improve our odds of getting asked to dance."

"Well, what are we waiting for?" I asked, then linked Wendy to me by the crook of her elbow, and together we ran to the other end of the dance hall, tipping our weight back on our heels as we slid into the middle of the floor, spreading the newspaper shreds, then spun around laughing, doing it over and over again. Pretty soon the group caught on! We were all in the middle of the dance floor, laughing and spinning and dancing and singing at the top of our lungs. As one song ended and another began, we just kept moving our feet. I was so happy!

"Hey, Amy, let's go get a drink," Wendy said, grabbing my arm and pulling me toward the drinking fountain through a set of heavy double doors. My face pounded from dancing so hard, but I didn't care. I loved it! I took two giant gulps of water, and then ran my hands over my face to get rid of some of the sweat before rubbing them dry on my jeans.

"Boy, is it hot in there," a guy said, two steps from the drinking fountain. He had sandy blond hair that curled in all the wrong spots, but he had a cool boy-next-door flavor to him and a boldness that caught my attention right away. *And* he was looking in my direction.

Where is WENDY? Is he talking to me? Wait…this can't be happening! "No doubt. Hot with a capital *H*!" I said, still wondering if he had meant to talk to me. *Oh my gosh, I am such a nerd. Why did I just say that?*

He opened the door that led back into the dance hall, but he stopped me before I could go through, touched my arm, and said, "Do you want to dance?" The spot on my arm tingled, and my eyes and smile lit up like a switch had just been flipped on for the first time.

"Sure," I said, wondering how exactly did one slow dance? Just hug for two minutes?

I remembered watching Katie at a stomp a few months ago, and it seemed like she just swayed back and forth and put her hands up on his shoulders in a relaxed kind of way. *I can do this*, I chanted in my head. *I can do this. Be cool, Amy.*

He led me into the middle of the dance floor and then put his hands on my hips. So naturally, I put my hands up on his shoulders. We stood there, swaying back and forth with four fists of space between us, and talked eye to eye. He didn't look down at my lips, and he even laughed at my quirky humor.

"What kind of music do you like?" he asked.

"Oh, whatever..."

"Do you like DJ Jazzy Jeff?

"Oh, yeah I do!" *Who is he talking about? DJ who? Oh, please don't ask me what my favorite song is!*

"Good 'cause I requested a song by him next."

"I can't wait!" *Dial it down, Amy, dial it down.*

Before the song ended, he had asked me my name—the most beautiful question a guy can ask a girl. And before the evening was over, he had asked me to dance three more times, and each time, I stood in total shock that he had repeated his request. So did everyone else. The pretty girls in my group didn't get asked near as much as me. Me! When I got home, I told Mom the story down to the final details, and she listened and laughed right along with me as her hands wiped the last of the dinner crumbs off the table.

The next day Mom and I took the drive to visit Dr. Thomas. His office smelled like leather and paint, and he had contemporary art on his walls in sea foam green and mauve. I missed the old familiar office of Dr. Broadbent with his children's books and worn-out toys. Dr. Thomas's office breathed the air of a much more uptown, sophisticated, and stylish place.

"Pssst! Mom, come sit by me and we can look at *GQ* together!" I said, still full of life from the night before. We laughed and talked while looking at the magazine like two best friends. Mom even scooted her chair closer to mine so she could get a better look at the glossy pages of chiseled, sexy, smoky eyed men.

"Oh, Mom! Look at him! Tall, dark, and handsome...mmmm."

"Oh, yes, and blue eyes, too."

Despite my happy exterior, deep inside I wrestled with emotions of anxiety. I wanted to know what news the appointment would give. I wanted the doctor to say my face was ready to be transformed.

"Amy Jo? Dr. Thomas is ready to see you now," the receptionist said.

"We can put down the *GQ* magazine now," Mom winked at me.

With each step to the examination room I tried to shake my nerves off. *This is no big deal. I will be fine. No matter what the outcome is, I will be fine.*

Dr. Thomas, in his lilac pressed shirt and white doctor's coat, looked as handsome as the men on the magazine pages. I sent a funny glace to Mom, trying to tell her that now we needed to be serious and listen. A whole year had gone by since our last visit, during which I had plenty of time to think about this appointment, and each time I did, I thought about the words of my sweet Dr. Broadbent: "Just trust him."

"I've decided I want you to take the bone from my skull for the bone transplant," I said, not even letting him greet us.

He shut the door, then turned and sat on his rolling black stool, moving toward the examination table. "That's a good decision. I'll put that in my notes."

Then he took a moment to talk to me, and in that space of time he showed the same kind of genuine care that Dr. Broadbent had always displayed. I felt as if I was his favorite patient. His plan for my surgery had changed little from a year ago. His only concern centered on whether or not the bone structure that supported my face had stopped changing. After a set of X-rays were taken, Dr. Thomas gave us the good news that we could schedule the surgery. Then my heart started to pound. *My day will finally come! Oh, thank you! Thank you! I will get my surgery!*

"You will have your jaw wired shut for six weeks. I know that it will be uncomfortable for you, but this is the only way to get the alignment we need and the structure in place."

"My mom is going to get me a blender of my own," I said, knowing full well that the worst part of this ordeal would be giving up my favorite food for weeks on end as I let my body heal.

"We will keep you in the ICU for a few days then move you to the main floor. I want you to be there for up to a week so we can monitor your progress."

Then, looking at Mom he said, "We'll need you to go to the blood bank and have them draw a sample of Amy's blood. We will likely have to give her a transfusion during the surgery." I batted my eyes twice, and then shut my lids for a brief second. *This will take courage, lots of courage. But I can do this. I know I can.*

Dr. Thomas finished giving us the details, then patted me on the knee, smiled a big smile, and said, "You will do just fine."

"Go ahead and have a seat," the billing receptionist said upon our exit from the examination room as she motioned to two chairs tucked up close to her desk. "Now then, may I make a copy of your insurance card?"

Mom sat down, pulled out her wallet, and handed her insurance card over. I fidgeted in my seat. I hated talking about the money associated with surgeries. The burden of the financial side of the surgery always took me off guard. It wasn't fair that so much of the precious resource of money in my family became dedicated to fixing my face. I cringed when the billing lady told Mom the estimated cost to expect despite our excellent insurance, circling the number with her fancy pen. Mom adjusted her weight in the padded seat before asking a myriad of questions—so many questions. Dr. Thomas saw three other patients while we were sitting there sorting things out. I tried not to notice him going in and out while we discussed numbers and payments. Finally, after what felt like an hour, we left the billing lady and discussed the date of the operation with his scheduling assistant. Mom thought June 19 would be best. That way I would have time to recover before we left for Alabama to see Jeannie in the national pageant. *June 19 will be the day I change forever.*

"Do you want to get ice cream?" Mom asked as we left, pushing the door open for me. "You know it's a tradition now."

Just the thought of Mom and me having a tradition that centered on sugar made me laugh right out loud. "You know I do!" We drove to the ice cream shop, the one that faced north, and ordered two flavors of ice cream, just like the time before.

"When you were born the doctor told me you wouldn't be able to sing," Mom said on the way home as I tuned into a country radio station we both liked. "And yet, here you are. Singing! You are truly a miracle." I smiled and sang as loud as I dared. All the while, I couldn't stop thinking about how this summer would change my life.

The next day I met Katie by our lockers, adjusting her mile-high hair in her mirror, concentrating on the height and depth of her bangs. I couldn't wait to tell her my good news! But before I could she was telling me her *own* good news. "My mom told me this morning that we're going to San Diego on our family summer trip!"

"Oh, cool. I'm so jealous! I want to see the ocean! What are you going to do?" I asked, now checking my own hair.

"SeaWorld, the zoo, and don't you know it, we are for sure going to the ocean..." she listed, on and on. "We leave June 15, and I can hardly wait."

"Oh, Kates! I am going to have my big surgery that week. You know, the one I've been telling you about? I'm going in to the hospital on June 19."

"You are? So soon? I didn't know it would be so fast. I am really sorry. I wish I could be here for you! I'll have to see if my mom will let me call you long distance while we're gone."

"OK. So you won't even get to come and see me in the hospital?"

"I guess not," she said making a frown, "but, I *will* come and see you as soon as we get home. I *promise*. Promise! You are gonna be one foxy lady when you are all done! As if you aren't already the most gorgeous woman I know!"

Her locker clinked soundly shut, echoing the ring for several long seconds, and I selfishly thought how miserable I would be, recovering without my best friend. I needed her! How could I do this without her? She was my best friend!

"Hey, Amy! Would you be interested in going on a blind date?" Jenny, a new friend, asked me between classes. "He's a total stud. You will have so much fun! A bunch of us are going. Please say yes! You are so fun! Please!"

"Sure! Wait, who is he?" I answered.

"He doesn't go to school here. He's my cousin, Mark. But you will love him! We are going to go to dinner and then maybe a movie or some of them were thinking ice blocking or bowling."

"OK, great. Yes! When? And what are you wearing?"

"Tonight! You always look cute! Wear what you have on! We will come and get you at seven unless you change your mind."

Another date! Ta-da! Life is great!

I organized my outfit choices when I got home, placing shoes and earrings next to each option. I settled on my acid-washed jeans and a neon shirt paired with a denim jacket and my converse high tops.

"Hey, sexy babe!" shouted Jenny from her car between honks. I danced out to the driveway, exaggerating my moves swinging my arms above my head. "You and Mark are going to sit in the back, we just have to go pick him and then my date up."

"Rad! Hi, Lindsay!"

"Lindsay is going to sit in the back with you and Mark; her date is meeting us at the restaurant."

"Cool! I'm excited!"

"You should be! My cousin is so cool. You are seriously gonna love him."

We drove through the city, connected to the freeway, and soon we were in Mark's driveway. When Jenny honked he came out the front door, taking long strides, his hands tucked in his jean pockets. He *was* good looking. Tall with brown wavy hair, and he clearly had great style. He even had on a denim jacket. *We are twinners!*

"You are sitting in the back with Amy and Lindsay. Amy is your date," Jenny said out the window.

He opened the back door, and the bright lights in the car came on. I leaned out, extended my hand, smiled, and said, "Hey, I'm Amy. You get to sit back here by us girls. Hope that's OK."

"Oh, hey. Nice to meet you," he said, looking right at me, far longer than I was comfortable with. He pulled his face up into a strained, polite smile as he got into the car. He didn't have to tell me he thought I was ugly. The space he created between us as he sat down told me, with crushing reality, that I didn't have a chance with him.

"Where do you go to school?" I asked, not allowing myself to soak in pity.

"Oh, just down here."

"Cool." I tucked my hair behind my ear, brushing his jacket with my arm. I felt him adjust his body into the door of the car so there was no chance of us touching. "It's a nice neighborhood. Looks great."

"Yup."

"So Jenny said that you like basketball?"

"Yeah."

"Cool, me too. How about the Jazz this year? Good, huh!?"

"Yeah."

"I've been watching them forever. When I was a kid I would sneak my parents' portable TV down to my room. Like I was watching something bad and would get in trouble if I got caught! Whenever I would hear my mom approaching I would hurry and turn it off and throw a blanket over the TV. It was just basketball though!"

"Huh, funny. Hey, Jenny, what's the plan for tonight?"

"We are going to pick up my date, then meet the rest of the group at the restaurant. Then I don't know! Have any great ideas?"

"Oh, OK. I was just going to say that I probably can't stay out very late. I have a lot going on this weekend."

"No way! You said you were free tonight!"

"I know, but something came up this afternoon."

"Party pooper!"

"Yeah, sorry about that."

We picked up Jenny's date next and the car soon filled with loud laughter and conversation. My date stayed silent. Five minutes later we were at the restaurant and joined the rest of the group.

"We just order at the counter and they bring it to us," Jenny said. "These guys have the best, best, best shakes and fries."

"Hey, go ahead and order," Mark said without looking at me when it was my turn at the register.

"Burger, no onions, strawberry shake, fries, and a large water."

"Are you two together?" the cashier asked.

"I'm paying for hers and mine," Mark said, lifting his chin my direction but keeping his eyes ahead.

I turned to see Jenny, Lindsay, and the rest of the group setting up napkins, utensils, and ketchup in a large round corner booth.

"You guys can sit right here," Jenny said, pointing to the end of the half-circle.

"Excellent!" I said scooting around so Mark would have enough space to sit by me.

He sat down, put both elbows on the table, and tucked his head down between his shoulders.

"Are you OK?"

"Yeah. Fine."

"Do you need a Tylenol or something?"

"No."

"Headache?"

"Something like that."

"Number 256," called the cashier a few minutes later.

"That's our order," he said, slowly getting up. A minute later he was back at our loud table. "Here's your burger, shake, and fries. And here's your water," he mumbled. "Do you want a straw?"

"Yeah! Thanks!" I said, aligning my food in front of me, making sure he had ample elbow room. But, he didn't sit down. He didn't put his food next to mine. He didn't offer any verbal explanation. Instead, he sent a message loud and clear that he didn't want to be paired with me. In a calculated move he turned his back and walked away from me to a vacant table to set up his own meal.

His stark action consumed me. *He would rather sit alone than sit by me. I am an embarrassment to him. He doesn't want to be seen with me. He must think I am a hideous monster.* I took a bite of my burger. The bun caught on my braces. I took a sip of water and scanned the group of couples over the lid of my drink. They hadn't noticed that my date had abandoned me. *I am better than this. No way am I letting him do this to me. Not now. Not after coming so far. I am beautiful. He may not see it, but I am. I know I am.* I moved to the edge of the round curved table and stood up.

"Hey, there's still room over here. I don't bite!"

"That's OK. I'm just going to sit here."

"What are you doing over there, Mark?" asked Jenny, standing up so he could see her.

"There wasn't enough room at that table."

"Hello! Yes there is! We will scoot more if you want."

"I'm fine over here."

I sat back down. Our matching denim jackets didn't seem so cool now. Inside I was crushed, but I couldn't let him win. "Wait a minute, I will come over and sit by you," I said, faking confidence as I stood, packing up my dinner on a tray to transport it to his table. *I'm not letting you hurt me. I know what you are doing. I can feel it, but I am stronger than you think.* "All right, see we both fit great at this giant table made for a family of six. Tons of elbow room!"

"Yeah. Right."

"How is your burger?"

"Fine."

"I am a bit of a fry connoisseur. These are some of the best I have had. Thanks so much for buying my dinner."

"No problem."

"So what else do you have going on this weekend?"

"Just family stuff."

"Soon summer will be here and you can be as lazy as you wanna be."

"True," he answered. I ate as fast as I could, dumped my tray, and stood next to the other table, joining in their warm laughter again. At the end of the night I pretended not to care when he opened the car door before Jenny had come to a full stop, walking fast to his front door. There was no mention of a second date. No hug or kiss to end the night. Not even a simple good-bye. I pushed the feelings of obvious rejection down into layer eleven and tried to forget the sting.

When summer started I made a mental list of who I would tell about my surgery, and I put Moose on the list—near the top. The message he wrote in my yearbook was simple and to the point, "Amy, you are awesome. We will always be friends no matter what." I knew we would, too, no matter what. I pulled out Jeannie's sophomore yearbook from two years earlier and placed it next to my shiny new one. I counted the signatures in mine, and then hers— they were nearly equal. Then I skimmed all the way to the back of her yearbook and looked up Ronald Jamon Eastland in the index. I found his senior class picture near the front of the book and placed my finger between the pages to mark the spot, and then found two more candid pictures of him. Flipping back and forth between the three pictures, I remembered the time Jeannie and I had seen him in the mall. And that smile. That amazing Hollywood smile, and the way he had looked at my sister with eyes that talked just like lips do. I stared at him for an eternity, thinking there was not a more attractive boy anywhere in her yearbook. She was so lucky to know him and to have gone on dates with him —*and* get rides home from school in his car. Boys didn't reject her. They worshiped her. Calling her days in advance, hoping to get one of her precious weekend slots. They treated her like a princess, and wowed her with their creative date planning and romance. They wanted her to be with them and to be seen next to them. I tucked my head into my pillow, then opened my own yearbook again and read Moose's message one last time before going to bed.

CHAPTER TWENTY

To "become" is to direct yourself to what you know you are inside: your hidden potential and all your magic. Yet many never reach high enough because it is easier just to "be".

    I can't breathe! I can't breathe! Someone, please. Please! Help me! I can't talk. I can't breathe. Why can't I move my arms? I'm trapped! Someone see me! My eyes…my eyes won't open. Someone!! Someone. Anyone. Can't you see me? I'm screaming, but I can't make a sound! My mouth. Why can't I open my mouth? My throat. The pain. Please…help.

    "Nurse! She's struggling, please get in here NOW!"

    Jeannie. Jeannie…. I can't talk. Is that you? Where are you? Please help me. Tell them.

    "She needs help!"

    "Straighten her breathing tube, check her stats. She's in distress," shouted one nurse to the other.

    I lay there, struggling and covered in panic. My toes were cold and my right thigh felt completely numb. My legs were shaking out of control. I could feel the nurse's warm hand trying to help me, her palm wrapped around my wrist, her other hand quickly checking my breathing tubes. She called for more help. Then three nurses and — at last — a doctor came to my side. They worked as a team, pulling the tape that held the tubes to my face and re-aligning them correctly. I sucked in a stream of air, so little air, but it was fresh.

"Nobody was even in here with her!" Jeannie shouted. "You can't just leave her all alone! I had no idea what to do, and there was no nurse at the station. I had to run down the hall to get help and leave her by herself in there!"

"She woke up and panicked, and her tube wasn't allowing her to breathe as much air as she needed," the doctor tried to explain.

"I need to know that you are going to take good care of her. She's my sister, and I just…I have never seen her like this before. Please just take good care of her." Motionless, I felt pain mixed with a strange combination of relief. *Thank you, Jeannie. Thank you for protecting me. Again.*

I tried to swallow, to open my eyes, to move my head, to lift my hand, or breathe in the scent of Mom, who must be near, and failed each time. My senses, all but my hearing, had been temporarily robbed. Slow motion encompassed my thoughts like a dream that I had dreamt before.

"Amy?"

I tried to speak, but the tubes made my voice impassable, and even thinking burned through my energy like an intense chore.

"Can you hear me?" Jeannie asked. "If you can, don't try to talk. You have tubes in your mouth, so just nod your head."

I made a slow "up" gesture, but then did not have the strength to move my head down.

"Are you OK?"

I shook my head, opening my eyes as far as I could to tiny slits. The room was dim, but the light from the hallway cast a fuzzy white glow into the doorway. A nurse flew by my weakened line of sight, her scrubs blurred. Next to me I heard the soft drip of an IV, and my body caved to the honesty of the situation.

"I am going to stay right here with you until Mom gets back. Are you in pain anywhere, or do you…oh, Amy, I am so sorry you have to go through all this. I really am…and there are so many tubes, and you look just… I have …never seen you this way before."

I tried again to open my eyes to look at Jeannie, but there was no energy left in me. So I kept them shut, just to rest a little longer. I wasn't OK. There was nothing about me that felt right.

"Are you asleep?" Jeannie asked, her voice cloudy.

I lay quietly without responding, concentrating on the weight of breathing through the tubes and fighting the pain that edged on.

"Amy?"

I was too feeble to answer, and I wanted to sleep more than anything. I kept my eyes closed, letting time pass and feeling the comfort of having Jeannie sit close.

"How is she?" I heard the nurse say, now back in the room.

"She fell back asleep," Jeannie whispered. "I'm going to stay with her."

"She will likely sleep most of the next twenty four hours. I will be back to check on her in just a moment," the nurse said before her footsteps faded into the background.

Jeannie's voice trailed off to a low tone, well below what I should've been able to hear, "I am having the hardest time in the world dealing with how you look right now, Amy. My heart aches for you, and ...I'm angry, too...so very angry. I don't know why you have to get all the pain...and I...I get all the glory."

I opened my eyes just the tiniest bit, long enough to see her near the foot of the bed, looking down at her hands, which were folder together. A small red light coming from the side of my bed gave off a glow. My mind grew heavy, and I fell back into a deep sleep.

I learned to swim at the age of nine, much later than my peers. Wearing tubes in my ears for chronic ear infections had hindered me from learning how to swim along with all the other kids. I feared water just as much as Dad feared snakes. Todd, Toots, and I were in the same swim class, and so all three of us learned to swim together. When our report cards came at the end of the lessons, Todd had easily outshined me, and he made sure to tell me so. I was so scared of deep water that even when the lifeguard offered to take me out and teach me in the five-foot pool, I was afraid. I was the girl holding on to the side of the pool, not going past where I could touch.

Early in August of the same year, Jeannie and I went to the pool together, riding our bikes, counting our change, and then running to the pool's edge. Jeannie was an expert swimmer. She was the girl with no fear. She was the girl who had saved a boy from drowning.

It was on that day in August that Jeannie convinced me to jump off the high diving board, into the deep end. A feeling of fear and exhilaration came over me as Jeannie coached me from the side of the pool, her body immerged all the way to her shoulders. I could see her face looking at me from what seemed like hundreds of feet, not just ten, below me. She told me exactly what to do, and then, over and over again, said she would save me if I couldn't make it. I stood on the edge of the board for several long seconds; the water cast my reflection far away below. I didn't know how to swim, even with all the lessons. I could hear Jeannie. She was encouraging me more than anyone ever had—loud, confident, and sure. She just *knew* I could do it.

So I jumped.

She swam after me when I struggled. Then we both got to the side of the pool and smiled and cheered about my victory.

"You did it!" she said to me enthusiastically that day. "You really did it! You jumped off the diving board!"

"I am so glad that you were here. I couldn't have done it without you! Did you see how high I jumped? I did it! I really did it!"

"Yes! You did! I'm so glad I was here! You did it, Amy!"

I often thought that Jeannie must have pleaded with God while we were still in heaven: "Won't you please send me first?" she may have asked. "Amy will need me. I just know she will. Let me go ahead of her. I will show her how to have courage, how to be strong, and I will protect her when she needs me. And, God, don't wait too long to send her to Earth. I'll be waiting to take care of her."

I am so thirsty. My throat...Oh, someone give me water, please! Why are my arms still strapped down? I can't move my legs. Where is Jeannie? Where is Mom? My jaw—everything—hurts so badly. Please, God, are you there? I promise—promise—that if you get me through this night, I will always honor you. Through every chapter of my life, from this day forward, I will do my best. I don't know if I can make it on my own tonight. I just...need you...like I never have before. This is more than I can handle. I can't do this.

I turned my head slightly and saw something shining back at me—the red light. I stared at it for a long time as I tried to absorb my confined condition. Then I fell back asleep, even with the pain, knowing God was near—He must be.

What time is it? How long have I been here? I need water.

I tried to sort out any memory of my surgery, but only fog filled my mind. Just one day earlier I had sat in my room on the edge of my bed and had written in my journal.

Sunday, June 18

One day before my surgery, and I think I'm ready. Gramp came over tonight to say a special prayer for me, and he cried all the way through it, hardly getting his words right. He gave me a kiss on the cheek, then he hugged me goodbye. We have to be at the hospital at 8:30 a.m.

The next day Mom had asked me to be the one to drive us to Salt Lake City for my surgery. My nerves were calm, and Mom needed to rest on the way down. Nothing was better in the whole wide world than being the captain of the van, although she was a lot of metal to handle once we got to the big city. Tight turns in a twelve-passenger van made me feel like I had skills behind the wheel. Luckily I only had to do a few left turns and one right turn. Once we were in my hospital room, I changed into a white cotton gown with tiny blue flowers on it, put my street clothes in a bag marked with my name, and let my mom tie the fabric strings together in the back. The anesthesiologist came by next and asked routinely if I knew of any drug I was allergic to. I shook my head "no" while at the same time Mom answered a sound, "Yes."

"She had a reaction to the drug Anectine when she was just a few days old…" she said, while glancing back at me. "She had a hard time coming out of the drug. We were afraid she might not ever wake up."

"Anectine is an older drug that we don't use much anymore, but I will note it in her paperwork," he said, while pushing up his glasses on his shiny, somewhat-bumpy nose.

After we were all situated, Dad and Jeannie arrived with Gram and Gramp in tow. All these years they had been to nearly every single surgery, starting with my first one at five days old. My heart was so full just seeing them there to support me on my big day. Auntie Julie showed up a few minutes after they had transported me to the gurney, and she came bearing the gift of laughter—my favorite comic book, *The Far Side.* I got choked up looking around at all the people I loved right there with me, each one rooting for a safe and healthy outcome.

Gramp came right up to me and put one hand on my shoulder, leaning down into the gurney as he whispered into my ear: "Just remember your ol' Gramp will be out here waiting for you when you're all done. We were here just like this when you were a baby. You've been through a hell of lot for one kid. We sure do love you." His eyes filled with tears, and his hands started shaking, just like mine. He made my own emotions well up, and I fought to hold back the tears. Echoed in love, I found myself having flashbacks to all the other times I had been in the same situation so many years before. A moment of fear struck me, out of habit, and I quickly dismissed it. This time, *this time* I was going to be brave. This time I would make all the nurses and the doctors laugh, and they would say, "This girl is amazing! This cranial facial surgery is not even *phasing* her!" Yes, this time I knew what to expect. *This* time I was prepared.

I said good-bye to my family and then the nurse pushed my gurney next to a wall in a hallway lit by large white lights. And there I waited and met fear—once again. My arms and legs started to shake with nerves, and then my whole body shook with tiny vibrations that I couldn't seem to control. *Pull it together! You can do this! Don't be scared—it will be over soon, and you will be back to normal. Stop shaking. Come on...stop...shaking.* Several minutes later Dr. Thomas arrived, his presence comforting my nerves.

"You won't feel anything during surgery, Amy. We will take good care of you." He looked me right in the eyes, and I couldn't help but trust him.

When he walked away, my eyes started to water, and I wanted to shout, "Never mind, nurses, doctors, and the lovely staff! I am fine the way I am! Take me home, please! Pull the van around, Dad. This is no longer going to happen!"

The anesthesiologist was at my side next, like a robot, putting the IV in my arm and taping it down with such force that I nearly spit, "Ouch!" Then he gave me a shot straight into the IV, and I felt the cold drug quickly kick in. The rush tingled from my limbs to my insides, and I remembered how much I liked falling asleep this way. Soon, all my brave thoughts and all of my fears were covered in relaxation so strong I couldn't—and didn't—fight it.

And, just like all the times before, while the doctor worked, I slept. And I felt no pain.

Until I woke.

Then the pain struck me with explosive and pessimistic force and dragged me into a place I didn't know existed. It was my kryptonite, and I had no choice but to let it win. I stared again at the red light, focusing in on the moment and hoping that time would speed up. I wondered how much longer it would be until I felt like myself again. A day? A week? A month? *Forever?*

"Amy, hi. My name is Jayne. I'm your nurse tonight, and I will be taking care of you. What is your pain level? Can you tell me by lifting one finger for OK, two for not good, and three for really bad?"

I put two fingers up. The pain was getting to be more than I could bear. I only knew that I needed some relief.

"I'm just going to take your vitals and clear your breathing tubes. When I'm done I'll give you more morphine, and then you can go back to sleep."

I tried to respond.

"Are you cold? If you are blink or nod."

I managed to blink twice to make sure she understood.

In a few minutes she was back with a warm blanket. She placed it on my knees, and then unfolded it down to the end of the hospital bed. The blanket was heavy and heated, and it felt so good on my cold toes.

"OK, Amy, this may be uncomfortable. I'm sorry. I need to clear your passageway so you can continue to breathe through the tubes. I will be using a type of vacuum suction, and you will feel a bit of sting." The sound of the machine broke my euphoric state, then the pain hit.

Wait! What are you doing? STOP!

The wretched throbbing amplified, shredding the nerves on my mouth and throat over and over again. Seconds felt like hours. I couldn't yell—my voice was paralyzed with the tubes in place—but my mind screamed loud and furious. *Will this never end? You are hurting me! Stop. Stop. Stop! I can't take it. Stop! Do you even know how this feels? Make it stop!*

"Are you doing OK? We're almost done" she said above the machine. "I'm sorry. I know that must hurt. The bad news is, we will need to clear the tubes every two hours."

My eyes wanted to cry. My head wanted to yell. I felt so vulnerable.

Reach, Amy…reach. Reach for your strength. This won't last forever, I told myself, feeling my body fighting to stop the unravel.

"All right, I am just going to change your IV bag and give you more medicine for the pain, and then you can go back to sleep." I nodded the best that I could. The claustrophobia of being trapped in a body that I had such little control over stole the personality that I so desperately wanted this nurse to know I had. I wanted her to see that I was tough and resilient *and* funny, but I only felt weak and drained—physically and emotionally.

When we were little, Jeannie and Todd and I used to lock each other in the boot box next to the back door as a game to see who could last the longest. The box was wooden and only four feet by two feet. I would scrunch inside and the other two would sit on top. The box was thick with darkness inside, and the air had a damp smell of wet boots and soggy gloves. Even if I pushed with all my might, I couldn't budge the hinged lid. I would lie there in the crippling dark thinking about the bravery it took to be smashed in a ball with so little air to breathe. Then the fear of never being able to get out would set in, and I would pound on the wooden "coffin" screaming, "Let me out! Let me out! I can't breathe!" Sometimes they let me out right away, and sometimes they would pretend they didn't hear me. I would get anxious thinking I would surely die a disastrous death right there, confined forever inside the smelly boot box.

"OK, you're all set," the nurse said. "You should start feeling the morphine take effect. I will be right here with you all night." The last of her sentence faded into the drugs. The red bulb next to my bed seemed even brighter, like the shade of the summer sky just before the sun sets, throwing off the last flashes of color. The red light was my constant refuge. My mind once again fell into heavy, wonderful sleep.

Two hours later, the hell of the suction therapy was unleashed again. It woke me from peace and stung the nerves in my sensitive mouth while cracking my already parched throat. The pain seemed unavoidable, and was so tangible I felt that it had become a permanent part of me, seeping into every cell and fiber. The nurse kept saying, "Just a few more seconds," but she lied. She didn't know what she was inflicting. How could she? The seconds spanned eternity, and there I lay, not able to make a sound—not one tiny sound—to show I had taken responsibility for owning the pain.

I woke at four in the morning and slowly looked to my left to find the bit of constant comfort I had found throughout the night. The light was still there. My head was spinning, and my right hip came alive with the sensation of pins stabbing into my skin; I was in need of another dose of pain medicine, and yet, I hated feeling so dependent.

A new nurse came into my room, and with the change in guard I felt surprisingly abandoned. This wasn't fair. I needed Jayne back! Jayne knew me, and she knew how to take care of me. The new nurse, Lori, started right in checking my vitals and

224

trading my IV bag with a full one. The nerves in my face stood up, awake. She succeeded in delivering the same level of pain while suctioning out my tubes as Jayne had. The hurt raged on, loud and intense. I was glad that none of my friends could see me now. I am sure I looked awful. I *felt* awful. My lips burned. They were raw and cracked from being stretched in surgery. The nurse must have read my mind. She took a white plastic spatula, not even two inches long, and spread Vaseline on my lips.

Out the door and down the hall I heard the cry of a young woman. Someone else, just like me, faced the pain. I wondered about all the stories hidden in the walls of the hospital of weak bones, mending hearts, failing organs—the fighting for life and even the giving in and letting go. The walls had heard the conflict of the human spirit and the prayers to God. I felt the calm of the medicine rocking me back into an unaware state. I liked it when the aching disappeared and let me rest.

By 6 a.m. I knew the suction was coming, and, it seemed, so did my body. I gravitated toward the comfort of knowing that it would be over soon and that I would be getting more air through the breathing tubes once they were cleared. I took a minute to inhale when the nurse was done, and I promised myself that when the wires were off my teeth in six weeks and I had my strength back, I would run as fast as I could, bringing my lungs to capacity with rich oxygen.

The first night recovering from surgery was the worst night of my life; the confined feeling and the tangible pain were paired to become a living nightmare.

"How is your pain level?" the nurse asked, her voice soft. "Do you need more medicine?"

I opened my eyes, looked at her, and tried to nod my head. I hoped she knew that meant I needed more painkiller. She did. I woke two hours later, knowing it was still morning, to the sound of Dr. Thomas speaking in his everyday volume: "Let's keep the breathing tubes in another twenty-four hours," he said to the nurse.

What did you say? Are you talking about me? Can't you see I'm fading? No, please! No. My throat is killing me. Please take them out now. I'm not strong enough to last another day like this.

I kept my eyes shut to avoid using energy I didn't have and to hide my emotion, and then I heard Mom. She was standing next to me. How had I not noticed her before now? I seemed to remember that she had been there all night long. Next to me? Down the hall? I wasn't sure.

"She is really uncomfortable with the tubes in. Is there a chance you can remove them sooner than that?"

Oh, thank you, Mom. Yes, please take them out. Please! Speak for me!

"I can understand that, and we will pull them out as soon as she is more stable. For now, it is best to leave them in," Dr. Thomas said. "The good news is her operation was successful."

It went well? So I am OK?

"We extracted the necessary sponge bone and transplanted it to the areas of her face that needed more structure," he said, adding, "I know she wanted us to take the bone from her skull, but I think in the long run she will be much happier without having to grow back her hair, so we took it from her hip. She will have about a three inch scar."

So that explains my hip pain and the numb feeling in my leg.

"We were able to successfully add several metal plates to her face which we screwed into the transferred hip bone for stability—twelve in all. The result will add a nice harmony to Amy's face."

"Did you have to do a blood transfusion?" Mom asked.

"No, in fact, she was lucky to not have lost much blood. I was pleased with that. She is a strong little lady," Dr. Thomas stated. Then he went into more detail about the surgery while referencing a plaster mold of my jaw and teeth. I tried to listen and comprehend, but his voice seemed so far away. "We also redesigned her chin, like we discussed, and placed a screw in it to keep the new placement intact. By moving her chin forward slightly, we gave her a more balanced profile."

"I see," Mom said.

"What did you use to screw the screws in?" Dad asked, standing what seemed to be near the back of the room. He, of course, would want to know the mechanics behind the operation.

"Actually, we use a power screwdriver," Dr. Thomas said, "but the screws are made of titanium." Dad must have been smiling. I was almost positive. "The last thing we did was change her jawline. We broke it, then shifted her teeth and bite, and finally, wired it all back together. This phase of her recovery will be the most intense and uncomfortable for her."

I lay there thinking how could anything be more uncomfortable than not being able to talk, or eat, or drink, or take a big gulp of air into my lungs. I craved sleep—the only thing I knew I could have. Without making much of an effort to let the others know I had been listening, I fell back asleep feeling thirsty and uncomfortable.

The nurse woke me soon after with the same horrible tube cleaning treatment that I had endured throughout the night. And this time, I cried. The pain descended on me too intensely, and it had haunted me too often during the night and into the morning. I couldn't bear it anymore. Then the nurse carried on with the routine of checking my vitals and changing my IV.

When the nurse was done, I opened my eyes as far as I could for the first time. I saw Mom and Dad standing next to my bed. In the hallway I heard my Auntie Debbie and Uncle Davie talking to Jeannie. I looked straight at Mom, staring her down to get her attention; I had to have someone listen to me even if I couldn't talk! It didn't take long for her to notice and soon she leaned over me, and I desperately tried to communicate with her. *Someone* had to know how badly my throat hurt and how thirsty I had become. I lifted my hands and pretended to write on them.

"You want something to write on?"

I nodded my head and lay my head back on my bed, all of my energy gone.

"Do you have something Amy can write with? I think she's trying to tell us something," said Mom to the nurse. The nurse came back a minute later with a small white board and a blue dry erase marker.

"Here, she can use this," she said, wiping it clean. The effort just to hold the board upright and concentrate consumed me. Finally, I managed to write three words: "pain throat thirsty."

"She's thirsty! Can we get her some ice chips?" I heard Mom say.

"If she wants them, let's give her a few to try," the nurse said. "She'll have a hard time sucking on them with such trauma to her mouth and jaw, but it's worth a try if it'll make her more comfortable."

Mom tried to push a small piece of ice through the tangled wires that held my jaw together. At last a tiny wedge made it to my tongue, melting on my lips and giving me the smallest amount of relief. I took the board and wrote: "more." For the next few minutes Mom fed me slices of ice through my mouth maze, and then exhaustion set in, and I lay back on my pillow and rested, wondering how I could possibly lack so much strength.

"When you were just eighteen months old, we took you to the hospital for one of your surgeries," Mom said quietly, now sitting next to me in a chair by my bed. "The nurse told me to go ahead and leave you there, all alone, and that you would be fine. But when I came to get you three days later, you wouldn't have anything to do with me. I walked into the waiting area to get you, and you were riding a small red trike around the room. You never even stopped pedaling. You just looked up at me and scowled. You certainly knew that you had been left there alone! Of course, I should have known you wouldn't like being there by yourself. After we took

you home it took you days to stop being mad at me. I
decided that I would never leave you all alone to
recover in the hospital again." Mom patted my bed.
"I stayed here last night, just down the hall, but I
have been coming in all night long to check on you,"
Mom continued.

I couldn't speak the words that I wanted to
say, but just having her near covered me like a warm
comforting blanket. To do this all alone would
be...impossible. I needed her there, just like I always
had—right from the very start. I closed my eyes
softly and drifted away, once again, for what seemed
to me a long time. When I woke again, I heard voices:

"If she's stable we can move her out of
intensive care into a standard room within the next
few hours," the nurse said to Mom. *What?* I asked
inwardly. *So soon? Just leave me here. I don't want to go
to a new room. I like this room and the red light with its
faint glow.* But exactly two hours later, the nurse
stayed true to her word.

"Amy, I want you to try and swing your legs
over the edge of the bed, and then stand if you feel
like you have the strength. I'll hold the IV as we
move you to the gurney," she instructed, showing an
enormous amount of patience and understanding.

Oh I can do that. No problem, no problem. But
when I tried to do the simple task, my head started to
spin in a dizzy dance that ended with me having to
start all over again, and again. After the third try I
got to my feet. *Legs! Where are you? Stand! Come on,
legs! Why are you so weak?* The nurse grabbed my arm
in a firm grip to steady me, then twisted my body
and sat me down on the new gurney. I felt like I had

just run a marathon. Complete and utter exhaustion set in. My heart was racing and my head felt light and queasy.

My new hospital room was small, but it had a nice big window that faced west and allowed me to watch the sunset. The bed had several buttons on the side—one that moved it up, another that moved it down, and two that moved the head of my bed up or down. There was also a button with the word "nurse" printed on it—but there was no red glow.

"We'll need to give her a sponge bath," the nurse said to Mom as soon as I was settled in my new bed. *Sponge bath? Oh no, someone please stop this train wreck. Old people in nursing homes get sponge baths! Not me! Not ME!* But nobody asked my opinion, and, really, it wouldn't have made a difference anyway. The nurse lifted and turned my body, and with Mom's help it was over in a few short minutes. I pretended not to be embarrassed, but inside I was absolutely mortified. I firmly decided that nobody needed to know that I had had a sponge bath—nobody.

Night came soon and played out the same as the one before. Each time I woke to have my tubes cleared, I watched the second hand chase the minute hand—pushing the hours closer to dawn.

"OK, let's go ahead and take out her breathing tubes now," Dr. Thomas ordered the next morning.

I opened my eyes as fast as I could. At last a bit of relief! I moved the bed into an upright position, and tucked my hair behind my ears. Dr. Thomas called for the nurse to assist him, and then put one hand firmly on the back of my head and started to pull the tubes out. What I thought would be sweet relief was instead drawn-out, sharp pain as he slowly pulled out the tubes that were covered in a waterfall of blood and fluid. I could feel the sensation all the way down to my lungs in a piercing jagged pull. I coughed and gagged when the tubes broke free, but I felt helpless without being able to open my jaw. "You are healing well," Dr. Thomas said as the nurse wiped the blood off of my mouth. "Everything looks good. You should be able to go home in another five days if it all keeps going well, OK? I'll be back in to check on you tonight."

I looked at him and gave a single nod of my head then sunk back into the bed. "Amy, would you like to try to stand up on your own?" the nurse asked when Dr. Thomas had finished his assessment. I couldn't help but remember how I felt the last time I stood up, but I wanted to try again. I got up slowly and felt the same weak feeling I had the time before, but I stood for several seconds on my own, determined to make it to my in-room bathroom and to the mirror that hung above the sink. For two days I had wondered what I looked like now that I had *finally* had my surgery. With one hand I guided the IV tower, and with the other I used the wall to steady myself between small steps. Mom had stepped out of the room, promising to be back in a few minutes, and the nurse stood nearby filling out more paperwork. After a few steps my legs seemed to get stronger. My old self was coming back! I turned the corner to the bathroom and saw the mirror shining back at me. I had such a love-hate relationship with the thing, but more so, I was curious. I looked down at my feet, still covered in blue hospital slippers, as I took the slow steps all the way to the sink's edge. Then I put the IV tower next to the wall, placed both hands on the countertop, and looked up at my reflection.

"Amy? Are you in here?" I heard Jeannie call from the doorway of my room, but I did not respond—my eyes were fixed on my reflection. Staring back at me was a stranger who had puffy, fat cheeks, bruised eyes, tape across her chin, a stretched nose, and swollen, cracked, dry lips. *I look horrible.*

I lifted my upper lip gently using two fingers on my right hand and two fingers on my left. Inside my mouth was a tangled mess of wires keeping my teeth snapped together, lots of blood, stitches, and swollen irritated tissue. The sweeping feeling of claustrophobia melted over me again, landing in a mess right in front of me. I moved the IV tower to the other side of the sink and started to shuffle back to the bed.

"I'm here," I said to Jeannie through clenched teeth and a scratchy throat. With the tubes out, I finally was able to speak again, but even the smallest sentence hurt to say. Whispering was much more comfortable.

"Are you OK? Wow, I can't believe you're up and walking around!"

"Mmm hmm," I said, wondering silently if I would ever look like myself again.

"I brought you some slippers and socks with pom-poms," she said, helping me back to the bed.

She knew how I loved pom-pom socks. Gram always wore them. Jeannie had brought me a sparkly white pair with pink pom-poms. I sat down on the edge of the bed next to Jeannie, and she helped me take off the sad blue hospital socks and put on the happy new pom-pom socks. I was her little sister again, and she was taking care of me.

"Are you ready to try something to eat?" the nurse asked, coming back into the room wheeling a cart full of colorful liquids.

I nodded. *Eat? Food? YES! I am so hungry. Feed me!*

"I know that Dr. Thomas explained that you will be on a liquid diet for six weeks, so today we're going to try a little hot Jell-O and some broth and see how you do," the nurse said in a matter-of-fact tone.

Hot Jell-O? For lunch?

"You will want to try and suck the Jell-O through a straw on the inside of your mouth, next to your cheek. Because your jaws are wired shut, that will be the only real place for you to have enough room for the straw," she said while setting up a small cup and filling it with hot red Jell-O.

I placed the straw in right where she said, but it felt all wrong and so tight. I had no strength in my lips to wrap them around the straw, yet my stomach was growling eagerly. I managed to get a small amount from the cup to the straw, but it tasted horrible—like red, bloody acid. *Disgusting!*

"Did you get anything to go down?" Mom was back with me, helping to see that I got a little food in my system.

I shook my head feeling total and utter disbelief that I couldn't do a simple, menial task; I *knew* how to use a straw! Why were my lips failing me now? I was so disappointed in myself and so hungry. More than anything, though, I craved real food. The knowledge that six long weeks of a liquefied menu lay ahead felt daunting.

"Do you want to try the chicken broth instead?" the nurse asked. Broth *did* sound better. At least *it* came in a can, like soup, and was supposed to be eaten hot. I looked down at the brown translucent liquid thinking that my lunch was as bland as cardboard. Did anyone ever eat a bowl of chicken broth and say, "Wow, that was delicious!"? I put the straw to my lips again, and with full concentration and effort I was able to get several sips to go down successfully. The broth was warm, and it flowed easily from my swollen throat down the straight path to my stomach. I felt better, even if it was boring food.

Then I saw the last thing on the tray—apple juice! A beverage that was actually *meant* to be a beverage. I concentrated again, with Mom and Jeannie cheering me on, and I drank half of it— taking a whole hour to eat.

"I got you something at the gift shop," Mom said, handing me a white shiny bag. I opened it immediately. Staring back at me was a small brown monkey. My collection of monkeys had officially begun! Now I had three! One from Mom, one from Dad, and one I bought all on my own. He was a baby monkey with a diaper, a pacifier, and soft short fur. For a second I thought I was probably too old for a stuffed animal, but for some reason the little guy comforted me. I tucked him into my arms, pushed the button to recline my bed, and once again fell asleep—only to wake to the sound of the phone ringing loudly in my room. Mom picked up the receiver:

"Yes, she's right here. She can't talk very well, but I'll give her the phone." She handed it to me. "It's Katie," she mouthed. My eyes filled with tears at the sound of her name, my best friend. She remembered. I put the phone to my ear, and I tried to talk to her and tell her all about the surgery the best that I could. The wires holding my mouth together made it hard to show my excitement for her phone call; I sounded like a circus ventriloquist with a mouth full of tar. Still, hearing her voice was the highlight of my day. She sounded so happy as she told me all about the beach and swimming in the ocean and how the waves felt when they crashed into her.

The next day I got a bouquet of balloons from Dr. B and then a visit from Wendy, Christy, and a few other friends from school. Christy brought me a single pink rose. Moose didn't come to visit, though, and I kind of knew he wouldn't. Just the fact that he said he *might* come had meant so much to me in the weeks leading up to the surgery. Gram and Gramp and Jeannie were there nearly the whole week, checking on my progress. Dad went home after the first day to take care of the rest of the kids, but Mom—Mom stayed, just like she promised she would. She took care of my growing list of needs and worked hard to make sure that my pillows were fluffed and that I always had something to drink. She even helped me to the bathroom—I had lost all shame.

The days that followed were filled with the same routine: Dr. Thomas would come to check on me in the morning. Then I would try to drink some apple juice and hot Jell-O for breakfast, watch some TV, get a few visitors, drink some more hot Jell-O and Sprite for lunch, try to sit up, and — if I felt OK — read a few *Far Side* cartoons and tried not to laugh. After that I would walk around my room, watch more TV, get another visit from Dr. Thomas, have hot broth and apple juice for dinner, and finally go to sleep for the night. The nurse taught me how to suction my own mouth at night, and I felt mighty smart doing such a sophisticated job. I would wake up during the wee nighttime hours, fire up the controls, and clean out my mouth, and when I finished I could breathe a little better.

One night after cleaning my mouth out, I couldn't fall back asleep. I lay there in my bed, with the white sheets and two pillows holding me in a comfortable position, and I prayed. I was so grateful. During the last few days of recovery I had forgotten how lucky I had been in surgery; the procedure had gone just as planned. I was grateful for the skilled doctors, the nice nurses, all of the visitors that had traveled so far to see me, and I was grateful that the surgery was over and God had protected me. I was filled with a calm peace — heaven's own sleep-aid.

CHAPTER TWENTY-ONE

*Friendship ties together pain and struggle with laugher
and loyalty. A true friend will stand next to you in your
hardest hour and find a way to make it all OK.*

"Let's try going for a walk," Mom said the
next morning after my hot Jell-O breakfast.

I shoved the bed tray aside. "Really? But
where?"

"Just through the halls of the hospital. A nice
walk will do you good, and me, too."

I couldn't argue with that; my room had
assumed an atmosphere of staleness and
predictability. I stood up, had Mom check the back of
my gown to make sure I was all tied together, then
steadied myself with the IV tower and took the steps
needed to leave the room. Mom and I walked all
around the hospital, and I tried to smile at the other
patients and visitors that we passed, even though it
hurt to raise my lips in a friendly greeting. Most
stared at me. I expected that, but this time I didn't
even care! The walk felt so good, and I could feel my
personality coming back from hibernation.

Tracy Clead and her family came to visit, and
her warm friendship and laugh made me sit right up
in bed —I wanted to show her I was the same Amy I

had always been, cracking jokes and having a good time.

My last night in the hospital, Mom said her goodbyes and Dad stayed with me instead. He pulled his cot close to my bed. "Here is your water mug. I put ice in it for you," he said, adding, "Do you need another blanket? Are you cold? Do you know how to call the nurse if you need her help?" I answered all of his questions with a shake or a nod of my head, so happy to have him paying me his full attention. For a flash of an instant I remembered being a young girl at the dinner table and thinking someone had poured water into my glass of milk. I was upset, and although it was just a silly little problem, Dad took my glass and leaned it back and forth, attempting to see the water. In that one instant he was all mine, and nobody else's problems mattered. Having him next to me in the hospital felt much like that moment—multiplied by a hundred.

Sleep came slowly for me, yet Dad was snoring loudly soon after the lights went out. I worried I would wake him up once I fell asleep with my labored breathing and nurses coming in to check on my vitals, so I forced myself to keep my eyes open. I hadn't ever slept so close to Dad, yet there he was, near enough to touch. His dark brown hair was still combed in a part, almost undisturbed, and his face showed only a hit of stubble that had started to grow in since his morning shave. I couldn't remember a time in my life when I had studied Dad's face so closely. His lips were parted in the middle, but they touched on the edges as he filled his lungs with air. In and out, in and out, in and out. Oh, how I missed breathing so contently. I could hear the nurses out in the hall at their station, chatting quietly, and for a moment I thought that I might never be able to make it at home alone without them. The hospital room practically felt like it was mine! And I was just starting to get used to the liquid diet that they delivered three times a day to my bedside. Yet, I knew tomorrow the sun would rise, like it did each morning, only this time I would begin to face my recovery outside the walls of the hospital. At 2 a.m. when I needed to clear my mouth, I flipped on the machine—a nearly automatic reaction to wanting to breathe more clearly. The enormous sound caught Dad off guard, and he sat straight up in his cot, fully awake, hurling his blanket to the ground in a state of immediate action.

"Amy! What's going on? What's that sound? Do you need something?"

"I'm OK. I have to do this all the time," I said, my muffled voice falling short of his ears over the roar of the suction. A few minutes later I turned off the machine and lay back down in the bed before closing my eyes in an attempt to finally rest. Dad's eyes were still open and watchful when I drifted to sleep, real proof that he loved and cared for me.

The next morning Dad got up much earlier than I did, and he did so quietly. He prepared for the day without waking me, complete with his face magically smooth again after shaving off the night's whiskers. After my routine breakfast the nurse informed me that I could shower if I would like before being discharged. *Ah, a shower! Yes! It has been so long!* I felt a rush of joy at having that ounce of independence back as I stripped off the hospital gown and stepped into the shower, free at last from the IV and all of the hospital cords. I let the hot water run all over my body and even inside my mouth before I soaked my hair for several long minutes in the stream that felt like rain. I lathered to a full head of suds, digging into my scalp and rubbing the pads of my fingers in tiny circles. Then I took the bar of soap and scrubbed the spot on my arm that the IV had been taped to until the rolls of sticky residue dissolved away with the rest of the dirt. With a clumsy move I dropped the soap, and it smacked the puddle of water on the shower floor. It felt so good to be clean again, but the moment was short lived, and my body quickly betrayed me. The energy I had felt just minutes earlier ran off me as fast as the water did, down the drain and out of sight. My mind was left spinning, and my head was light and fuzzy. I knew that feeling. I had fainted once before, the dark cloud grabbing hold of me and taking me down.

I'm going to faint! I can feel it. What do I do? Think, Amy, think! I sat down right on the shower floor, next to the bar of soap that was getting smaller and smaller, the suds on my head washing over me and into my eyes. *If Mom were here, it would be different, but, not Dad. I can't ask him to help me. I have to figure this out. Come on...think, Amy.* I put my hands out in front of me. They were shaking, and my breath was short and fast. *I don't know if I can do this. I don't think I can. I need to, though. Come on, body. Please. Please don't make me ask Dad to help me. Or a nurse. Please fight back and give me a minute of strength.* I stood up with my legs shaking and my mind spinning. I steadied myself under the showerhead and rinsed myself. Then I wrapped my body in a clean white towel and, with a final effort, lunged to the hospital bed. My eyes went black and the spinning continued for several long, drawn-out minutes as I waited for my body to reset. I was so glad to be alone—to have faced that tiny mountain without any help. My legs hung off the hospital bed, shiny with water, until I had gained enough strength to stand on them and get dressed. When I had put the clothes that I had worn to the hospital nearly a week earlier back on, tied my shoes, and finished packing my belongings, Dad came back into the room, smelling faintly of bacon and eggs. And then it hit me. I was going home.

The head nurse brought a wheelchair to my room while Dad went to pull the van around to the front of the hospital. I sat down, putting the small monkey from Mom in my lap, and the nurse gave one mighty push to get the wheels rolling. All the way down the hall, I made jokes, and all the way down the hall the nurse's laughter echoed like beautiful music.

"Do you want to stop and get a milkshake?" Dad asked as we headed home on the freeway. "Mmm hmm," I answered back, thinking that there *were* some delicious benefits to being on a liquid diet. He pulled into McDonalds, and the smell of fries surrounded the van. I had no idea how I would survive without fries for the next several weeks— lovely, beautiful fries. "Two large vanilla milkshakes," Dad said to the girl through the ordering receiver. *At last, something that I really like.* But the straw was too big for the strength in my lips, and I couldn't suck even the tiniest bit of shake up

and into my mouth. I set it down in the captain seat
drink holder and rested my head back on the seat,
grappling with the hunger that persisted in my belly.

The smell of Mom's cooking greeted me as
Dad and I came through the front door. But instead
of feeling joy, the scent of ground beef browning
with onion and spices in her large frying pan let me
down—I ached for her home cooking. "Are you
feeling OK?" Toots asked, making her way from the
chaos of my brothers playing to where I stood frozen
in the middle of the kitchen floor. I tried to answer
Toots back, but my voice felt weak, silenced by the
wires that bound my jaw together and even more so
from the reaction that was starting to gather around
my thoughts. So I just nodded my head up and
down. Inside though, I was struggling. Mom came
over to me, took the hospital bag out of my hand and
gently persuaded me to sit down in Dad's big
recliner.

All the kids grabbed a plate of food, with
Todd piling his sloppy joe so high it overflowed. He
had toasted the bun and was layering the meat sauce
with cheese, which melted to strands of gold—the
image was pure torture. Mom was busy getting
plates for the rest of the kids, so I got up out of the
chair and went to the fridge, my head fighting the
dizzy spells. My options weren't numerous—milk,
juice, water. Oh how I wanted a toasted sloppy joe! A
crunchy, delicious, hearty meal!

"Your eyes are kinda bruised." said Todd
through bites, the red sauce dripping from his lips.
"Does it hurt?"

"Kinda," I said, glad that he cared. Justin and
Darin each stopped long enough to look at me and

then continued to chase each other around the table. I settled for a strawberry energy drink made for old people with no teeth who frequently had sponge baths—a geriatric smoothie. I sat back down in the chair and watched my family move around me with their full, content bellies.

"Your face looks fat and puffy," Darin said, voicing a fear of mine that the surgery didn't help at all.

"I have twelve screws in my head," I fired back to him. I stood up to walk to the bathroom and on the way, saw the mail that was stacked up high next to the phone. In the bathroom the laundry overflowed the basket, spilling onto the floor. The lingering housework was evidence that Mom had been missed here at home while she'd been helping me in the hospital. The world, it seemed, had gone on just fine without me here, though. I was hardly missed at all, yet I was strangely uneasy about being tossed back into the normal throws of disorder at my home. It was so different from the quiet atmosphere and all the attention I had received at the hospital. The mirror in the bathroom bounced back a reflection at me, but I was avoiding all mirrors for a while. My stomach started to growl again, the strawberry energy drink holding no weight in my stomach.

"Do you want to try your new blender?" Mom asked when I rejoined the family in the kitchen. "We can put in a sloppy joe and you can drink it right up!" I raised my eyebrows, partly in disgust and partly in famished curiosity. All I could think about was Todd's lunch plate and how badly I missed real food.

244

"OK," I said, hopeful that it wouldn't be too bad. But the meal was worse than I ever thought it could be. I closed my eyes and put the straw to my lips, not looking at what I was drinking while gulping down the strange texture. At least my stomach was satisfied.

"It all goes to the same place. You just don't have to do any of the work to get it there," Dad said, rubbing a bit of sarcasm on my attempt to eat my lunch. My mouth felt like a prison, but I had done it. I had made it through the surgery, and it had been a success. I would survive.

During the next several days, I rested, blended up anything I could find (from doughnuts to cold cereal), and waited to get better. One afternoon the doorbell rang, and on the front step was a note and flowers from a secret admirer, wishing me to get well soon. My heart jumped as high as the power lines! I wondered all day who could've left them.

Finally Katie came home from California. She came to the back door and completed her famous secret knock, then came into the kitchen area where she found me sitting in Dad's recliner. In her arms she held a pink-and-green-striped gift bag. "I got you a souvenir from my trip," she said, handing me the bag. "So how do you feel anyway? Does it hurt?" she asked. I pulled a giant pink brush out of the bag, big like a paddle, and tried to smile.

"I love it! I love it," I said, trying hard to show her that I loved it despite my stiff expression. "I was in a lot of pain in the hospital," I said, taking a moment to pause. "I'm glad it's over, but it wasn't too bad. I just don't like blending up all of my food. It's pretty gross. Tell me all about your trip!" I said, moving to the couch so we could sit by each other. Katie grabbed the brush and ran it through my hair, starting at the ends and working her way up my air-dried curls. While she brushed she told me all about the ocean and how blue it was, and how salty, too. She stayed a long time that day, and then came back the next day, and the next. My surgery and recovery had been a long ordeal, and I didn't see the end in sight for several more weeks. But with Katie near, things weren't so bad—not so bad at all.

CHAPTER TWENTY-TWO

Sometimes it is best to forget we have flaws. Everyone has scars. The difference is some are hidden on the inside, and others are on display for all to see.

My stomach roared a mean, angry growl. I dug my fingers into the skin around my empty tummy and sipped on my blended chicken noodle soup, dreaming about crackers to go with my lunch. It had been nearly four weeks since my surgery, and the pageant in Mobile, Alabama was two thousand miles from our home and mere days away. My strength had been compromised during my recovery, and having to travel in an RV-caravan of relatives for nearly thirty hours to get there sounded daunting. I felt weak and utterly exhausted. Mom made the case to Dad that she, Toots, and I should all go by air and meet the rest of the family there. He agreed with the plan. It was going to be my first time in an airplane! I finished my liquid lunch and went to my room to begin pre-packing. I laid out all of my cutest clothes, including my favorite cream and red trimmed hat that one of the teachers at the high school said reminded him of Princess Diana. I packed books to read, my journal, my camera, a notepad to draw on, and lots of straws, then rested as much as I could until the day of travel arrived.

"The best part of flying is the take-off," Mom said as we waited to board the plane. I stood next to the large windows and watched the aircrafts leave one after another into the morning sky. I believed once that I was meant to fly on my own when Dad brought home army parachutes, and we ran fast through the backyard, catching air behind us in the thin fabric, making our feet feel light. When the parachutes disintegrated into threads we pretended we had wings of our own and filled them with our imaginary span, running up and down the small hill in the backyard.

"Whoooopie, here we go, up, up into the air," Mom said laughing as our plane lifted off the runway and pointed its nose upward. "Pretty fun, isn't it, girls?"

"Feels like a roller coaster!" I smiled back, wide and happy, showing off the wires holding my jaw together, "Toots, look out the window!"

Up in the air I couldn't get over how brilliant and white the clouds were. The fluffy ones looked just as they did below on the ground—soft enough to sleep in. The other passengers closed their window, but not me. I kept it open and stared at the clouds so long, my eyes started to hurt from the intense bright white. Once we were airborne, all of the passengers were served a hot lunch, so I loaded my portable battery operated blender full of Salisbury Steak and potato wedges. Then I blended, the sound ricocheted throughout the craft as the blades battled to grind up the airplane food. To mask the sound I stuffed the blender out of sight below my knees, "Mom? Pass me a blanket to put over my blender. It's so loud!"

Within minutes a stewardess was leaning over our row, eyeing down Mom. "Excuse me ma'am. Can you explain to me what is going on back here? We have passengers reporting that a terrible noise is coming from this area, and some are concerned it's the engine, which I can *assure* you it is not. What are you hiding down there?"

"Oh, nothing to be concerned about, that's the sound of my daughter's portable blender. See here, her jaw is wired shut and she has to liquefy all her food before she can eat it." I lifted the blanket to expose the struggling blender. The stewardess looked at me, nodded once, and let the blending continue. I covered my mouth to hold back laughing, thinking about all those people fearing the worst— and me, drinking the worst.

"Wow! Look at this! Mobile, Alabama, here we are. A city of grandeur. My goodness it looks like a southern post card," Mom said as we made our way by taxi to the hotel. Old, giant mansions lined the streets and each was surrounded with a manicured yard. Mature trees towered over the landscape, flowers colored the beds with optimism and hope, and it seemed each front porch was waving an American flag. Our hotel room had two queen beds trimmed in gold and forest green comforters, a big window, and a stiff couch that beckoned to me as we entered. "I have to sit, Mom. I'm so tired. I might faint. I can't breathe so good."

"Oh, dear. Sit down right here on the couch. I am going to walk to the front desk and see if they have something we can give you to blend up and drink. I am sure you are just plain worn out after our day of travel."

"I am."

Toots unpacked her luggage, while I sat and waited for my energy to surface again. Mom was back soon with a drink and delightful tone in her voice. "The staff is just wonderful. I told them all about your situation and they said they would do anything they could to make you more comfortable."

"Good. Thanks, Ma."

"And, they said there is a reception in an hour in the lobby for all the families of pageant girls. Here, drink this down," she said, handing me an orange juice.

"Thanks," I said, taking a sip through my bendy straw. "I am going to sit here for a minute longer. My head is spinning."

"I think we all could use a good, long rest. We've had quite the day."

An hour later the hotel lobby was humming with family support teams, including lots of cute teenage boys, all to cheer their sisters on in the pageant. I spotted one tall boy wearing glasses. He was about my age with dirty blond hair that made a giant surfing swoop before it feathered out. I made my way to the refreshment area, tracking close behind his steps, grabbed a drink, and introduced myself. "Hey, I'm Amy. Is your sister in the pageant?"

"Sorry, what did you say?"

I moved the muscles in my mouth and throat just right to annunciate my response back to him, "Oh, uh. My jaw—is wired shut. I can't talk very good." My voice was lower, but not sexy lower—more like scary lower. I wanted to scream, *"Hey! I am cool! I just can't talk normally right now! Have you ever dated a girl with a portable blender? It's pretty awesome! Come on, give me a chance!"* He was polite but moved away from our conversation as quickly as he could.

"Mom, will you walk with me to the McDonald's on the corner?" I asked when we didn't have any pressing tourist plans the following day. "I'm craving fries. I just have to have some. It's all I can think about."

"Well, we'd better go get you some then! Do you feel good enough to walk that far?"

"Yeah. I will be OK."

Mom and I strolled along the sidewalk, where she did most of the talking. The street was lined in trees with branches as old as the hills, the sunlight showering the leaves. I wanted to sit and rest, but wanted fries more.

"I need a large fry and a small vanilla shake," I urgently said to the cashier once we arrived inside, the pangs of hunger attacking me.

"Miss, you are gonna have to speak up, I can't understand a thing you are sayin'."

I focused and tried not to get frustrated. Mom could understand me, why couldn't she? "Large fry. Small shake."

"I still don't get it, Miss. One more time, please."

"Large fry. Shake."

"OK, was that a *large fry* and a shake?"

I nodded up and down, knocking my dangly earrings around.

"For a minute there I thought you were saying 'argfry,' I didn't have a clue what you meant.

Glad we got that figured out! If you step to the left we will call your number when your order is ready."

Back at the hotel room I immediately plopped the shake into the bottom of the blender and covered it with fries. When the blender sounded, I could feel my taste buds going crazy, watering ridiculously. *This is it!* I thought. *I will have fries again!* I poured myself a glass of fry-shake and sat down on the couch in our hotel room and took a long, happy, sip. I grimaced. It was a horrible mix of oil and ice cream. *How could fries just turn on me like this when I need them most?* After two more sips, the rest went in the garbage, and I was back to dreaming about crunchy, salted fries. The hard couch offered me no comfort, but I was so tired I couldn't stand.

Finally it was Jeannie's big night. "We can't believe that you made the trip all the way from Utah just a few weeks after major surgery," one mom of a contestant said to me before the pageant. Another lady grabbed my cheeks with two hands and said, "You are just so beautiful! We are so glad you're here!" Her clenched fingers dug into my tender tissue and set my nerves on fire for the next hour. I tried not to cry like a baby who just got pinched, but I felt like a baby. I was hurting, and hungry, and tired.

Jeannie ditched her original talent of singing to a donkey and traded it for the new-and-improved talent of "dancing with a dummy" —that is to say, a mannequin man dressed in a tuxedo. When she and "Edward" twirled into the spotlight to the song "In the Mood," the audience thought she had broken the rule that only the contestant could occupy the stage.

He dipped her, he spun her, and he moved her across the floor in smooth, gliding rhythm. Once the audience realized that *Jeannie* was doing the work of both dancers, the laughs and cheers grew louder and louder—she had wowed them all! I screamed from our seats in the upper balcony as loud as my limited mouth could, putting my hands around my mouth and yelling her name, "Go EEEEnneeeeEEEE." My head steamed to a dizzy haze after just a few shouts, and I fell back into the arms of the chair long before the applause from the audience had died down. *This is such a rip-off*, I thought. *I can't even cheer, and I am good at cheering! I can't even hear my own voice, it's so small right now. I'm sure Jeannie can't hear me either.*

"Look at all the *gorgeous* dresses," Gram exclaimed, smelling of flowery perfume as she leaned into me. The stage was soon jam-packed with stunning young women in glittering gowns, their lips covered in glossy pink and red shades. All of them had figures that would rival Barbie herself. "Oh my heavens. They sure are pretty girls. Every one of them." She tapped her polished fingernails on my knee. "Amy, look there, at the one in the peach dress. My word, she looks like a Miss America."

"I like that color, too, Gram."

"Look at this one here," she said pointing to the far end of the stage. "I don't care much for her short hair; she looks like a boy. There's Jeannie! Now, doesn't she look nice, just marvelous. She really does! I sure am proud of her."

Jeannie radiated—beamed! Her beauty dwarfed all the other girls as she moved with refined class. She wore the crystal ring just like she had last time, carrying luck around her finger. She had borrowed a dress from a friend, expressing to Mom that she needed something sparklier for the big national pageant; Mom had agreed. I crossed my legs and tucked my left hand between my knees, then bounced my foot back and forth taking advantage of the physics of motion. In my mind I pictured what I would wear if I were out on the stage: shattering deep blue? Envy green? Gram's favorite color, peach? Yellow, the color of sunshine? The girls on stage lined up in a half moon shape, standing with their arms draped at their sides, their left feet set in a diagonal to their right heels to gain a slimming appearance. Then it hit me. I stopped moving my foot, keeping it still as I announced in my mind the most fitting color of all for my dress. *I would wear white.*

One by one, each took her turn at the microphone, speaking with flawless eloquence. As I listened, I escaped to a place in my mind below the skin, where my own beautiful was. My gown was made of marvelous challenges, laced together with stitches of endurance, beaded with bravery, and crowned with a halo of possibilities. My stage had been the hospital, doctors' offices, and speech therapy sessions, my judges surrounding me at each turn of life, some harsher than others. I relaxed into the chair and listened to the next contestant, thinking quietly that *my* beauty had been born in the fight for my first seemingly impossible breath, and had lived in each day of persevering thereafter.

"Amy is in a pretty fragile state," I overheard Mom say to Dad during the intermission as he snacked on a Snickers bar that was packed with devilishly crunchy peanuts. But I didn't feel fragile in spirit right then. I felt strong—stronger than I had ever felt. I was surrounded by girls just two years older than me, girls more beautiful than I had ever seen with features more perfect than I would ever experience. All night there were reminders that I was not one of them. And yet, there I stood with my jaw wired shut, my crooked top lip, deep scars on my filtrum, a flattened nose, and twelve new screws buried deep inside my cheeks, smiling my best smile and cheering my best cheer—despite it all. I *was* feeling strong, oh so strong.

Jeannie finished off the night by winning two awards, one for talent and one for poise. Our section stood and applauded again, each of us so proud of her for taking first place in two categories. She had been a favorite of the crowd, and certainly was *our* favorite. Disappointment raced over me, though, as the judges favored someone else as the National Junior Miss winner. *How could they? She is the best! Don't you know that there is no other girl in the world like her?! Nobody! She is more than all of those other girls put together.* I heard Gram let out a sigh of frustration, "Oh my land. For heavens sake. Why did the judges pick *that* girl? Jeannie was the prettiest and smartest one up there." My relatives all sat speechless in our balcony seats, thinking there must be some mistake. Within minutes the atmosphere of the pageant was over, the house lights were up, and the audience was making their way out the doors.

"I am really proud of how I did," Jeannie said to our small group of supporters as we met up with her in the reception area. "I stayed true to myself throughout the whole pageant. I don't have any regrets." Other pageant girls soon filtered out. The girl with short boy hair was stunning up close. "Hey everybody I want you to meet my roommate," Jeannie said, pulling the girl into our circle.

"You have an amazing daughter," she said to Mom and Dad, shaking their hands in genuine interest. "She influenced all of us with her faith in God. That's what I will remember the most about her— well, and the fact that she danced with a dummy for her talent!" They hugged, promising to keep in touch.

"Hey, Utah! You did great out there! When you started dancing with that dummy, I tell you what, I have never laughed so hard," said a hefty man with thick hands as he reached around and shook Jeannie's shoulder. "You were our favorite by a long shot!"

"Ours, too!" answered back Auntie Julie with a crack in her voice.

"I'm starving. Let's go get some dinner," Jeannie said. "I haven't eaten much since morning."

Mom put her hands together, "I think a celebration is in order. We survived! You did great, Jeannie! And now we won't have to worry about you going all over the nation traveling and speaking. I was a little concerned with that idea if she had come out the winner."

"Let's scotacklica," rallied Dad. "We saw a good steakhouse not too far from here." I felt the hunger pains gnawing at my insides, eating away the last of my blended up lunch.

The waitress introduced the specials then brought us a basket of out-of-the-oven rolls. The fluffy texture with the pat of butter sliding down the hot curve and onto the plate below was almost more than I could bear. I pulled out my blender and placed it quietly under my chair. I sat next to Auntie Debbie and watched her hands spread the soft butter on her roll in such a careful manner, then raise the bread to her lips. I could hear her bite into the crust, crunching and scattering bits of crumbs to the plate below. "Well, Jeannie, you did our name good out there," Uncle Davie said, taking a roll from the basket. "We're darn sure proud of you." The rest of the relatives chimed in, talking and eating rolls while praising Jeannie for a job well done. I shuffled my feet and knocked the blender over, the lid falling off and clattering to the hard floor. I reached down and stood it upright feeling a wave of dizziness attack me. The main course came out after the salads had been served. Sizzling steaks wrapped in bacon, grilled chicken smothered in savory teriyaki sauce, baked potatoes with a side of sour cream, and vibrant vegetables that colored the plates.

"Now *this* here is what I call a good dinner," said Dad. "I'm sure glad we came to Alabama to see you in the pageant so we could come here and eat afterward and have this here steak." He cut into his hot potato, snapping the tight skin with his sharp knife, letting a puff of hot steam escape. I took a sip of my juice through my straw while I watched him mash the insides of his potato, mixing it with sour cream and topping the mound with fresh ground peppercorn.

"Amy, do you want to try and blend up some of my chicken?" Mom asked, looking my way. "We could mix it with a little soup."

"In a minute. I'm not hungry right now. I'll just keep drinking my apple juice."

Auntie Debbie buttered another section of roll, tipping her hands just right and giving me full view of her next bite. But this time, it wasn't the roll that caught my eye. She had the most beautiful ring on. It was mesmerizing. The centerpiece was stretched out to nearly an inch, and it rippled in a soft fashion. It was cream and blue in color, looking like a mix of the ocean and a sandy beach. Each time she lifted her hand for another bite of roll, I got a new glimpse. *I must have a ring like that one day*, I thought to myself. *I must. Look at it! Amazing!* And then it occurred to me—*this* was the ring. This was the ring Auntie Julie had told me about! The ring with the deformed pearl. The ring I thought nobody would ever want. Auntie Julie had been right. It was beautiful. Unique, one-of-a-kind, beautiful. I reached below my chair and grabbed my blender. "Mom, yeah, I think I will try some of your chicken." I fired up the blender and thought past the dinner, focusing again on Auntie Debbie's ring. Her imperfectly perfect ring.

"It hurts so badly when I try to yawn," I said to Mom as we left Mobile, Alabama the next day and headed to the airport. "My jaw cracks and pops and makes a horrible sound." I was utterly and completely exhausted. The strength that I had felt the night of the pageant was all gone, and in its place was raw sensitivity. I hated feeling beat. I wanted to escape from the pain for a day, from the wires, from the stares.

"Amy, you have been a real trooper on this trip," Mom responded. "I don't know how you've done it all with such a good attitude. I know that it's been tough." I let a tear slip out without anyone seeing while I watched the lines on the street disappear into a solid blur. I had tried so hard not to be jealous of Jeannie and her charmed life, but it all seemed so unfair. There we were, two sisters on two ends of the spectrum—two opposite experiences, two different lives. My weakness in both mind and body started to play tricks on me, and I felt deeply sorry for myself—and helpless—with my *own* poise nearly gone.

I was glad when our plane landed back home and I could go down to my room and rest in my own bed. I covered myself in familiar blankets and fell into a deep sleep. When I woke up the next day I made a list of all the food that I would eat as soon as I could. Ah, cheesecake, pancakes, mashed potatoes, chicken nuggets, grilled cheese, tacos, spaghetti, and—oh!—chocolate chip cookies, Rice Krispie treats, jelly doughnuts, toast, scones, hot bread, corn on the cob, pizza! And of course, my loyal friend, fries.

Gram and Gramp stopped by as soon as the RV caravan made it back to Utah. "Oh, Amy, I know this is no fun, but just think how good you will feel when it is all over with." Life was nearly opposite as it had been the summer before—the summer of the Rebels. Instead of spending hours laughing with my friends, I spent my days hoping I didn't laugh since the movement made me feel as if my jaw were breaking all over again. Instead of staying out late into the night wandering up and down 100 and 150

East, I spent hours resting in Dad's recliner, and instead of making plans for the next day with a group of friends I adored, I spent a lot of time alone trying to tolerate the hours as they ticked by ever so slowly.

The last week of July, on a Tuesday, Mom and I went to Dr. Thomas's office to get the wires cut off my jaw.

"How are you feeling?" he asked, checking me over before giving me freedom again.

"It's been a little hard," I answered honestly.

"She's lost some weight," Mom contributed. Dr. Thomas took a pair of cutters off his tray. First he cut one wire, then the rest. With each cut a little more relief was granted. I slowly opened my jaw, and the ache felt *so* good. I moved my jaw slightly from side to side, at the request of the doctor, and then back into a closed position.

"The bone graft and jaw look good," Dr. Thomas said. "Just what we wanted to see. Start with eating soft foods for the next few days. Your mouth needs some time to adjust."

"When should we do my lip and nose surgery?" I asked. Dr. Thomas had told Mom that I would have to have at least a few surgeries on my lip and nose once the cranial facial and jaw surgery were out of the way.

"Not until winter. We want to give your tissue enough time to get back to normal. It is still fairly swollen."

"Maybe we can do it over Christmas break," Mom said, looking at me.

"Sure…yeah, that would be great."

Mom and I stopped by our ice cream shop on the way home, just like the times before. I got ice cream, but this time it was packaged in a giant waffle cone. I carefully took a tiny nibble from the edge with mild apprehension that I would break my jaw if I over-enjoyed the experience. The bit of cone tasted like heaven.

As the days went on, the summer seemed to slip away as though someone switched my life to fast forward. I spent less and less time looking things over in front of the mirror each morning as the swelling went down and I started to resemble myself again. I didn't feel like I looked much different on the outside. At times I would run my fingers along the lines of my face, curious about where the surgeon had put the screws and metal plates. My face did have a nicer, more balanced rhythm to it, but it was subtle and natural. Nobody said, "Hey, Amy! Is that hip bone and screws I see in your face? They have turned you into a real swan! You look magnificent!"

One sunny morning, while riding my bike as fast as I could, the wind caught my hair and pushed it behind my back, and I started to feel freer than a bird. Being all locked up and tied to the inconvenience of recovering from surgery during the first part of the summer made me appreciate even more the joy of just living. The feeling I had while watching Jeannie the night of the national pageant returned to me. *My strength comes from my challenges,* I thought. I peddled faster and faster, and as I did I realized that perhaps Jeannie and I were not so different after all. We were both sisters, both beautiful. I knew I would have dark clouds appear in the days ahead, but those days would make me strong. I would have shining moments, too! I'd already had so many! More were certainly ahead. I only needed to choose to find them. I was charged with an exhilarating rush of confidence as I coasted down 100 East toward home with my hands resting on my thighs as I balanced the bike against the road. I resolved that I wouldn't change a thing about my personality or who I was—not one thing. I parked my bike next to the side of the house and smoothed my hair back away from my face before walking in through the back door. A smile grew inside my heart. My surgery was behind me—I'd done it.

I shut the back door and in its wake, heard a shocking explosion of screams. One, then another, loud and intense! They shattered my thoughts like fragile glass, sinking like a pit to my stomach. *Where is that coming from? The basement? What's wrong? What's wrong??* I started running as fast as I could carry my feet down the stairs to the basement. I couldn't tell where the sound came from. I whirled my head back and forth. Someone was hurt and needed my help—and right now! The cry sounded again, laced with agony—and somewhere in the pain, I heard my big sister.

"Jeannie? Is that *you*? Where are you? Jeannie? *Jeannie*?" I ran through my room, and then her room, moving swiftly, yet I still couldn't see her. I raced through the laundry room, the bathroom, and back to the family room. Then I heard her cry again, a deeply rooted sob that was uncontrolled and angry.

"NO! NO! No. No. No…." And at last, I found her. She was at the corner of our house, deep in the basement, pacing the storage area next to her room; her blonde hair covering her tear tainted cheeks, her haunting energy chilling my veins.

"Jeannie! What happened? Are you ok? What…what's the matter?" I scanned the room for blood or any sort of wound on her, searching for any indication of where her pain was coming from. But I found nothing. My body shuddered. She was my rock. My *Jeannie*. And yet she looked as if someone were physically scratching at her heart and pulling it into a million pieces. With each heave of her chest she left me wondering what could possibly cause such suffering, the tears flowing so fast down her face that there were no signs left of her signature makeup. Then like thunder cracks a quiet storm, she spoke the words and shocked me with the news: "He died…Ron is dead," she said in a near whisper, taking my breath and suffocating the room. "There was an accident. The car he was in rolled off the road down the mountain…" She trailed off with a sob. "He died."

No…not Ron. My thoughts reeled in my head. *Not the boy with the flat top hair and movie-star good looks. The boy who made Jeannie light up like nobody else ever had. No…there must be some mistake!* I couldn't speak. This was too much! Too much. Her struggle was in motion, locked deep inside, tearing her apart. She fought the reality, beating it up with her mind and losing control by screaming the word "No!" until my own heart felt the piercing of love and friendship lost. I thought the whole world must have heard her. Waves of the unknown mixed with the heavy emotion in the room made me ache for my sister — who loved this boy — and for this boy who would never be back. The room filled with drowning sadness. Jeannie had been the one to teach me everything, but not how to take care of *her*.

"What…can I do? Is there…anything…Do you…want to...talk?"

Her actions were a dizzy mess as she shook her head over and over again. Smashing into me with riveting pain. I tried to find the right words to share with her, to instantly heal her broken heart. I wanted so badly to change what the past had so swiftly made the future. I felt helpless and lost. In one emotional effort Jeannie pounded her palms against the wall between her room and the bathroom and sunk her head deep between her shoulders. Then, almost as if I were invisible, she pushed through her door and ran up the stairs to the outdoors. A trail of heated tears followed her footsteps. I sat down with my legs flat against the cold cement of the storage floor where I could feel the draft coming through the bottom of the door, knowing there was nothing I could do to relieve her broken heart. I had let her down, I couldn't rescue her like she had done for me. Upstairs I heard Justin and Todd fighting. Outside cars drove up and down our street, and high up in the maple tree next to the window I heard a bird singing her happy song—all completely unaware. I quietly thought to myself again, this time with a somber heart, *My sister and I are not so different—no, not so different at all with the scars we must bear.*

CHAPTER TWENTY-THREE

For centuries stars have captured the minds of those who seek guidance and direction. But for others, stars carry wonder and mystery—and a place to wish on.

I went with Jeannie to Ron's funeral just a few days later. I stood in line with her, not sure whether to fold my arms or keep them at my side, looking at pictures of him and absorbing the sorrow that she and the rest of his friends felt at the weight of his passing. The sting of his life cut short stayed with me for days. Jeannie wasn't the same after Ron died, rarely speaking about him in the weeks that followed, almost as if talking about him would give others tokens of his memory until there was nothing for her to remember.

She left for college in the late summer, and when she did, the room next to mine felt still and vacant. I would sometimes sit on her bed and pretend I was talking to her while she got ready for a date. But there was no alarm clock going off in the morning, or shower running all the hot water, just an empty feeling. She packed up her clothes, too, leaving behind only a few rejected outfits hanging in her closet on wire hangers. For the first time in my life I was without Jeannie. I didn't know whether to love or hate the new feeling. *Who will protect me now? Who will show me the way?* I was left to try and be myself all on my own, without her there to catch me if I needed her. I missed her just like I had when she left on the big yellow school bus when she first went to kindergarten and left me behind at home. I pulled out my yearbook, her message that she had written to me two months before took up a full page: "Amy, I want you to know I am going to miss you next year. You are a very special sister and I love you very much. I wish I knew better how to help you with your operation. I hope you feel like you can talk to me about anything. I hope your high school years are fun and worth remembering. Remember to be a good friend to *everyone*, and don't judge people too harshly. You are a very pretty girl, both inside and out. I love you! Your big sis – Jeannie."

I was determined to make the next school year the best yet, and to take all of Jeannie's advice. In mid-August, before high school started back up again, I made my way over to Katie's house. I unlocked the chain link gate between our two yards and walked up the small hill to her back porch. The sun beat hot on the deck at the back of her house. I jumped as fast as I could up the cement steps, careful not to burn the bottoms of my bare feet. I knocked three times on the sliding glass door, just loud enough to get Katie's attention. She was sitting at the bar eating half a grapefruit. "Can I try a bite?" I asked, pulling out a bar stool and sitting down next to her.

"I thought you hated grapefruit."

"Does it taste better with sugar on it?"

"My dad puts salt on it," Katie said, raising her eyebrows.

"I'll try some, but I want sugar on it, please."

"Well this is a first!" Katie said as she slid me the glass container of sugar and then cut out a single slice of grapefruit, which I did not hesitate to cover—

no, drown—in sugar. And when I ate it, I sort of fell in love with the crazy fruit.

"Registration is already next week," Katie said, cutting me another piece.

"I know. Our junior year! We won't be the youngest anymore."

"Do you want to go together? We can get our lockers and see who we have for teachers. I can see if my mom will let me take the van."

"Surely!"

"Shirley? That's my aunt's name you know! Ha ha!"

"Now I just need to figure out what to wear and how I am going to do my hair."

"Don't you already have that figured out?"

"Well, yeah, I have a few options," I said, winking at her. I stayed at her house all afternoon, and by evening the Rebels gravitated to the top of 150 East, just like old times.

"Hey, you guys! I met him! I met him!" Moose announced, unfolding a story for all of us to hear while catching his breath. "I met Chris LeDoux!"

"You did?! How? Tell us everything!" I said, shocked that *our* Moose had met a celebrity country singer.

"He was going to his tour bus after the concert last night, and my buddy and me followed him and then climbed to the top of a chain link fence so we could get a better view," Moose said as he acted out climbing over the fence, complete with huffs and puffs. "We scaled it as fast as we could, then shouted his name again and again. We didn't think there was a chance he would hear us, but then he stopped, turned around, and came toward us! At first, we thought we were going to get in trouble for following him. We jumped to the other side of the fence, and he came over and talked to us. Then he signed our cowboy hats and told us to keep working on our music. Best day of my life so far!" Moose finished his story with a laugh and bent his head back to stare up at the night sky, waving his cowboy hat high in the air.

"Moose, you are so lucky!" we chimed in.

"Who wants Twizzlers?" Katie said, opening a bag of chocolate licorice.

"ME!" I shouted as if there were any question at all, while pulling two out of her bag.

"Amy, you know what song we really need to learn sign language for?" Wendy said, grabbing my arm.

"Wait, *real* sign language?"

"Oh yeah! Kathy, you know, who was in choir with us? She knows sign language for the whole song of *Right Here Waiting for You*."

"By Bryan Adams?"

"No, no, Bryan Adams doesn't sing it, Richard Marx does!"

"Oh! I love that song! We totally need to learn the whole thing!"

"*Oceans apart, day after day…*" she sung while I made swooping waves with my hands.

"Do you think she will teach us? For real?"

"Totally. Then we won't have to be posers anymore!"

"We are so cool. Oh yeah! Oh yeah!"

"I can't wait to actually know what you are saying! Ha ha!"

"As if you couldn't already read my mind."

We all stayed there, at the top of 150 East, far longer than we should have. Our friendship had faded during the school year, but none of that mattered, and soon we were right back to where we left off the summer before, gathered close together talking and laughing and feeling the warmth of the summer night. We would always be the Rebels. Of that I was certain.

When the swelling from my surgery finally went down, I could see the subtle improvements to the bone structure in my face and in my chin, too. Dr. Thomas was a genius! Dr. B put a new set of braces on my teeth. Still, I never saw my teeth move into a nice straight row, and I was quite certain I didn't even have enough teeth to make a row. But at least the braces were helping to hide the giant gaps where I had missing teeth.

Katie and I had two classes together—first hour English and fifth hour history. They were the best two hours of the day.

"Hey, Amy!" Dusty Dusenberry called to me when I walked into my class.. "Sit by me, right here, in this vacant seat." I had known Dusty most of my life. He lived in a large custom built home with a steep driveway and double doors to the main entrance, by far the nicest home at the bottom of 150 East. He was a year older than me, same age as Tracy Clead. He was my height with a head of bright blond hair and a frame made up of long wiry limbs. Dusty was clever and adventurous, drawing friends of all types with his charming chatty personality. "This is how we are going to survive class: we are going to whisper all the way through the lesson and not pay attention," he said once I sat down next to him. "Are you good at taking notes?" I nodded. "Don't do it, don't take notes, then we will have to listen. If we listen we can't whisper, and if we can't whisper we have to listen."

The next weekend he invited Wendy and me and a few others to go hot tubbing at his house. I tried on two different swim suits before I left for his house, and both of them made me look flat as a board, even when I arched my back and rolled my shoulders. I decided I would wrap my towel around me until the last possible second, then leap into the hot tub and keep my shoulders underwater until it was time to leave. When we all arrived at Dusty's house, Wendy was in a cute, pink suit with yellow ruffles along the top and no concealing towel. *Ugh!* She looked sensational! I held on to as much dignity as I could and stepped into the hot tub while Dusty was busy looking the other way. After sitting low in the steaming water for just a matter of minutes, I wanted to get out. The heat was taking me over! I felt like my chicken legs would soon be edible, but I didn't want to risk Dusty noticing what I didn't have! In a moment of desperation, I turned my body 180 degrees, put my knees on the bench and my back toward the group, and cooled off. *Relief!* Then, slyly, I turned back around again, with my arms folded, to get back in the hot water. The motion turned out to be horribly unnatural and unattractive. Next to me sat Wendy, who was making the group laugh by poking her painted toenails out of the water for

Dusty to grab. They flirted and flirted and flirted, and I sat there with my shoulders under the water, thinking I should have painted my toenails, too.

"Look at all the stars out tonight," Dusty said after his Dad had brought us all mugs of hot cocoa. "We all should make a wish." I had been making wishes my whole life. I'd made them on stars, on dry chicken bones, and while going over the railroad tracks near my home. I closed my eyes and made a wish—the same one I had made for years, the same wish I'd never spoke out loud. I wished that a boy would pick me to be his girl and see me like I see myself, past the ugly on the outside, and into the pretty on the inside.

CHAPTER TWENTY-FOUR

Kisses to the air, on the back of a hand, or on lips are never wasted. And the first kiss, no matter how brief, is never forgotten.

"Jeannie won model of the year!" I announced to Katie as we walked to English class the next day. "She got a $100 certificate!"

"Holy cow! Awesome!" she answered.

"OK, so tonight for the fall stomp what time should we leave?"

"I don't want to be the first ones there, you know, like when we were sophomores? We need to show up a little late now if we want to be cool. What are you wearing?"

"I am going to wear my black leopard-print skirt that ruffles to my knees and my black jacket with fringe. Will you help me with my hair tonight?"

"Um, hello, YES!"

"Yeah! I will be over after dinner. Is Wendy still picking us up?"

"That's the plan, Stan."

When I got to Katie's house she was ready with her set of tools: a ratting brush, hairspray, and her three-way mirror, which I avoided. "So how you get your hair really big is that you rat, then spray, then repeat. Otherwise, once you start dancing your hair will just go flat."

"I don't want flat hair. I want it to look like yours."

"I am growing my bangs out so I have to make mine even higher," Katie said while working around me. "You will look good, I promise. Cover your eyes, I am going to spray again."

"How does it look?" I asked after several minutes of ratting and spraying.

"So good! You're going to have the best big hair ever, Amy Jo."

"Thank you so much!" I nearly shouted, feeling unstoppable as I reached up to feel the creation.

"Don't touch it, and don't move. Come in and sit on my bed and let your hair dry while I finish getting ready."

Wendy came and got us, and all three of us crowded into the front two bucket seats of her small car. She turned up the radio nearly full blast as we traveled the few blocks to the school. Wendy got out first, then I tried to scoot out the door on her side, but I was stuck. Totally and completely—and so was Katie. Our hair had somehow meshed together on the ride over with the heater blowing on it and all of us crammed in such a small space, not to mention all of that hairspray.

"Pull, but not too hard, I don't want to wreck our hair," Katie said. I moved ever so slowly.

"It isn't working. I can't seem to free my bangs. I think I'm stuck to the top of the car, too."

"Hold on. All right, on the count of three let's both move our heads the opposite way. Ready? One …two…three!"

"Owwwwwwwchiiiiees!" I hollered.

"Oh! That worked! Freeeeedom!" Katie yelled. We all started laughing so hard we nearly turned blue from lack of oxygen.

"That was a close one!" I said, still laughing. "Wendy, do I, *ahem*, look OK?"

"Flawless! We are going to own tonight!"

Once inside, I just stood next to Katie who was tracking down guys. Her eyes were like an eagle's, scanning the collection of potential dance partners back and forth. A distance away my eyes caught and stopped on the bully. He was dancing with a short girl with blonde hair, his arms around her, content. I moved my gaze away from him, happy he ignored me now when we passed in the halls. Dusty started walking toward me before I could finish forgetting about the bully.

"Hey! Dusty! Don't you have some homework you should be doing?"

"My lady," he said holding out the crook of his arm, "let's dance."

"Dance?"

"Yes, I request your presence on the dance floor before the song is over." I put my hands up on his shoulders, ready for bear hug dancing. "No, no. We are going to dance the proper way. Give me your hand," he said using a fake accent and positioning me into a ballroom dance carriage. "Now this is how we ought to all dance, instead of the glorified three-minute hug."

274

"I don't know how to dance this old-fashioned way," I laughed. "Maybe you should have been born last century."

"Hold on, I'm going to dip you!"

"Wait!"

"No waiting for dipping, now hang on!" My hair moved in an upside down mass, holding good form as he dipped me low.

"Whew! That was fun!"

"Next time, let's see if you can do it without keeping your back stiff as a board. You nearly tipped me over."

"Hey, listen, I am a first time dipper here."

"Big dipper?"

"I would say more like a skinny dipper. Oh! No, I mean, a little dipper."

"Right. OK, here comes another dip, now bend!" I arched my back just like I used to in gymnastics, then paused there until he pulled me up, just in time for the dance to end. "Much better. Next time we really should try dancing a whole song," he said as he spun me around one last time.

The rest of the night I watched him make his way around the dance floor, asking a different girl to dance for each new song that played. He flirted and dipped, swayed and then moved along. I waited for him to come and find me like he said he would, so we could dance a full song, but his strategy involved quantity and variety. Lots of variety.

The next Thursday was historic as the Berlin wall started to come down in the morning, filling the school with a buzz of energy. Dusty was waiting for me when I got to class. "I think we should actually listen today," he said.

"Wait, and learn something?"

"I'm not so sure we have learned *anything*."

"Did you know I learn by osmosis?"

"Prove it. I'll make you a bet that you won't know the next answer the teacher asks."

"I bet I will!" I answered, trying to figure out flirting, "What does the winner get?"

"A kiss!"

"A kiss?" A thousand thoughts flew through my mind: *Is it safe to kiss with braces? Will he do it? Kiss me? He won't want to kiss MY lips, will he? Does he like me? For real? Dang it! I should have practiced more on my hand!* When I won the bet he leaned in to give me a kiss right there in the back of the classroom, then faked to the left, grabbed my hand, and gave me a quick kiss above my four fingers, which he held in his. All day long I held my hand close to me so nothing would disturb the tingle where his kiss lingered. Throughout the remaining days of fall I listened for the phone to ring, or for him to pass me a note, or ask me to a school sponsored dance, but it didn't happen. Instead, he told me all about the foreign exchange student, Andre, from Germany who was living with his family for the year. But the kiss on my hand, the first one, would always belong to Dusty.

CHAPTER TWENTY-FIVE

The magic eight ball has twenty answers inside of it. Ten illuminate the window with an affirmative response. The rest deliver information that can seem too honest. But only a fool would shake the ball only once if the answer wasn't favorable.

"Hey, Amy?" Jeannie called to me from upstairs. "Are you ready to go?"

"Hold on a minute," I hollered back. I was in the bathroom, quite positive that I had *finally* gotten my period. I had been waiting for this day ever since fifth grade when Mom had to join me at school for a horribly embarrassing assembly on "blooming". By waiting, I mean I had prayed in fear that I would not be one of those girls who "started" at school while wearing white jeans. *I don't feel any different,* I thought as I looked at myself in a full-body side profile and pulled my shirt tight against my chest. *My boobs aren't any bigger. Hmm, but I am a woman now…right? One day I will be a mother! I'll have kids of my own! I am a woman! A WOMAN!*

Thankfully, because of Katie, I knew exactly what to do. But I decided not to tell anyone. This was such a personal experience. I smiled though, at the thought of reaching such a milestone. And in secret, too! Nobody knew! I met Jeannie upstairs waiting to take me with her to her college town for the weekend. We both got situated in the Ford Escort, then Jeannie tossed me two blankets.

"You'll need these. My heater doesn't work, and it's freezing in the canyon." I tucked one blanket under my legs and wrapped another around my shoulders, feeling a blend of maturity and adventure. "When we get there," Jeannie continued, "the first thing we are going to do is go to a sorority house. Lisa and I have to go through some silly initiation. Then we can go to my apartment and get something to eat and get ready to go to the student dance."

Ahh, YES! I thought excitedly. *I can't wait to go to my first official college event! I wonder if I look old enough to pass for a college girl now. Hmmm, I hope at least one guy asks me to dance. There is no place else I would rather be right now than with Jeannie. I can't wait to dance!* The drive up to Logan was forty-five minutes from home to Jeannie's place. And she was right; it was freezing in the canyon. I was glad that she was prepared and glad, too, that she had looked out for me. Still, the blankets were not quite adequate enough, and I found myself wishing for the toasty warm heater of the van.

"OK, Amy. Now what I need you to do is look out the window for me for the next few minutes—*very* closely. Your job is to look for deer eyes. They'll look a little green, and if you see them you need to warn me so I can slow down."

"On it," I said, watching the curves of the dark road. I knew all about the deer in the canyon. This route was the same one I had taken years ago for speech therapy lessons. Now, to think that Jeannie was a student at that very school and that Mom was an alumnus, it all seemed to come full circle. I almost wanted to see deer, just so I could warn Jeannie and she could say, "That was a close one, Amy. Without you here something terrible might have happened." But only darkness stared back at me. Not a single reflection bounced off of the car's headlights. After we were out of deer danger, Jeannie's mood changed; despite being in a safe zone of roadway, she almost seemed *more* serious. I thought she might have still been watching for the deer, or maybe she was just too cold to laugh. But something was on her mind.

"Amy, it might be a while before you have a boyfriend," she said, her words icing my body even further. "Guys can see that you're special." My energy rolled off of me and dripped right out the car door. The excitement of showing up at the university with Jeannie was immediately gone. I didn't know how to respond.

"Oh, OK. Right, yeah, I know it won't be the same as what you have," I said, trying to believe that what she was telling me was meant to help me and not point out the obvious.

"When a boy finally does ask you on a date, it'll be because he sees the real you," she said, turning briefly to look me straight in the eye. "You came into this world in a miraculous and remarkable way, and he will see that you are different and unique." I nodded, feeling emotion hit me in my core. I could only keep staring out the window, pretending to look for deer. "The boys won't want to hurt you 'cause they know that you've felt some level of that rejection your whole life, and if things don't work out, they won't want to add to that."

Stop talking to me about this, I pleaded with Jeannie inwardly. *I don't want to start crying! I just wanted this weekend to be fun! Dancing! Music! College guys!*

"People look at you, and they're amazed by who you are and by your optimistic attitude. And you are *funny!* Who knew you were so funny? And my friends love you. They think you're so great. I am so lucky to have you as my sister."

I tried to think of something to say back to her, but I couldn't find the words. The rest of the ride I was quiet. The anticipation of going to a big dance and showing off my moves to a whole new group of *older* students was gone.

At the dance I swayed slightly, back and forth, to give the illusion of movement—of dancing—but my soul stood still. Why would I want to give up energy dancing if I was just going to be passed up time and again? To see the real me someone would have to be quite desperate. And maybe Jeannie was right about the guys not wanting to date me because they knew that I wouldn't be able to handle any sort of rejection. I was like boy repellant. I hadn't even been on a real date yet, unless I counted the two blind dates or the drive to get fries with Moose. The worst part was that, in my heart, I knew I had so much to give. So what if I got hurt? I could take it! I wanted the chance to at least fall in love.

As we walked back to Jeannie's apartment after the dance ended, I felt hope fade. Winter could be so cold, and I found myself dwelling on Jeannie's words again. I had three guy friends, but none of them ever showed any interest in me "that" way. Instead, they talked to me about the girls they were going to take to the next dance—the cute ones. Or, worse, they asked me about Jeannie. "Is she dating anyone? Does she like college?" Or even, "Your sister is such a fox!" I wondered, then, how long would I have to wait for someone to notice *me* and not be afraid to uncover what was beneath *my* skin? Jeannie said I was special. Maybe I was. I *felt* like I was. I nearly burst with awesomeness just waiting to get free—so much to share, so much to give, no boy to give it to. I lay in the makeshift bed Jeannie had set up for me that night, so still, for a very long time and allowed myself to cry. Jeannie didn't have a clue about how rejection felt. She hadn't missed a single weekend of dating since she turned sixteen. I let the tears fall from the corners of my eyes down to the pillow in a slow meandering stream. I sat up in bed, and rubbed my eyes, wondering if all this emotion was me, or the new hormones rushing through my body. Through Jeannie's bedroom window I could see the moon, hanging high in the sky without a care in the world. Wouldn't it be great to be the man who lived on the moon? I bet his only job was to sit and watch the world below. And eat small bites of moon cheese.

Then I thought about God, sitting up there higher than the man on the moon, looking over me. He certainly understood what I was going through, and I bet he even had a great plan in store for me. I trusted that he did, anyway. I didn't want to be anyone but me. I got out of bed, knelt down, and thanked Him for all the good things in my life: my family, my friends, my home, and even my trials.

CHAPTER TWENTY-SIX

Attraction cannot be predicted, measured, or contained. Its power draws forth a response that is magnetic, fascinating, and—luckily—completely invisible.

"Can you believe it's already the first of December?" Katie asked as we walked the long sidewalk up to the doors of the high school. The early morning fog still hadn't quite burned off, and the frosty sidewalk was slick with ice and lines from the freshly shoveled snow. "This year is flying by! What do you want for Christmas?"

"Uh, Katie? Did you just see that? Did he just wave at me?"

"Who?"

"Jamie…Jamie Acton. I think he just looked at me and waved—but I'm not sure. He just went inside the school through that side door."

"Seriously? He waved?"

"Yeah, I mean, there's nobody else around, so it was to us, and if you weren't even looking….wow…that was… cool. He's so popular!"

"He *is* popular! What kind of a wave was it?"

"He raised his arm halfway up and did a once over like this," I said, demonstrating.

"Holy cow, yes! He *did* just wave at you!"

"Maybe, Kates," I reasoned, "he just thought that *you* were looking. I bet it was actually for you."

"No way. I wasn't even looking! He waved at you! He's in our English class," she said, pulling open the front door of the high school.

"I know…I've seen him…" my voice trailed off. I tried not to pay attention to the guys who were out of my league, and Jamie was definitely out of my league. I replayed the event as Katie and I walked to English, hiding inside the feeling of intense butterflies. I could see him ahead of us, my eyes catching fragments of his dark hair and rust polo shirt as his body zigzagged between the steady stream of students. He was tall, dark, handsome, and mysterious with a blast of edgy good looks, far outweighing the men on the pages of GQ. A surge of reality hit me; maybe he thought I was OK. What if he *had* waved at *me*?

The seats in our English class were arranged in a two-layer-deep horseshoe shape. He sat down, across the room and diagonal from me, pulled out *The Grapes of Wrath,* and put it on his desk. I turned my head to look at the teacher, but moved my eyes to Jamie's desk, hoping he didn't notice. I could see his hands, beautiful lengthy fingers, with slightly protracted knuckles. He held a number two pencil, twisting it between his fingers before tapping the eraser against the desk in a soft calculated beat.

"Class, quiet please," said our teacher, Mr. Moore, who was rumored to be a millionaire. "Reminder, please listen up. All of you will need a copy of *Hamlet* by the first of January. I am giving you a fair amount of time to find a copy, so no excuses." He stood and started walking around the room. "What I love about *Hamlet* is how Shakespeare uses elements of tragedy to tell the story through powerful drama. You should be thrilled we are reading such a classic." *Oh no. I hope there aren't any talking donkeys in this Shakespeare book.* "Hamlet is a story of betrayal, one of my absolute favorites for character sides. For now, class, let's continue where we left off last time with *The Grapes of Wrath*. I need to see books on desks, people, come on! Keep up!"

I pulled out my own copy of *The Grapes of Wrath* and opened it to chapter thirteen, then tilted my head sideways as if to be studying the far corner of the room. But I was watching Jamie's hands again. They seemed to be alive and quiet all at the same time. Music lived within his palm, right in his fingertips, right in the arteries that carried blood back to his heart. I followed the length of his forearm up to his biceps and back to the crease in his elbow, seeking out the anatomy in his arm that I had learned in physiology—extensors, flexors, and tendons. He arched his thumb and the abductor pollicis longus muscle moved. The simple energy stabbed me with a pang, and yet there was nothing unusual about his motions. I stretched my vision ever so briefly to his face. Deep, distant eyes the color of singed amber set off his tussled hair. His features were symmetrical, molded with precision and handsome accuracy. His nose was artful, prominent cartilage, showcasing a strong profile above a set of masculine, full lips. He moved one hand along the edge of his desk, leaving fingerprints as a reminder of his presence before he slid comfortably into the back of his chair. When class ended he disappeared through the door, back into the rush of students getting to their next class. I couldn't wait to see him again.

"Save me a seat for the assembly today!" Katie hollered at me as we left English class. "I'll see you in a few hours."

"OK, but don't be late. We want to get good seats so we can see Moose in his first ever performance."

I optimistically determined over the next few hours that Jamie had waved at me. The feeling lifted me to an unfamiliar plane that caused my mood to surge.

"Come on, sit down. It's about to start," I said to Katie, who made it to the assembly with just moments to spare.

"I had to run back to my locker and put all my books away. Good seats, Mouse-Woman!"

The stage of the auditorium was set low and felt more like an arena than a performance stage. As soon as we sat down we twisted our necks looking for any other possible friends that might sit by us.

"Down here!" I shouted to Wendy. "We're down here! Come sit by us!" She bounded down the stairs, her hair moving back and forth over her shoulders.

"Is there room? Scoot down a seat. No, two, scoot down two seats. Oh, can you guys believe Moose is in the assembly? I'm so nervous for him!" Wendy said, looking up and down the aisles to try and spot Christy. Maybe nobody else knew how much Moose wanted this fame and fortune, but we knew. "Christy! Christy! Come on!" Wendy yelled with her hands cupped to her lips to magnify the sound. Soon, we were all sitting together, waiting for Moose's big debut. Wendy leaned forward, her elbows on her knees and her hands holding her chin. Up and down and up and down went her ankles in a nervous motion.

Back in Junior High, Wendy and Moose were an item brought together by feelings of insane puppy love. Feeling like a third wheel was nothing I was ashamed of, so I'd tag along as we three would walk the distance home. I had to listen to them flirting with one another as Moose shuffled his feet at the slowest pace imaginable, which bought them more "together" time. Rumor has it they used to go into his basement to practice kissing. I never confirmed that with Wendy. I just assumed it was more mindless gossip. When we finally made it to the top of Moose's street, I would wait for an eternity for them to say goodbye. Hugging, then walking away, then hugging again, then stretching their arms out until only their fingertips touched, all at the top of 150 East. I was so jealous of what they had!

I don't think Wendy ever got over Moose, and who could blame her? She would probably always have feelings for him. Her eyes worked the stage anxiously, back and forth. "There he is! Look! That's him! This is so exciting!" she said, nearly jumping out of her seat.

"MOOSE! MOOSE! MOOSE!" I chanted with Katie and Christy joining in.

He walked out on the stage dressed in a cowboy hat, Wranglers, and a bold striped western shirt. Behind him four back-up singers, all dressed in a similar fashion, helped him set up the microphones and guitars. Moose—all this time I knew he could do it! To think it all may have started as an air concert somewhere in his basement.

"So this is my first time doing anything like this," he said, the microphone making a horrible high-pitched shriek, "but here goes nothin'."

Then, with a single strum of his guitar, he started singing "Friends in Low Places," and the crowd erupted into rowdy applause. His voice cracked the first two measures, and then he found his rhythm and shook off his nerves. His smile filled the stage, and he belted out the song so loud the auditorium echoed his voice off the back wall.

"Stand up! Everyone stand up!" I shouted to Katie, Wendy, and Christy.

"Get up! On your feet!" Christy yelled to the rest of the row.

"I can't believe he's doing this! "said Katie as she started to dance right there in the tiny space between the seats. The more he sang, the more I believed that one day he would be famous. There was something about Moose that all would love. When the song ended, the audience wanted more. The Rebels jumped up and down as we shouted his name like he was a famous celebrity—and to us, he *was*. He had done it! Moose had made all of us so proud with his first big performance.

I sat down and looked at Katie, both of us winded from spontaneous dancing. "OK, that was pretty dang cool!" I said to her between laughs. "So *fun!*"

"I think Jamie is playing the drums next," Katie said.

My heart stopped. "Jamie...Acton?" Katie nodded.

"I heard from someone that he was going to play the drums in the assembly. See? Isn't that him?" I strained my eyes down to the now-darkened stage, and a streak of electricity raced down my spine.

I could see the drums now, being pushed out from the corner of the stage. His tall frame was partially hidden behind the set.

"Katie! It *is* him!"

"He's been playing drums since junior high; I think he's pretty good, too." He positioned himself behind the drums, checked the height of the set, and then, with a drumstick in the air, he signaled that he was ready. A lone spotlight focused on him, and for a split second the students in the audience were stone-cold quiet. Including me.

Jamie broke the silence suddenly with the aggressive but simple beat of his drums, progressively amplifying with each boom, boom, boom, boom. He started out slow, then gained speed and quickly moved to an unthinkable beat, keeping faultless rhythm while pounding every angle. His eyes were focused on a place far away from reality, and his hands moved the drumsticks in a motion that nobody would ever believe possible. The sound traveled to our ears fast, amazing and unsettling, and we soaked in a beat that drenched the audience. Faster and faster he hit the crash cymbals and toms, until the veins on his arms were visible to me even ten rows up. Tiny drops of sweat formed on his forehead, reflecting the lights. I never knew the drums could be a single source of music, but watching him play and listening to him create the sounds, I was convinced. The harder he played, the more energized the crowd became, and soon every last student was on their feet cheering as loudly as they could for him. On he played, crashing the sticks into the drums and throwing his head back and forth in time with the beat, shambolic with wild rain. I watched his arms, his hands, and his mind work together. He hit the cymbals with beautiful force until one of the sticks snapped in two. He didn't hesitate. Instead he tossed the half stick across the stage and kept playing—with only one hand. The audience screamed even louder, making the auditorium shake.

"Katie...he's amazing!" I screamed over the roar.

"Told you!"

"I mean, no. He is beyond good! Did you see that? His drumstick broke! He's playing with one hand!"

"I know!"

When his number ended, the crowd went crazy one last time, and as hard as I tried not to stare, I couldn't help it—I was captured.

The rest of the day and into the night, I thought about him and how his hands had filled the auditorium with riveting music, how he had played from his soul with magnificent intensity. And how maybe, just maybe, he had meant to wave at me. When I wrote in my journal, it wasn't about the outfit I wore or what was for lunch. Instead, I wrote about Jamie—the boy who played the drums.

CHAPTER TWENTY-SEVEN

A smile lets others know you are alive. Hide it, and there is nothing to tell. Show it, and the world can feel your happiness.

"There's a mouse in here somewhere!" Mom proclaimed two weeks after the assembly, not even glancing up at me as I walked in the door. "He keeps poking his head up through the gas burner."

"On the stove?!"

"Yes, the little guy is going to be in trouble if I can't get him to cooperate and come on out of there so I can put him outside where he belongs."

"Have you tried giving him some cheese? Or peanut butter?" I asked, staring at Mom with my eyebrows raised. She was holding a Tupperware upside down, and she looked every bit the part of a tough hunter.

"Yes! I tried all of that, and he's so sneaky that he grabs it and goes back into the hole. But he *must* come out! We can't go on like this!"

I could hear the tension mounting in Mom's voice; she was serious, and she meant business. She had a crew of kids and a hungry husband to cook for and didn't have time to mess with catching a mouse.

"I think if I turn on the burner he'll *have* to run out. Then let's catch him and toss him outside!" she said, still clutching the Tupperware in her right hand. It sounded like a fair plan, and Mom did say she had tried *everything* else. On the count of three, Mom turned the burner on, igniting it to a full blue flame, and lickety-split, out came the mouse, running for his life.

"Get him! Get him!" I screamed at Mom as he raced back and forth across the stove. "He's trying to run away. Oh no, NO! He's going right for the—Mom, get him! No! Oh no!" Mom tried to turn the stove off, but the poor mouse's tail caught the fire—but only until mom smacked it out, killing the mouse and the fire at the same time. We both looked at each other. "Wow, Mom, you just killed a mouse. That wasn't too nice."

"Well, I had no choice! He was in my stove-top!"

During dinner, I couldn't help but be solemn. Mom didn't bring up the mouse again; she was convinced that if there were other mice, they soon scattered after the "incident," moving outside where they belonged. I had to believe her. Had to.

When Christmastime rolled around, Mom and Dad bought me a new nose, which was just what I asked for. I woke up at 4:00 a.m. the day of the surgery, and Mom and I traveled the familiar road to the hospital.

After the surgery was over, the nurse put me in a wheelchair and pushed me to the recovery room, where I was greeted by my reliable support system: Mom, Dad, Gram, and Gramp. And Jeannie. She was there, too, guarding me like a lion, taking it on as her duty to protect me.

"Amy did great," Dr. Thomas said to the group while I was resting. "We transplanted cartilage to her nose and made her a more prominent tip, which will significantly improve the structure of her face. We also changed the left nostril and tightened it up so it is not as big, and inside her nose we widened her breathing passage, so she should be able to see a noticeable difference once her healing is complete."

"She'll be sore on her lower lip for several days—we took quite a bit of tissue out to help keep her lip from sagging. The sutures will dissolve in ten to fourteen days. In the meantime she'll be fairly uncomfortable as that area heals. The swelling for this type of surgery doesn't go down fully for almost a year, so keep that in mind."

When I got home Jeannie changed my bandages and put Vaseline on my swollen lips. Then she brought me a bowl of soup and a slice of banana bread. My lips were numb, and my nose was in a brace to keep it from being bumped, the inside of my nose stuffed with gauze. But I was content.

"Dad, will you please come take a picture of me?" I said one afternoon, thinking I would want photos to document my recovery. Dad was in the garage, working on a car.

"'Course, A-mouse." He put down his tools and rubbed his big boots on the rug in front of the landing that came into the kitchen. He snapped six or seven pictures with his camera, and then he did the same thing the next day, then twice more. Each time he would say, "I think you're looking real good, A-mouse. Just remember it'll take a while for all the swelling to go down." My hair stayed pulled back, out of my eyes, and I ditched my makeup in favor of my more natural multi-color, purple-and-blue bruised look. Mom propped up my bed so I could sleep better at night, but sleeping was horrible. I couldn't breathe at all through my nose, and getting air through my mouth created a different problem—the sutures in my lips dried out and ached. My lips stayed numb for several days, making eating and talking difficult. I was glad when the stitches on the inside of my lower lip started to dissolve a little at a time. At last, I could see the changes in my nose and lips. They were obvious and fantastic! My puzzle was starting to become a complete picture.

Mom went with me to Dr. Thomas's office a week later when I got the bandages off of my nose. He pulled off the brace and the sticky tape, took out the gauze using his long tweezers, and then held my chin in his thumb while he moved my face from side to side and up and down.

"Much better," he said. "What a nice profile. You have a tip on your nose now, see?" he said, handing me a mirror. I took it with both hands and looked at my nose.

"Oh, it does look better," I said, feeling glad that the flat slope was gone.

"This is a big improvement over what you had," he continued, "and you'll also notice that your breathing will open up."

After the appointment Mom and I went into the lobby bathroom so we could have a better look.

"Your nose is so cute now! Look at the nice slope you have. Oh, Amy, it does look good," Mom said as I leaned in as close as I could to the mirror.

I could see right away the biggest difference of all: "Mom! I have a nose with cartilage! Look! Cartilage! Oh, happy day!"

CHAPTER TWENTY-EIGHT

Vulnerable moments teach us about our core strength and challenge us to embrace the truth.

Mr. Jim Jones, my physiology teacher, stroked the blond hair on his arms with his meaty hands—back and forth, back and forth as he waited for all of us to find our seats.

"All right, who is ready to learn today?" he said, bellowing a hearty laugh. "You don't have a choice, each of you will learn, and I will teach. That's your job, and that's my job."

His arrogance didn't bother me in the least; I loved his lessons. When he had taught us about eyes and the thousands of rods and cones responsible for light levels, I became fascinated with vision. The day we all had to prick our finger to see what our blood type was I discovered my blood type, O+, was normal. *Normal!* He used games to help us learn the names of proteins, a plaster skeleton to help us memorize the bones, and stories to get us to relate to illnesses. Physiology was way more fun than math.

"Everyone open your books to chapter nine," Mr. Jones ordered, still rubbing his forearm as he looked over the heads of the students as if he were studying the back of the wall. "Today we are going to learn about congenital defects and anomalies." I had often wondered what Mr. Jones was like in high school. Popular for sure. Athletic, no question. Smart, yes. Handsome—still.

"Congenital birth defects. Where do I start? Here's the thing folks, our bodies are amazing. Think of all the coordination between the cells to create a whole limb or a functioning brain. Most of the time things work great. Sometimes though, the cells goof up, and things go wrong. Take, for example, a baby born with Down syndrome." I kept my eyes on Mr. Jones, glancing down at my paper long enough to scratch notes only I would be able to later decipher. In his class I sat near the front so I wouldn't miss a thing.

He continued, "Down syndrome is also known as Trisomy 21. It's the most common congenital anomaly in the world. Let me back up. In a human's developmental stage, there's what's called meiosis, the process in which cells divide and replicate." *Meiosis...divide and replicate. OK, got it.* "During normal meiosis, the chromosomes go through a phase called dysjunction, or in simple terms: each pair of chromosomes divides and splits into two identical chromosomes and goes into the different spots of the dividing cell." He paced back and forth in front of the class, reaching his hand up under the sleeve of his polo shirt to scratch his shoulder. "Essentially what happens with Down syndrome is that one pair of chromosomes didn't divide and the whole pair goes into the same spot in the dividing cell, making an extra chromosome." *Wow. Such a little mistake.* "Down syndrome babies are identified by a few characteristics at birth: round face, their palms have a simian crease line, they have lips and tongues that are larger than normal, and an up slanting of the palpebral fissures. Who can tell me where that is?"

"Right here on the eye," answered a student one row over from me.

"Correct. Palpebral fissure is the anatomic name for the separation between the two eyelids. Now, let's talk for just a minute about spina bifida," he said, pulling his black stool over to the front of the class and reaching one foot up to rest on the bar, as if to stretch out his calf muscles from the constant pacing. "Spina bifida occurs when the embryonic neural tube doesn't close and part of the spinal cord protrudes through the opening in the bones. Everyone put your fingers on your back and feel along your spine. See how the backbone moves and bends?"

I leaned forward toward my desk and traced my spine, then looked up at Mr. Jones and nodded.

"With spina bifida the vertebrae don't form properly around part of the baby's spinal cord. Most of the time surgery can correct this birth defect, but in bad cases, it can make walking or physical activities hard to do without some added help."

"Moving on," he said, standing, then adjusting the height of the stool before sitting back down, "the most common type of birth defect is congenital heart disease." *Birth defect. Ugh. I hate that phrase.* "The interesting thing about congenital heart disease is that although present at birth, many times there are no symptoms. In fact, sometimes you may never have a problem and lead a completely normal life. I've known people who have lived with a congenital heart problem their whole life and not slowed down one bit."

A hand shot up near the back, "My sister has that."

Mr. Jones nodded, then dove back into the lecture.

"Finally, let's talk about a deformity of the face: cleft lip and palate. This is a congenital defect caused by abnormal facial development early during pregnancy." My lungs caught— I sucked in a quick puff of air and held it there, hoping he wouldn't continue. *That's me. That's what I am. He is going to talk about me in front of the whole class! Oh, I should have seen this coming! Birth defect. My birth defect!* "A cleft means fissure or opening. In other words, it's a gap. It used to be that the condition was called a harelip, because of the resemblance to a hare, or rabbit." I kept my eyes steady on Mr. Jones, trying not to flinch or show that I was affected by the sound of the word "harelip" the bully so often used on me years before, rubbing in my face that I looked more like an animal than a girl. "So really, this defect has great range. Some are born with just a tiny notch in the upper lip and others have a split that carries from the nose to the back of the throat. The defect can occur as a cleft lip or together with a cleft palate. Then there are single and double cleft palates. A double obviously is the most severe. Amy?" he asked looking right at me.

"What was yours? A double or single?"

"A double," I said, not dropping my eyes from his even though my face burned hot and loud.

"In her case," he said lifting his chin toward me, "she probably had surgery to close her palate, called a palatoplasy, somewhere between nine and eighteen months." I nodded a slight yes. "The number of surgeries to correct this condition depends on the severity. Some are performed by plastic surgeons to aid in the appearance of the face. The worst cases could be nearly a dozen surgeries by the time the condition has been corrected." I thought briefly of the many surgeries to put my puzzle together. "There are of course many complications with a cleft palate, hearing, eating, breathing, talking."

"How does it happen?" asked a student near me. I didn't turn my head to see who was curious. I could feel eyes burning into my back, associating my defective face with every word Mr. Jones said.

"Here's the deal folks. Cleft palate is one of those conditions we aren't exactly sure why it happens. Could be genetic, although that theory is patchy. Other research points to cleft palate being caused by lack of folic acid. If we look at third world countries, where they lack proper nutrients, sometimes you will see two or three siblings with a cleft palate."

The weak part of me wanted to put my head on my desk and hide. The strong part wanted to shout to the class, "This is me! This is who I am! I am not ashamed! Please don't feel sorry for me. I like who I am!"

"In combination with issues from birth, many born with a cleft palate have learning disabilities, specifically in having difficulty learning to read." *Learning to read? I didn't make that up?* I thought, remembering the great private struggle from elementary school as the words never added up to sounds. Mr. Jones stood up from the stool, stretched his arms up to the ceiling, sat back down and said, "Most babies born with a cleft palate, with proper care, end up leading normal lives." *Normal?*

He finished with his lecture, then slid his black stool under his desk, but my thoughts stayed close to the pain of my flaws. I shuffled my papers slowly as the students passed me by, pretending I was organizing something of great importance in my Trapper folder as I waited for the last student to leave the room. "Hey, didn't mean to put you on the spot," Mr. Jones said, wringing his dry hands together. "You come off as a confident young woman so I knew you wouldn't mind me using you as an example."

"Oh, it's fine," I answered still feeling how his lecture had grated at my tender pain.

"Are you done with your surgeries?"

"I had my cranial facial surgery last summer, and over Christmas had my nose and lip done."

"Good to hear. You've obviously had some skilled doctors; they did a nice job on you."

"Thanks," I said, stacking my folder on top of my book, hanging onto his compliment. "My mom and dad worked hard to make sure I had a team of good specialists to help me, the best in the area."

"I would say to you then that you are lucky to have such great parents. You ought to thank them when you get home." He turned, walked to his desk, and over his shoulder stated in a booming voice, "Not every kid is as fortunate. In some areas of the world babies born with cleft palates are abandoned."

"I know, I've read about that. Thanks, Mr. Jones."

Something in the last comment Mr. Jones said about thanking my parents flipped my perspective and made me want to run down the steps of the high school to Dad's classroom, throw open the door, and shout my gratitude to him. And Mom. She didn't abandon me. She wasn't ashamed of me. Minutes after I was born she held me tighter. Loved me deeper, and breathed beauty into my being by telling me I had the "most determined little expression on my mouth." I was her delightful prize, and she was mine.

CHAPTER TWENTY-NINE

When a prayer travels to God with faith, even the smallest one is heard.

Mrs. Jensen picked me up for a last minute babysitting job and before we had even reached her house I calculated I would earn six bucks for the night.

"Were the kids OK?" she asked three hours later as I climbed into the front seat of her car.

"Oh, yeah, just fine," I answered while bucking my seatbelt. "They're super, so cute,"

"Super cute little monsters, right?" she laughed while glancing in her side mirror as she backed out of the driveway. "Thanks again for coming on such short notice. I want to treat you to a shake or item of your choice. Do you have time to go to PJs?"

"*Do I?* Yes! Of course! Thank you!"

"It's my pleasure," she stated as she turned on the radio. We chatted over the songs that played as she drove the few miles to the popular eatery. We talked about everything from my surgeries, to school, to homework, to boys. "Do you care if we get our food from the drive-through?"

"Fine by me!"

"Get whatever you want," she said pulling up to the outside menu. "Mamma's got the checkbook tonight!"

"Can I get a scone? I mean, may I get a scone?" I asked, analyzing the price and hoping I wasn't being too greedy.

Mrs. Jensen looked at me, rolled her bottom lip into a frown, raised her eyebrows, and asked, "Really? Is that it? No shake to go with your scone? We need to put some weight on your frame, Amy!"

"OK, two scones!"

"Now we're talking!"

"With honey butter!"

"Whoa! See! I knew you had it in you!" she laughed as she pulled forward to the window to place the order.

The stalky blond guy inside used both hands to shake the window free before he leaned forward, hanging his wrists out in the cold.

"Hey guys. What can I get you tonight?"

"Two scones and a chocolate shake."

"Pssst...and honey butter!"

"Yes! And honey butter!"

"OK, cool," he mumbled. "Hold on and I'll have your total."

I scooted forward so I could see through the window and into the patches of light coming from the back area of the restaurant. The mysterious air coming through the window smelled of used cooking oil mingled with the scent of fresh baked pizza. "Let's make a gigantic straw," I heard a guy say from the belly of the kitchen. "How many do you think we can put together and still drink from a cup?" His deep voice was familiar.

Another answered him, "I've put twelve together before, so beat that!"

"You're on, Donkey Kong!" the guy said. "I will take your twelve straws and raise you three more."

He passed by the window, and in a flash, I knew why his voice struck home with me. It was Jamie.

"Holy crap! I know that guy!" I whisper shouted to Mrs. Jensen.

"Oh, the guy that's supposed to be making your scones?"

"He's pretty much the most popular guy in school. He's so good looking! He also plays the drums. Like, really good!"

"Do you want to talk to him? I can honk this horn and get him to come to the window! Say the word!"

"Oh, no, no, no. We're not really friends, we just have English class together," I answered, trying to control the nervous wobble in my voice.

The stalky blond returned to the window. "$5.69."

Mrs. Jensen ripped the check out and handed it to him while I unsuccessfully strained to see Jaime one more time—but the stalky blond blocked the view.

"Go ahead, dig in," Mrs. Jensen coaxed as she turned out into the street. "No need to worry about making a mess in this car, nobody would know the difference."

"OK, thanks," I said, ripping off a hot edge, then dipping it into the small cup of honey butter, wondering why butterflies danced in my tummy for a guy I'd never even spoken to. I pictured him there in the kitchen of PJs, making my scone with the very hands I stared at during class, the same hands that turned the beat of a drum into music. Mrs. Jensen carried on a one-way conversation the rest of the ride, while I nodded along, already thinking how I needed to talk Katie into going to PJs again with me soon.

"Who's going with me to Gram's house?" Dad asked the next day, after the Sunday dishes had been washed and laid out to dry.

"Wait for me, Dad, I'm coming."

Gram was in her housecoat when we arrived, pulling tall glasses out of the cupboard.

"Hi, Gram," I said, passing her on the way to the living room.

"Amy?" she asked, turning to look me in the eye. "Do you have a headache tonight?"

"No, not tonight," I said, giving the same answer I had for the last two months. "I feel just fine."

"Oh, that's good, honey. Now go on in and sit down."

"Right here, A-mousie," Gramp said, patting the couch next to him. "Did you spend all your money again this week?"

"Gramp," I started while kicking off my shoes and pulling my legs up beneath me, "I spent every last dime yesterday. Unless I get a babysitting job I only make fifteen dollars cleaning my neighbor's house on Saturdays."

"My hell. Is that all the money you make in a week?"

"Why do you think I look for cheap finds at the thrift store?"

"I'll tell you what we need to do. You and I need to go into town one of these Saturdays and you can show me around," he said, twisting a worn toothpick between his bottom gold rimmed teeth. "I'll even take you to lunch afterward. Cause you sure as hell can't afford lunch if you're only making fifteen bucks a week."

"You've got a deal, Gramp. I'll take you thrift store shopping and you can buy my lunch."

"Aims, have you got a hot date to Prom yet?" asked Auntie Julie while nibbling on the insides of her cheek.

"No hot date for Prom. No hot dates pretty much ever."

"What about all those guy friends you're always telling me about?"

"Most of them have their dates already and a few don't want to go 'cause it costs so much money. One of my guy friends is having me help him figure out what to wear, you know, so he can match his date's dress." I tilted my head and pulled all of my hair over my left shoulder. "Katie got asked at the first of the month, so I am kinda helping her look through magazines to find a dress she likes."

"Who's she going with? Anyone we know?"

"His name is Tyler. She's been dating him a little bit. He's big! And tough! He asked her really early because I think that he wanted to make sure nobody else asked her. She has two boys fighting over her right now."

"That's a good problem to have! Maybe she can share, and one of them can take you," Auntie Julie winked. "Where are they having Prom this year?"

"At the capitol. That's where they had it last year, too. I've heard it is really pretty."

"All the way down in Salt Lake? We had our Prom in the high school gym. In fact, we were the last class to have our Prom at the old high school," she said, looking up and to the right as if recalling the day. "My dress was yellow tiered taffeta with white polka dots."

"Pretty! Tell me more!"

"It had long sleeves and was a bit poufy. I actually still have it."

"Julie was the Prom Queen," Gram said balancing two glasses filled with iced Pepsi, her elbow skin flapping back and forth as she walked into the room.

"You were? Wow! That's so cool! Prom Queen!" I said, thinking that Auntie Julie must have been the prettiest girl in her high school. "How did you do your hair?"

"Oh, let's see, I wore it curly. Big, full curls. My hair went all the way down my back."

I wrapped my finger around a strand of hair next to my neck. "Katie is going to do her hair to the side with a bunch of tight curls. At least that is what she is thinking she will do."

"That sounds pretty cute! Now, Aims, don't give up. Some lucky boy will ask you to Prom."

I raised my eyebrows, shrugged my shoulders, and replied, "I hope so, but I don't know. There isn't much time left. It's fine though. I mean, no big deal."

I watched Auntie Debbie, sitting across from me in a comfy chair, take a ball of yarn and crochet the beginnings of a hot pad.

Katie and Wendy had dates, and Christy didn't care if she went or not. But me—I had wanted to go to the Junior Prom as long as I had known it existed. *That* was the dance of all high school dances, the crown jewel of the dating world, the nod of true acceptance. "Have you been asked to Prom yet?" girls were asking one another in the hallways, followed by, "Who is taking you?" and, "Have you gotten your dress yet? What color is it? Do you have matching shoes? How are you going to do your hair?" The more the girls who had dates talked, the more my heart ached for their same experience. "Amy, are you going?" friends would ask me, "Oh, no, and it's fine," I would answer, trying to be positive. "I, you know, I don't really care." But I *did* care. I wanted a date to Prom more than anything. I had to go. I just had to. I watched Aunt Debbie change to a new color of yarn, wrapping the crochet needle in and out of tiny pockets of nothing, until she had made *something*. She nodded as she assessed the edges. And just as soon as she had completed one hot pad, she started on another.

On the drive back home I came up with a plan. I would wear my cutest outfits all week, smile at every boy that I passed, Nair my legs, and shine, shine, shine! Monday morning I put on my bright blue rayon shirt paired with my cutest jeans. I walked down the halls of the high school swinging my books next to my hips like the cool kids, smiling at each new boy who passed me, thinking to myself, *Pick me! Take me to the dance! Please…just look at me, smile at me, see me! Don't look away. Pick me. Please. Ask me! Like me! Give me a chance—please...someone...pick me.* A hollow feeling escaped my stride on the way home as I considered the fact that not one boy had given me the smallest hint of attraction. Mom was there when I got home, assuming her usual spot in the kitchen, but I only stopped briefly to visit before I went to my room to re-group.

On Tuesday I pulled out all the stops and wore my new leather mini-skirt, the color of worn, soft chocolate, coupled with a cream silk top. "Oh my fetch! You look so pretty!" Katie said as soon as I got to my locker.

"Does my skirt look OK with this top?"

"Um, hello! Miss Fashion! You look so cute!"

"Whatever! Look at you! I love that Esprit shirt on you!"

"Thanks! It's my sisters. See you at lunch!"

I smiled at the guys before class, after class, and during lunch. Katie said I looked pretty, and I *felt* pretty, yet I received the same response from the potential dates as I had on Monday—a sharp look away as soon as I made eye contact. My confidence fell flat. Not even a whisper of hope surrounded my thoughts. I was a reject.

"Amy Jo! Are you coming to History? You know you're going the wrong way, right?" Katie laughed as I walked the opposite direction from our classroom, my leather mini-skirt sticking to my legs with each step.

"Yeah, in a minute, I just need to go to the bathroom."

"OK, meet you there, woman!"

I dipped into the girl's room to check my makeup—and to let my face relax from the constant smiling. A few seniors were standing near the mirrors talking about preparations for the dance in agonizing detail—one said she didn't want to go to a dance that was sponsored by the junior class. I shut myself in the end stall, locked the handle and leaned my back against the inside of the door, waiting for them to leave so I could be all alone. When they did I put my hands on my thighs, exhaled, and hugged my insecurities so close to my soul I struggled to stand. I shook my head back and forth, trying to eliminate the swell of pain that rocked through my body from something so stupid as a dance and something so big as being wanted. I focused on the floor, running my hands to my knees, digging the heels of my palms into my muscles to divert the pain I felt overpowering my being. The bell rang, and I heard lockers start to slam, the cold sound echoing through my body.

I unlocked the stall, and turned to look at myself in the large mirror. My eyes were wet. My heart was weak. The years of this trial compounded and started to break at my fragile confidence. I had only one path left. I took in a calculated breath, which filled my chest and lifted my shoulders briefly—and then I prayed to God like I had never prayed before, desperate with him to hear my selfish prayer, asking him over and over in my mind to grant me the wish I had been wishing for my whole life. *I am begging you to please hear my prayer today like you have so many other times. I am not asking you to make my lips as they should, or make my nose perfect, or give me a cupid's bow, but... I am pleading with you to please soften one boy to look past my face of scars. I've carried this trial and tried not to complain. I need this prayer answered more than anything in the world. Please. I won't ever again in my life ask for something so trivial. Just…today…right now. I need you to hear me…please hear me. Nobody else knows how I feel or the depths of what I have been through but you, so today I am begging you, God, to please give me this one request. Please just let someone see beautiful me and ask me to the Junior Prom. Please.* I closed my eyes, then opened them and smiled at myself in the mirror like I always did, but my lips turned down and I hid my face in my hands, surrounded by quiet conflict. I ended my prayer, trying hard to suffocate my tears, by expressing gratitude for all the blessings that I *did* have—and I hoped that God was still listening.

I sat quietly through History class, nodding when Katie asked me if I wanted to go to the basketball game with her. I ate lunch without making conversation and slipped through the rest of my classes unnoticed.

For dinner mom made crunchy tacos loaded with seasoned beef, cheddar cheese, and diced tomatoes. I didn't tell anyone about my great request to God. It was personal and mine alone.

"Huh. Exxon Valdez has been indicted on five criminal counts," Dad said, taking a large bite of supper, bending the newspaper with his free hand. "I still say the captain is to blame. He never should have gotten drunk and left the third mate in charge of the ship."

"Seems one is pointing a finger at the other," answered Mom. "It's a shame. The whole mess is a shame."

"Ouch! Oh! Oh! I am in painnnnn," hollered Todd, rolling around on the couch holding his foot. "My ingrown toenail is keeping me from life! From living! It hurts so bad I can't even think! I'll never walk again!"

"My fetch, Todd, you act like someone just took out your liver."

"It hurts, Dad! You don't understand!"

"Look, come sit down and eat. After dinner I will find some salve for your toe," Mom said from her corner spot at the table.

"No! I can't wait, I need urgent help now! I can't think! Make it stop! Listen to me!"

Toots ate her dinner, then returned to the table with a stack of paper and a box of crayons, ready to create another masterpiece. Justin went downstairs to play his new video game, Bayo Billy, and Darin ran around the kitchen table—around and around and around. Finally Dad stopped him and said, "You're making everyone crazy!" So Darin went around one more time, just to test Dad. Mom got up from her warm dinner plate to take care of Todd's toe. I went to my room unnoticed, opened *Hamlet,* and tried to concentrate on the reading assignment for English class. An hour passed; then two, but my mind was somewhere else. It was absorbed in layer eleven. I couldn't help it. I tried to claw out of the darkness, but it covered me in heavy mud and kept me down where I couldn't get out. My appearance held me hostage, and there I sat, staring at the same page and not reading at all. I turned the book upside down, lay the pages against my stomach, and ran my fingers along the spine, as if by some measure I could reverse my condition by avoiding it. The fight to be normal seemed far too out of reach, the secret of the first impression eluded me, and the thought of rallying one more time bore the burden of an exhausted journey.

"Amy?" Toots called, coming into our room. "Amy, the phone is for you. I asked his name, and he said it was Jamie."

"Jamie?" I asked, sitting up so fast my heart started to pound.

"Yeah."

"Are you sure?"

"Yup."

"Did he say what he wanted?"

"Nope."

Jamie? Jamie? My thoughts instantly hurt, *please don't be a prank call,* I pleaded. *Please, Jamie, don't say mean words to me. Please don't do this to me tonight. I can take it any other night, but not tonight.* My heart tumbled at a fast pace from the intensity of adrenaline.

The short walk to the phone reminded me all too well of the last few times I had picked up this same phone, this same time of night, and heard a boy's voice on the other end cutting me and pouring salt in my wound. I braced myself to hear something mean, hoping with all my might that I would be wrong, and maybe he would be calling about the English homework instead. The phone was lying there just where Toots had left it—on the freezer chest with the receiver turned upright. I wanted to run away, not pick it up and face the conversation. I took a deep breath, and then paused just briefly before saying, "Hello?"

"Hi, Amy? This is Jamie Acton—from English class?"

Oh, OK, whew! He's just calling about our English assignment. Oh, thank you, thank you for not being mean.

"Oh, hi, how are you?"

"So, I was just wondering if you are going to Prom. Do you have a date already?"

Wait, what? IS this a prank call? Oh, come on. Please, no! I felt panicky, but I managed to answer. "No, I'm not going." *I'll show him,* I thought, feeling my resolve harden. *I'll be cold and tough, and I won't let him bring me down.*

"Well hey—would you like to go? With me? Be my date?"

I was speechless, torn in two with astonished hope and clenched confusion. *Huh? Me? Do you have the wrong number? Don't you just want to talk about the English assignment? This can't be right. You can't possibly have chosen me. There are so many girls that like you. I am nowhere near pretty enough.* I was sure now it was a prank call, but I heard myself saying, "Uh, yeah, sure."

"OK, cool. I'll see you at school tomorrow. Thanks, Amy."

I clicked the phone back on the hook and let my shoulders drop. I stood there, my heart racing out of control, and wondered what I should do next. It didn't *feel* like a normal prank call, I mean, he did say his full name. *Prom? Me? Could he have been serious?*

Then it came to me crystal clear—*Jeannie* would know what to do.

"Mom, can I call Jeannie? Long distance?" I asked, my voice shaking.

"Sure, why?"

"Umm...I ...just got asked to Prom, and I don't know if he was serious. And Jeannie knows Dave, who's a friend of his, and I just...I need to know if it was a prank call...or—you know—not." I dialed Jeannie's number with my hands shaking out of control and hope bursting out of my skin, drenching me in a hot wave of blush. "Is Jeannie there?" I abruptly asked the roommate who answered the phone. "I need to talk to her right now." A few minutes passed, and then I heard Jeannie's footsteps as she walked toward the phone.

"Amy? Are you OK?"

"Jeannie! I don't know. I'm stressing out. I need your help! I just got a call from Jamie Acton—to go to *Prom*! But, I don't know, Jean—I think it might have been a prank call. He's so popular, and I don't know why he would want to go with me."

"Whoa, Aim. Slow down. Who did you say called?"

"You know, that drummer guy? Jamie? HE called me! And asked me to Prom!"

"What! When? Tell me more!"

"Just now! Two seconds ago!"

"OK, calm down. I'll call my friend Dave since he is friends with Jamie and ask him if he knows anything. I will call you *right* back. Stay put."

"Please hurry!"

I waited right there in the kitchen, standing over the same heat vent that kept me warm when I was small as I watched the white bees fly safely to the ground. I held my shaking hands together as I rolled from the heel of my foot to the tips of my toes, then paced in circles around the heat vent, staying close to the phone. Each minute that passed brought doubt, but my heart beat on. I craved with all my might that the doubt would be extinguished and her news would be positive. More time passed. Longer than should have, and my hesitations seemed real. This was a big, fat, ugly joke. He was too popular, too good looking, with too many options to pick me. My head was still spinning, blurring my thoughts into a confusion of uncertainty. Still more time passed. Just as I started to dip into layer eleven again, the phone rang. I pounced on it, answering fast, ready for whatever answer she had for me. "Hello? Jeannie?"

"AMY! Are you ready for this?"

"Yes! What took you so long! Tell me!"

"He was serious! You are going to Prom with Jamie Acton!"

"He *was*? I *AM*? Are you sure? *Me*? Oh, Jeannie! I'm going to the Prom! I can't…I can't believe this. I am going to the Prom! It's real though, right? I mean, you talked to Dave. What did he say? I need to know what he said, all of it!"

"It's real! You are going! You are going to Prom!" She shouted echoing my triumph, then continued with the details of the conversation. "Well, I called Dave, and he wanted to make sure that the call was real—so he casually just called him to find out what was going on and if he had made his decision on who he was going to ask, and he said he had just called you! Jamie told Dave that he had noticed you in English class and that he thought you were cool, and he wanted to take you to the dance."

"Oh no! I was so rude to him on the phone, Jeannie! I just…I didn't think he was serious."

"Well he *was*, Amy! And now you have your Prom date. I will totally come down and help you get ready and do your hair for you. I am so excited!"

"Me too, Jean, me too. This is the best day of my life. I can't—I can't believe it. I am so happy right now! Thank you for helping me. I've got to call Katie and tell her! I can't stop shaking!"

Like simple harmony being played out one key at a time on a piano, I could feel God telling me that I was loved. I was his child. He knew me well enough to grant me my wish—the one wish I had wanted my whole life. I went right to my room, knelt down on the scratchy red carpet, and prayed with deep gratitude right through my core, not even forming a word in my mind. I stayed there on my knees with my heart pounding and my whole body shaking for strings of minutes, hoping that God could feel my thanks. When I finally stood my knees were raw. *He answered my prayer. He knows me. He knows me!* Happiness in my life had been plenty, but this—this was pure joy. The joy of someone choosing *me*. I found my yearbooks from Junior High and flipped to the individual class pictures. There he was. The first picture. I stared long and hard into his eyes and wondered what could have possibly prompted him to choose *me*. The space in my heart filled with security—all the doubt disappeared. My mind could hear no words. I simply *felt*. Felt as if I was falling. Time was another dimension, and I wanted to stop the clock from ticking so I could be immersed in the feeling forever. I forced my eyes to close, pressing deep into my pillow, wondering if this was a dream or a sudden new reality.

CHAPTER THIRTY

The essence of a woman is grace in motion, fine-tuned by the experiences, good and bad, that show the world she is complex and human.

"Hey! Amy! I heard Jamie Acton asked you to Prom? Did he *really*?" probed a popular sophomore girl as soon as I opened the doors to the high school. "I mean, I heard it from someone I know who's sort of friends with him, so I don't know if it is a rumor or what, but, you know, I'm just curious."

"You heard right!" I smiled passing her, then spun around on the balls of my feet, and half jumped into the air as I shot back my response, "I said yes!"

I heard my name humming through the sounds of lockers shutting and bells ringing, ricocheting through the air, spoken by unfamiliar girls pointing at me and whispering to their friends. And this time, I knew why. Some wanted to know about the details and how the event unfolded. "How did he ask you?" Others had their friends ask my friends to see if the rumor was true. "Wow, she is so lucky!" "Are they dating?" I could hear the chatter and feel the energy—positive, crazy, unthinkable, spinning energy. I walked down the hall toward my locker, passing other girls like me, who were smiling as big as I was, happy I had been given a chance.

These same girls had fought their own battles of outer challenges, rarely selected by the masses. In my heart I started singing the anthem of hope for *all* of us. I was their mascot. Their lucky, sprinkled-with-sudden-cool dust, I-hope-this-happens-to-you-too, happier-than-I'd-ever-been mascot.

"Amy! Come talk to us!" shouted a group of my close friends, motioning to me with their hands. "Come here! Come here! Is it true?! Do you have a Prom date? Is it really with Jamie Acton? You have to tell us how this happened! Are you so happy?"

I pushed my way into the corner of the hallway and didn't curb my enthusiasm. "Happy! Yes! He called me last night and asked me!" I answered with genuine joy, thrilled to have common news to share with them.

"Oh! That's so cute! And traditional! I didn't know you two were such good friends," one girl said.

"No, really, the thing is, last night was the first time we have ever talked. It was great though!"

"I want a dance picture!" one said.

"Me too!" shouted the rest in unison.

"I only get eight, I think, but I promise I will do my best to give you each one," I grinned.

"Oh my heck!" Katie said, bursting onto the scene. "Good morning, Miss Popular!"

"Kates! This is crazy!" I yelled, breaking away from the group. "Everyone already knows! How does everyone know?"

"Good news travels fast," she joked.

"I'm still shaking from last night. What do I do if I see him?"

"Um, say hi!" she laughed throwing an elbow into my ribs. "Come on, let's get to our lockers. You know we *do* have to go to class at some point!"

Before I could put the combination in my locker Jamie was coming toward me, his unmistakable tall frame forming in my peripheral vision. I wasn't ready to see him yet. I hadn't checked myself in the mirror or made sure my hair was still together. *What is my locker number? Think, Amy! Think! Scratch that. Just keep spinning it he's almost...* "Hey there."

"Hey there to you," I answered, taking note of his paisley shirt and the way it contrasted with his light washed jeans and braided brown belt.

"First, thanks for saying yes," he said, his eyes darting to and then anchoring on mine.

"Oh, for sure, yeah."

"Second, as soon as I find out when we are leaving and where we are eating you will be the first to know."

"OK, great, no problem."

The bell rang. He put one hand up into a wave and said, "See you in class, Amy."

And then I knew. The girls watching us knew. And those passing by us knew. The rumor was true. I had a date to Prom with the hottest guy in the whole school.

"Mom! Mom! Today was the best, best, best day ever!" I said throwing open the front door after school and running to the counter. "Like I was instantly popular! And he came and talked to me at my locker and everything! It was so cool!"

Mom looked up from here dinner preparations, her eyes reflecting my bliss. "We'd better go look for a dress soon!"

"Can we go tonight?"

"How about tomorrow night?"

"It's a plan!"

I was thrilled. *A dress! Mine! This time the beautiful gown will be for me.*

"I want to buy the dress for you, so pick anything you want," Mom said as we drove into town the next afternoon.

"Let's go to the mall. I am sure as soon as I see the dress I will know it is for me!"

"You lead, I will follow," Mom said as she parked the van.

At each shop we went into, I stopped in the middle of the floor and spun around, looking up and down at all of the dresses. "Nope, it's not here," I would say, and we would hit the next shop. We walked all the way down one side of the mall and then turned to walk down the opposite side. And finally, from a distance, I saw my dress two storefronts down. It was hanging on the top rack, high enough that I couldn't reach it, but it was most certainly my dress.

"Yes, that one, the white one with the lace top," I said to the sales clerk, who got a large wand to pull the dress down.

"Do you want to try on any other dresses?" she asked.

"No, thank you," I answered with a steady tone. Mom and I went right to the dressing room, where she took a seat outside the door. I fell in love with the dress before I even put it on, and I couldn't imagine one reason why it wouldn't fit. It was pure white with three tiers of satin ruffles. The top was lace with a built-in bodice, and the back neckline was cut into a V.

"I need help zipping!" I said, opening the door.

"Oh! Amy! That *is* beautiful!" Mom said, zipping the dress up. "It fits you just right." I looked at myself in the mirror, and for the first time I saw my long legs that the dress showed off so well. They were fantastic! "I love it, Mom, but there's only one problem," I said patting my chest. "I need boobs for this dress."

Mom stood up, moved her glasses down to the end of her nose and examined the inside of the dress, "I can sew a padded bra right in the lining for you, and nobody will even know."

"Oh! Mom! Really? Then it's *the one*! This is the dress I want!"

"Looks like we will need to get you some matching shoes, too," Mom said while unzipping the dress.

"Cool! I want to see if we can find some high heels in white lace."

We went to the first shoe store we saw and I confidently walked up to the clerk and said, "I need a pair of white lace high heels."

"We just so happen to have that very thing," he said, going behind the counter to look for my size. "Now, what color would you like us to dye them?"

"I don't need them dyed. My dress is white, so they are fine plain, just like that."

"Plain white?" he paused. "If you change your mind and want us to dye them to match your dress, just bring them back."

"Nope, white, just like they are."

Mom and I rode home, past the doughnut shop and up 100 East with Old Ben looking back at us, the peak still covered in snow. "Amy, I am so happy for you. All that you have been through, the surgeries, the hours of speech therapy…"

"…the bullying," I added, finishing her sentence.

"Bullying? What do you mean *bullying*?"

"You know, how I was bullied so much in elementary school, and then, in junior high, the boys would throw food at me during lunch?" I asked matter-of-factly while flipping through the radio stations.

"Well, I guess…maybe I don't know exactly everything," she said, clearly hesitating to recall my childhood. "I do remember you telling me some boys in your class didn't like the way your face looked, but my goodness you always had so many friends, you didn't seemed bothered by any of your challenges."

"I have always been grateful for my circle of friends, and my sisters, too. Jeannie protected me in elementary. She once beat up one of the bullies. Did you know that?"

"Yes, well, Jeannie was good at telling stories back then, it was hard to know how much of what she said was true."

"That part was true, Mom."

"You know, Amy, if you would have told me how bad things were I would have run right over to the school and talked to the principal and made things right."

"I know you would have, Mom," I said, looking straight ahead. "It was just easier to not talk about it. Anyway, it was just a few mean kids, no big deal."

"I am *so* sorry," she said, stopping at the red light and looking toward me. "I should have spoken to you more often about what you were going through. I never would've imagined you were struggling, not with the kind of confidence that you gave off and still do!"

"It's OK, Mom, really. The teachers didn't like us to tattle."

"Certainly the bullying wouldn't have been classified as tattling," Mom said, putting her foot heavy on the gas.

"Besides, you always enforced the positive and good in me. It was like you only saw the best of me."

"Of course! You are my daughter! And a miraculous one at that."

"Thanks, Ma." I glanced briefly at her, feeling the relief of an exposed burden.

When I got home I tried the dress on again in my own room, falling in love with it all over again. Once it was off, I carefully hung it on a foam hanger and zipped the plastic cover over the top of it.

"The phone is for you again," said Toots, coming into our room as if calls for me were a regular occurrence. "It's that boy again."

I skipped through the basement and eagerly answered the phone, "Hello?"

"Amy?" Just the sound of his voice made my knees weak. "Hey, so I know I just asked you to the dance a few days ago, but do you happen to know what color your dress is going to be? And, no pressure."

"Yeah, it's white. We just bought it tonight, so I know for sure."

"Cool...that's easy to match, white is good. You ready for your Hamlet speech?"

"I give mine later this week," I answered, wishing my voice didn't sound like it was moving over railroad tracks. "Memorizing a whole paragraph is harder than I thought!"

"I do mine this week, too. I'll see you in English tomorrow morning, OK, Aim?"

I smiled at the shortened version of my name and felt golden sparks of fire light my soul, elevating me to strange new heights. "I'll be there," I answered. I hung the phone up and danced all the way back to my room.

Jamie found me the next morning in English, turning my name into beautiful music as he spoke it. I hadn't felt this way before, so totally and completely taken. His dark hair matched his eyes, and when he was near me I fell into a daze—a stupid, out-of-control, no-idea-how-to-handle-myself daze. "How about I pick you up at six? We are doubling with Scott Kolts and his date."

"Six it is!"

"We are going to Mulboons for dinner, and then we will head to the dance."

"Sounds great," I said, putting my book on my desk.

"Can you come over to my house tonight?" Katie whispered to me when she arrived in class, seconds before the final bell rang. "We can study for our history test next week."

"Sure Kates." I answered, happy for the invitation. "Did you see him talk to me? Just now? Before class?"

"What? No! I missed it! You *have* to fill me in tonight!"

"Deal!"

When I got to Katie's house her mom had just made phankuken, a traditional German dish that tasted a bit like cheesecake, only smoother and with a woodsy flavor. It was my absolute favorite treat her mom made. "Go ahead and cut yourself a slice," her mom said, handing me a plate. Katie got out a tray, put two drinks on it, two forks, and our phankuken, and down we went to her room to study.

"I wish you were still going to the Prom," I said.

"He was a jerk. I'm not wasting any more time thinking about how he treated me."

"I know. And I don't want you to go with him after how he acted. But I wish someone else would ask you before it's too late."

"Me too," she answered, "but it's OK. I am soooo excited for you! Are you nervous?" She put a mixed tape of our favorite songs into her boom box and clicked it shut.

"Yes! Way nervous! And excited, too! We're going with Scott Kolts and his date, and we might be meeting some other couples at the dance. Remember Scott from elementary school? I always assumed he was a spy because he just showed up one day out of the blue then practically became the best break dancer in the fifth grade," I said, taking another bite. "He's so cool. His date, Charlene, came up to me in dance today and told me that Jamie likes me!"

"No way! AHHHH! Cool!" Katie situated the tray between us. "So can you believe he's been nominated for Prom King?"

"I know! Prom King! How awesome would that be if he won?"

"OK, what happened this morning? What did I miss?"

"He came and talked to me right before English class started and he said we are going to eat at Mulboons. I never know what to say to him!"

"Mulboons! That place is the *best*. They bring out this shrimp tray as an appetizer. They're famous for it. You're going to have so much fun, Amy! I can't even be jealous because I'm so happy for you. I know how bad you wanted to go."

"Thanks, Kates," I said, downing my last bite of phankuken. "Wait, did you say shrimp? So, will I have to peel them? Do I eat the tail? Will they be cold? I am so afraid to eat shrimp! I wish we were going somewhere else."

"You should have your mom get you some shrimp so you can practice eating them. But no, you don't eat the whole thing. Just watch what the other girls do and you'll be fine. Oh, and remember the fork rule. You know, the outside fork is the one you use first—for your salad."

"There's more than one fork at Mulboons? Ahh! I don't know if I can remember all of this."

"Amy Jo, I'm going to tell you something, OK?"

I nodded, setting my plate back on the tray.

"I have always known something great would happen to you. I mean, really great. I don't see your flaws, I never have. I only see your beautifulness, and it starts from the inside of you and radiates through *all* of you. We have been together from the beginning of our lives, and I have seen everything you have gone through. Ya know? And I know it hasn't been easy. You amaze me with how positive you are and how you never complain. So guess what? It's your time now, Amy. Go and show them who you are! And have the time of your life!" She lifted the tray off her bed and placed it on the floor. "And don't worry one bit about me. This is how it was supposed to work out."

"Oh, Kates. You are the bestest friend I could ever ask for."

We sat there for over an hour on her bed with our history books open, studying the moments of our *own* history—the characters, the timelines, the conflict, and all the resolve.

"Amy?" Katie's mom called down the stairs. "Your mom just called. She has your dress all ready for you to try on." *No way! That was so fast! Oh thank you, Mom! Thank you!* I smacked my history book shut, ran up Katie's stairs taking two at a time, rushed out the back door, and sprinted through both yards until I made it home. Mom was there in the kitchen, next to the sewing machine, holding the dress up and messing with the inside bodice.

"You should be all set! Go try it on." I took the dress and immediately grabbed the bust line. *Ahhh, padding!*

"Thank you, Mom! Thank you, thank you, thank you!" I stripped down as fast as I could, then took the dress and carefully stepped into it, pulled it up over my hips, and put my arms into the lace sleeves before lining up the shoulder fabric. I stretched my arms to my back and zipped it up all on my own. I walked out into the kitchen for her to see. "Mom! It works great! You can't even tell that you sewed the bra into the dress!"

"Spin around, let's take a good look," Mom smiled back at me. "Looks like that did the trick!"

"I'm going to turn on some ABBA!" I said, wanting to celebrate by dancing in my finished dress.

I found my favorite album, put the needle softly on the record, and listened to the pop and crackle before the song started. Then, pretending my thumb was a microphone, I belted out the lyrics at the top of my lungs, *"Friday night and the lights are loowww, looking out for the place to gooo…."* Soon Toots was standing in the kitchen, watching me dance and sing, and right behind her was Justin. I had an audience! *"Where they play the right music, getting in the swing, you come in to look for a king.* Prom King! *Anybody could be that guuuy*–Toots, come dance with me! Justin, you too! Ready? Now sing!–*Yoooou are the dancing queen, young and sweet, only seventeeeen."* I pointed to Toots, then to Justin. "This is *so* my song now! Everyone sing with me! *Having the time of your life, see that girl, watch that scene, diggin' the dancing queen!"*

CHAPTER THIRTY-ONE

Every fairy tale ends with "Happily Ever After," — but real stories, the ones with the best endings, live as a legacy long after the book has ended.

The big day—Junior Prom—finally arrived, and I met the morning early since I'd hardly slept while waiting impatiently for the sun to rise.

"There's a big storm coming in, A-mouse," Dad said to me, reading the weather headline from the paper. "Should be here in two days, probably right on your seventeenth birthday. They say it could bring ten inches of snow with it, just *exactly* like the day we brought you home from the hospital when you were a baby. That was the worst blizzard I've ever seen, and there we were trying to drive you home safely through all that snow, our car flippin' all over the road." He smiled as he flashed through the memories. "It was such a mess, with traffic lights out and the power out in our little house for a few days. You didn't even care. You were just happy to be a baby and to be out of the hospital, heading home."

My white bees? Coming to see me on my seventeenth birthday? I thought about the bees, and how close they had been to me all of the years I'd

needed them most. Right there, protecting me —
giving me strength. How fortunate I had been to
know them and to feel their power as they quietly
took up space in my heart. I did secretly hope that
the storm would come in on my *very* birthday, not
the day before or the day after, but on *my* day.

Jeannie came down from college just after
lunch, keeping her promise to help me get ready for
the biggest date of my life. She brought her tools of
the trade: her makeup bag, her spiral rods, and lots
and lots of affirmation.

"So we're going to do your hair first, and then
your makeup, and *then* you can put on your dress,"
she said while setting a pillow in front of the full-
length mirror in my room, running her hands
through my frizzy mess of hair. "OK, sit down so we
can start getting the rods in. So what I'm thinking is
that we'll put small spiral rods all over the top, and
on the bottom we'll use the bigger ones." I nodded
my head, of course. It all sounded great. "Now, when
Jamie gets here you are going to need to pin his
corsage on his tuxedo," she said, taking a section of
my hair and pulling it up high and tight before
taking a spiral rod and wrapping the hair around it
over and over again. "It's tradition for the girl to pin
the corsage on her date."

"Jeannie, that just makes me feel panicky!
There is *no* way I'll be able to do that without
stabbing him, and I know he's going to be wearing a
white shirt, so I don't want to make him bleed."

"You won't. It's easy. You just need to grab
his lapel then take the pin and push it straight
through the bottom part of the flower. I've done it a
bunch of times, and it's easy."

Sure. But I haven't done it a bunch of times, I worried. "Will you do it for me? I don't think I can!"

"You want me to pin the corsage on your date?"

"I do. Please? I don't want to mess it up."

"Let's just see how it goes. I'm sure you'll be fine," she said taking the last of my hair and wrapping it onto a large spiral rod. "There. Now we just need to wait for your hair to totally cool down. In the meantime, let's do your makeup. Turn and look at me." I spun around on the pillow and pulled my knees up close to my chest, then closed my eyes and waited. "You can open your eyes. We're going to start with the foundation first." She took a small triangle sponge and dabbed it in foundation. Then she lightly covered all of my blemishes before mixing the color out toward my neckline. "The biggest mistake people make with foundation is that they don't blend it out," she said while feathering the sponge into my hairline. Then she gave me an all-over dusting of powder. "Here comes the blush. We want to add color to your face so you look refreshed and alive all night," she said, swishing the color high up my cheekbones.

"I think that's a good idea. You know I don't normally stay up past ten! I'll need to look as awake as possible!"

"And now for the eyes—I want to make them stand out." She used an array of eye colors to come up with the right combination. Each time she added a shade she would stand back away from me a little as she looked me over. "Close your eyes again. I'm just going to fix something." With a Q-tip she blended the colors together into a soft combination of spring. Then she carefully added mascara, starting at the inside lash line and working her way out. I kept as steady as I could. "Open your eyes and look at me," she said after several minutes of pumping the mascara tube and applying it to my lashes. "Oh, wow, Amy. Your eyes look amazing. I don't want you to see until I'm done with your hair, too, but you look *so* pretty. The last thing we need to do is put on lipstick," she said while searching her bag for a shade of red. "When Jamie gets here you'll need to ask him to put your lipstick in his pocket since you won't have a way to take it with you."

"What? No way! I don't dare ask him that. I can just do without."

"Amy, you are *not* going to the Prom without lipstick. You will for sure want to reapply after dinner. All the girls ask their dates to carry their lipstick."

"They do? I haven't even worn lipstick before! I don't know what to do."

"Well, it looks great on you," she said, finishing applying it. "Now rub your lips together, and then put this tissue between your lips and get off the extra. See? Easy."

One by one she took each of the spiral rods out of my hair revealing a tight bouncy ringlet that had replaced my frizzy natural hair. She ran her fingers through the curls to break them up, then heated up a curling iron and added extra curls before spraying my hair all over with hairspray. "*Now* you can go put on your dress, and then we'll paint your fingernails," she directed.

I stayed as far away from the mirror as possible. I wanted to see the reveal all at once, like a real life Cinderella. I first put on my white nylons. I slipped my dress up over my knees. I had tried it on so many times that I had it down to a science. Even zipping it up was a breeze. I put on my high heels next. I felt so tall and beautiful, spilling with confidence and a sunny soul. How could such a miraculous thing have happened to me? *Me?* I stood up and smoothed the silky ruffles in my dress. Then, with my head held high, I walked out to the full-length mirror.

"Amy? AMY! Oh my goodness! You look gorgeous!"

"KATES! You came! You're here!" I shouted, nearly wanting to jump up and down on my bed, I was so happy.

"You think I would've missed you looking all glamorous and ready for the Prom? I *had* to come over. Wow, Amy. You look amazing! Really!"

"Aw Kates. I will miss you tonight! We have done everything together! We should both be getting ready for our Junior Prom—together."

"Nope. This is your night. I already told you that, Amy Jo. But you dang well better remember all the details and come and tell me first thing in the morning! You know I won't be able to sleep tonight!"

"I will, Kates," I smiled, finding comfort in her true friendship. "You really think I look OK?"

"I am standing here in amazement. You look like a goddess."

"You do look stunning, Amy," said Jeannie, now back in the room. Her words carried no frills or added excitement, but instead, awe.

"Amy Jo, I am going to leave before Jamie gets here, but don't forget to remember everything! You are beautiful. I'll love you forever, woman!"

"Ditto, Kates! Pray for me! And the shrimp!" I joked as she left the room. Then I turned and looked again in the mirror, and staring back at me were the same blue eyes I had always known—clear, bright, strong, happy. Mine. Then I saw the rest of my reflection—the dress, the hair, the makeup, and the slim long legs, and I hardly recognized myself. But it was me—it had *always* been me.

"Jeannie…thank you. Wow. I feel…so pretty. Look what you did for me. You…transformed me." I turned to look right at her.

Before I knew it the doorbell had rung, and my date had arrived. I stood on the top landing of the stairs, hidden in the shadows that led to the basement while Jeannie answered the door. She had told me it was a good idea to make your date wait a few minutes and not appear too eager. "Oh hi, Jamie, come on in. Amy is still getting ready. I'll go get her." Jeannie nearly ran back to me, her feet skimming across the linoleum. "He's here! And he looks so good!" she whispered in her excited voice.

"How long should I stand here? I don't know what to do!"

"Shhhh! A few minutes at least. I'll stay with you." We stood next to each other, not saying a word, waiting for the minutes to pass. My sister—my friend. She was as much a part of me as the blood that raced through my heart. She, too, had lived my experiences in her own way, taking on far more than I ever would know. She voluntarily changed her own life to help me along the way. I carried a picture in my mind from years ago when Jeannie and I were both small, long before we went to school. Mom had dressed us in homemade jumpsuits. Jeannie's was blue and mine was patchwork brown. Jeannie was standing next to me, looking straight ahead, confidently holding my hand, smiling. She would guide me, protect me, and teach me through the hardest years of my life. But in that picture, she didn't know that. She only knew that she was my big sister, and she loved me.

Mom greeted Jamie, and from where Jeannie and I stood we could just make out the conversation. Mom was telling him that she wanted to take pictures before we left to go to the dance. *Oh, good call, Mom! I want to document this!*

"Now can I go?" I asked Jeannie.

"Not yet. Almost, though."

After a few more minutes, Jeannie gave me the go-ahead signal. I took one step all by myself, listening to the sound of my own feet making a clicking sound as the heels hit the floor. Then I took another, and another, making sure that I wasn't walking too fast. I knew he heard me coming. I hoped he thought I looked pretty.

I turned the corner and saw him standing there with three red roses in his hand, a black tuxedo framing a crisp white shirt, and a red cummerbund and bow tie. My breath was taken away. Completely. I had never seen anyone in my life look so arresting. He was my tall, dark, and handsome.

338

"Hi, these are for you," he said, handing me the roses. Katie had once told me that red roses meant, "love" and that three red roses meant, "I love you." I pretended he knew that, too.

"Thank you." I smiled back, but in my mind I said, *You changed the future of my life. YOU! Thank you for being the one tonight who I needed more than anything. Thank you for being daring enough to give me a chance when nobody else would.*

Then, there was Jeannie, at my side again, getting the boutonniere out of the plastic floral box. "OK, now Amy is going to pin this on you, and then we're going to take some pictures."

"Actually, uh . . . Jeannie, I think you should do it," I said, my hands shaking so badly I knew I would be dangerous with a sharp pin. The headlines the next day would read, "Girl Injures Potential Prom King while Pinning Boutonnière, Sad Ending."

"Are you sure, Amy?"

"Yes, you know what you're doing, Jeannie. Go ahead."

Mom came back into the room with her camera out in front of her as she tried to figure out how to attach the film. Jeannie pinned the boutonniere on Jamie's lapel, and made it look so effortless. She was wearing worn-out blue jeans along with a plain T-shirt, her hair pulled back in a simple ponytail, her face colored with a tiny bit of makeup. I couldn't help but wonder if she had downplayed her looks for me so I could be the one shining.

"Oh boy!" said Mom shutting the camera door. "Let's get some pictures of you two." Jeannie posed us by the fireplace, and then by the piano, while Mom snapped a few pictures.

"Now, Amy," Jeannie choreographed, "take the roses and put them in your other arm, and put your free arm through Jamie's." *You want me to touch him! What if he thinks I'm being too forward? Jeannie, no!* But my arm did what she said, and I tried to act as cool as possible. *Just relax,* I told myself. *Have fun. Don't be so worried about what you usually worry about.* "One last thing before you go," Jeannie said as we went out the door. "Amy wants you to hold her lipstick for her."

"What?" asked Jamie. I forced a smile. *See? I knew you were the only one that did that, Jeannie!*

"Here, take her lipstick and put it in your pocket. She'll need it later," she said, handing him the tube. *OK, that was embarrassing. Just look at him and nod.*

Jamie opened the front door for me and led me out to his car. Then he opened the passenger's side door, just like I had seen the boys do for Jeannie.

"Sorry I'm three minutes late," he said.

"Well, that just means you'll have to bring me home three minutes late," I laughed back, hoping I sounded clever.

We took the short drive to pick up Scott and his date, Charlene. She was dressed in a brilliant blue, the color of a precious sapphire, and wore her hair long and in loose curls. Scott's mom insisted on taking her own set of pictures, waving us back and forth, telling us to stand here and there. I loved it. Each time a new picture was taken, I became braver, inching ever closer to Jamie. The faint scent of cologne that I smelled in the car became stronger the nearer I got to him. He was masculine and powerful standing next to me.

"You look nice tonight, Amy," Scott said from the back of the car as soon as I got situated and fastened my seatbelt.

"I was going to tell you the same thing," Jamie said. He glanced in my direction. "You look really pretty."

"Well, thank you." I smiled. "You both look very handsome."

I caught my new reflection in the side mirror, while Jamie and Scott made funny quips back and forth. When Jamie drove over the set of railroad tracks on the way to the freeway, I lifted both high heels above the floor mat, closed my eyes, touched a screw, and made a wish—just like I always did. "You know, Aim, that never actually works," Jamie said.

"It does for me," I said, wondering if he would ever have a clue how many times I had wished for this very night.

The Prom was to be held at the state capitol building. The girls who had been to Prom before had talked about how beautiful the building was with its marble stairs and rotunda that towered over one-hundred-and-fifty feet into the air. The drive into the city seemed long, and I regretted not asking Jeannie about conversation topics. She probably never had the problem of not knowing what to say next.

"Oh, no," Jamie said as we neared the city, his fingers fumbling in the pocket inside the car door. "Ah! This isn't good. Hey, guys, I umm…forgot the Prom tickets."

"Wait. You *forgot* them? As in they are still at your house?" asked Scott. "If we turn back we won't have time to get to our dinner reservation, but if we *don't* turn back then we'll miss the dance."

Turn BACK! I pleaded silently. *Do it! Come on, turn this Camry around! I don't need to eat!*

"Oh, geez, how could I have forgotten them?"

"We should just ditch the Prom and go get food!" Scott said, leaning up to the middle console.

Wait, you're kidding, right? I can't believe you're considering this. This can't be right!

"No, we should go get the tickets," Jamie said. "I'm sorry, guys. I thought I had them, but I don't."

Yes! Get the tickets! I breathed a sigh of relief. We turned around at the next freeway exit, and then Jamie pushed the Camry to drive as fast as she could go.

"Come on, Betsy! You can do it," he said, patting the dashboard.

At last, the ice was broken! Jamie hopped out of the car as soon as we pulled into his driveway, ran up the sidewalk and into his house, and before we knew it he was back again.

"Got 'em!" he said, stretching back to hand one keychain to Scott. "This is for you," he said handing me the other keychain. "It's our ticket into Prom. I want you to have it." The keychain was clear, and printed in cursive was the word "Somebody", the theme of Prom. I put it in my hand, holding it tight against my skin. *I am somebody! Me! I can do amazing things that take lots of courage, and now look at me! I am some boy's "somebody" tonight. When I get*

*home I'm going to put this in my butterfly jewelry box.
This is the kind of thing that should go in there.*

"My mom just told me that I resemble the one
and only Abe Lincoln," Jamie said once we were
back on the freeway.

"Wait, isn't his Adam's apple at least a
quarter inch lower than yours?" laughed Scott. "Hey,
I'm just being *honest.*"

"Shoot dang, if only it were a quarter inch the
other direction, think of the resemblance!" Jamie
jabbed back.

When we finally made it to the capitol
building, we collectively decided to eat after the
dance. The news didn't disappoint me—in fact, just
the opposite. There would be no shrimp disaster!
Charlene and I waited in the car while the boys got
out to open our doors. Jeannie had taught me how to
exit properly like a lady, but I had only practiced it in
my head. *Scoot to the edge of the seat, legs together, then
ease your legs out of the car keeping your ankles close, and
before you stand make sure you have your footing.*

"You got out of the car so good," said Jamie,
clearly impressed.

"Thank you," I smiled back, and thought,
*Wow! Jeannie was right! I am SO glad I listened to her!
And I'm getting the hang of this dating stuff. I am!*

The inside of the capitol was an architectural
wonder. Massive marble pillars lined either side of
the entryway, and there was a staircase cascading
down to the main level in mighty expansion. The top
of the staircase ended at a landing with two more
sets of stairs going up either side, giving access to a
higher level. At the base of the stairs couples were

having their pictures taken, and soon we got in line for the same experience.

"Stand close together; put your arm around her back. Now point the roses toward me so we can see them," the photographer directed us. "No, no, you need to stand closer." We moved together and I felt the fabric of his tuxedo brush against my arm, sending chills the length of my spine. "Now that's a good looking couple," he said. I smiled, just the same as I used to when Jeannie would take my picture.

The rotunda was filled with couples, all dancing close, each girl in a unique gown. The colors filled the hall with an artist's palette. "Amy! You look so pretty!" the girls said to me over and over. "Wow, I love your hair! And your dress—it's gorgeous!" *Do I know her? Or her? I don't think I do. Just smile, be polite, have fun!*

I caught a glimpse of the boys who I had gone to elementary and junior high with—the boys who teased me and tried to tear me down. They were looking at me differently though—with new eyes—as they danced with their own dates.

For a flash of a moment I was back in fifth grade. That was the year I chose to be part of an early morning square dance team. I knew it would be challenging to try, but I wanted to go, and I was excited to learn to dance! Katie and I talked about it for days leading up to the first class, wondering what it would be like and how, exactly, one dances in a square.

"You girls are going to have so much fun learning how to square dance. This is a great opportunity," Katie's mom said while she drove us to school early in the morning for the first class. The sky was gray with tiny streaks of pink—dawn, the best part of any day. I was shaking with nerves mixed with the chill of morning. "The great thing about square dancing is that there's someone calling all the dance moves for you, so all you have to do is listen to what he's saying." *I can do that. I can listen. This will be fun!*

When Katie and I walked into the gym, it was filled with a large group of fifth grade boys and girls, all casually lined up with their backpacks thrown up on the stage. Katie and I joined them, standing next to one another and waiting for further instruction. The cafeteria smelled of the beginnings of lunch, and in the background the echo of the metal cooking trays filled the air.

"Kids! Listen up. If you are here it's because you want to learn how to square dance," the teacher shouted out. "We've assigned each of you a partner who you will come back to after each dance sequence. When I call your name, stand next to the partner we have selected for you so we know if all students are in a pair." I waited along with the rest of the kids and watched as the boys high-fived the girls they were paired with, but when my name was called out, my partner was immediately horrified. He wouldn't look at me. He wouldn't stand next to me. He was humiliated to be paired up with me. As the music started, he wouldn't hold my hand. To add to my pain as we switched through partners, I met up with my bully face-to-face just as the caller said, "swing your partner." The bully grabbed my arm, digging his jagged fingernails into my skin and then swinging me so hard that I spun to the ground and across the shiny gym floor—the smell from his sweaty hand lingering stiffly in the air. I landed in a pile of crumpled legs and arms. His laughing pierced me. The tears stung my face. Even still, I got up. I danced.

"Amy?" said Jamie, bringing me back to the present. "May I have this dance?" I stumbled to collect my thoughts. *Tonight I am dancing the way I have always dreamed of—because of you.*

"Yes, I would love to dance."

Jamie's arms folded around me with his fingers locked at the curve of my back. I was so close to him I could feel his breath brushing past my cheek, my chin hovering just over his shoulder. Towering high above us was the grand rotunda with images of painted seagulls flying through the clouds. And we danced. I thought to myself that Jamie had set me free. I knew then, even before the first song had ended, that I loved him. Deep in my heart where hurt meets hope, that was where I loved him. I always would, too. *I will always love you, Jamie. For saving me. You have given me freedom—freedom from the stares and freedom to release my confidence. And this feeling is just like flying.* When the next song started, he asked me again if I would dance with him, and again I said yes—and then again—and again. Each time the butterflies filled my body exponentially. With each turn of my feet, I caught girls looking at me, wishing *they* were me.

Between the slow dances, the songs were upbeat rock music, but I wasn't totally certain that my regular dancing could sustain avoiding another "bra incident". I didn't have a backup plan if, for some reason, the sewing job Mom did didn't hold. It was too high-risk! All night long I tried to remember each moment so that I could tell Jeannie and Katie every detail. *I have to tell them we danced the slow dances, how total strangers said I looked so pretty, and how I felt like a real live princess at a ball. Oh, I wish so badly they could be here!*

"I'm sorry, Amy, can I steal your date for just a minute?" the student body president said as we left the dance floor to get a drink. "I'll bring him right back. I promise."

"OK, I'll just wait for you over here," I said, pointing to a marble bench. Jamie was gone for several minutes. I sat there on the bench, next to Scott and Charlene, sipping lemonade and waving at all my new friends. I was a celebrity! A high school star!

"Would you like to dance again?" Jamie asked when he found us.

"I would love to," I responded, standing up with the help of his hand.

When the song was over, the music stopped dead to silent air. Then the screech of a microphone turned up too loud rang through the rotunda.

"Hey, Weber Warriors! Are you having a good time tonight?" said the student body president, to which the crowd screamed back cheers. "First of all, thank you for coming. This has been a great Prom. One for the ages! Next, we would like to crown our Prom King and Queen, and finally, during the next song of the night, the royalty will dance together to the theme song of the Prom. Then we will have the final dance—and please drive home safe. All right, for Prom Queen the student body has selected...Krista Baldwin!" The crowd clapped and a few shouted her name. Krista was petite with fluffy light curls that swayed away from her face. She was always smiling, and I knew that night, somewhere in the crowd, she was smiling again. "And now—for Prom King, by a wildly popular vote, please join me in congratulating Mr. Jamie Acton!"

"You won! You won!" I said, grabbing his arm between the cheers of those on the dance floor. "Go find the queen! You won!" The excited crowd and those near us parted to let him pass—my date, the king. As the music started I listened to the words of the theme song, "Somebody" while I stood tall on the marble floor. "*I want somebody to share, share the rest of my life…*" the song started.

"Amy, you should go find Krista's date, so you can dance to this song," said a girl from the popular crowd as she passed me on the way to the dance floor.

"No. That's OK. I just want to listen to the words. I am fine just to stand here," I said, then thought, *The only person I would want to dance with is Jamie anyway.* The song continued, *"Someone who'll help me see things in a different light…"* I thought, *I will be forever changed because of this moment.* In fact, I could feel myself changing right there on the dance floor, beneath the towering rotunda, waiting for my date to return. My inner confidence was moving outward, catching all of the positive energy of the evening and pushing it to my lips—which were smiling—smiling for the love of a good life. Jamie had shown others that it was possible to see me the way I had always seen myself. Soon after the song was over, he appeared again, as Prom King. My Prom King.

The final dance was just for me and just for him, though not necessarily for *us*. I lay my arms parallel to his, reaching my hands up to hold his shoulders, so grateful for a fairytale ending. I thought of all I had been through—the teasing, the surgeries, and the headaches—and how each painful moment was worth it for *this* dance, for clarity. Mom had made me beautiful the first day I lived, holding me close and having faith that everything would work out. Jeannie had made me beautiful by fiercely protecting me and taking on more for me than a sister should ever have to. The Cleads had made me beautiful by being true and loyal friends, and my dearest Katie, my best friend, had made me beautiful by cheering on the greatness she knew was within me. The Rebels, too, had made me beautiful by accepting me, and each of my siblings had made me beautiful by finding a part of me in them and ignoring my scars. Dad had made me beautiful with his strong confident character, Gram with her timely kindness, and Gramp with his raw and untrained love.

And God, He had made me beautiful by making me just the way he intended.

Every time we turned around on the dance floor, there was someone new slapping Jamie on the back to congratulate him and someone hugging me and telling me I looked more beautiful than they had ever seen me.

"I feel like I just got every joke that has ever been told to me, and I can't stop laughing," Jamie said when the final dance had ended. And he *did* laugh. Longer and happier than any boy I had ever heard—genuine exultant laughing. I had a smile on, too, one that came from layer eleven, the richest of all places. Finally, I could let go.

As we walked down the outside steps leading from the grand capitol building to the vast lawn below, I looked straight ahead as I stepped down each magnificent step. My heels met the steps in unison to his, cracking the cool air with synched tempo. There, with the horizon perfectly in my sight, I caught a glimpse of my future laid out right there before my mind, calling my name. In an instant the memory was recorded deep in my soul. My heart filled with gratitude, overflowing; I couldn't believe that this was my life. My life! Right now. Right this moment. This was it! Yes, today was the beginning of the rest of my great days. I couldn't help but laugh right out loud in front of Jamie and our group. Never would I doubt who I was again, or the lovely grace of God. My stomach exploded with tiny firecrackers that danced all the way through my limbs, bursting at my fingertips and toes. I looked up to the clear night sky, and there was not a white bee in sight. Not a single one.

I paused, thinking about how they had missed the greatest finale of all—my big moment. But just as the thought left my mind, another entered, and I knew exactly where they were. My white bees had flown on to find another little girl—just like me. She sat curled up on top of the heat vent, looking out her sliding glass door to the distant storm, and there she waited for them—her *own* white bees.

And when they started to fall, she counted each one.

white bees

Twenty-one years later....

EPILOGUE

I clicked my high heels confidently up the steps toward the high school. Twenty-one years had passed since the magical night at prom, yet the feeling had never left me. Katie and I set our sights on college directly after graduation, leaving behind the streets of 100 and 150 East in the fall of 1991. That first night we sat next to each other on the floor of our shared dorm room, offering each other comfort, eating cold cereal for dinner, and assessing our plans for making it in the big world. By the end of the week we had gathered a crew of new friends and spent Friday night dancing in the foyer—bursting with youth and independence. After that first year, Katie moved back home, and I missed her with an ache that only softened when she came back to visit.

One day as I was working my way through college as an employee at the local bookstore, a mother approached me, her young daughter in tow, hidden behind her back. She asked me how I did it, how I held my head so high, and what was my secret? How had I become so sure of myself? Did I date? What was my life like? I peeked around at the girl and saw her face branded with a cleft lip. I realized the mother just wanted me to tell her it would all be okay. I smiled and said, "Last week I had six dates with six different guys, and I'm just getting started." Then I put my hand on her arm and finished by telling her, "The hard days will end, and the good days will be plenty. Just you wait. Your daughter will be fine."

Three years and a hundred adventures later, I earned my degree from the very university that—years earlier—had taught me the art of speaking.

As I got ready to leave the night of my twenty-year high school reunion, Maggie, my youngest, wobbled around on her small legs, tugging at my side and looking up at me with her big blue eyes. I couldn't help but be overcome with gratitude.

When I reached the front door of the high school, I pulled it open and entered a warm frenzy of former classmates, shouting hellos and wrapping hugs around me. Within minutes I found Katie, now a mother of five and married to a physician's assistant. She looked healthy and radiant, and with her typical flair she instantly filled me with feelings of affirmation as she stood back and admired my new outfit. We both scanned the group, pointing at those we recognized and shaking our heads in disbelief that time had really eaten up two decades since graduation.

Moose would have loved the party, but life had taken him too soon, too young. I could almost hear his contagious, hearty laugh echoing through the common area of the high school. His guitar was a permanent reminder in my home of the best summer of my life. The rest of the Rebels couldn't make it to the reunion, and it didn't feel quite the same without them.

Jamie had emailed me the day before, saying that for half a second he'd considered driving through the night from Los Angeles just to join me and our other friends in the celebration. Now a successful drummer in a band, he had just returned from a tour in Europe and was wrapped up in a commitment at a recording studio. I promised him I would take loads of pictures and fill him in on the details.

In the absence of the Rebels and Jamie, however, there was one person at the reunion that didn't bring back pleasant memories. The bully. From the minute I saw him, I knew it was time—for both of us—to resolve our conflict. He stood alone along the side of the wall, looking at pictures of past alumni. He was handsome and bore a kind, genuine aura. There was no trace—no, not a shred—of the boy I'd known all those years ago. He was just a kid back then, and like so many others he was only trying to figure out his place in the world. I approached him, and we exchanged small talk, but it was clear we were both ready to move toward a more meaningful conversation. When the moment was right, I looked him straight on and asked why he'd been so mean to me all those years ago. Tears immediately filled his eyes. He responded, balancing kindness and careful articulation, with the most sincere string of words I had ever heard—words I'd waited a lifetime to hear, and words, it seemed, he'd been waiting a lifetime to share. He told me he'd carried the guilt of what he'd done to me for years.

He'd taught his young boys to be kind and
thoughtful, yearning to make up for the past by
changing the future. He said he was relieved that I'd
come to talk to him, and he told me how beautiful I
was—and always had been. With each sentence that
he said, the wounds left inside me closed a little
more. At last! The heavy, heavy hate was gone. In the
void was compassion, and perhaps even a new
friend.

Then it was my turn. I told him thank you, wiping
tears from my own eyes. I realized that most would
think I was crazy for thinking it, but in a way I knew
he'd helped build my resilient character. Without
him, I might not have grown into the person I
became.

First thing the next morning, I called Jeannie
at her office at Utah State University and told her the
story. We both laughed at the liberation of a burden
let free. She, more than anyone else, knew that
forgiving him was another life changing event for
me.

Yes, epic moments do happen.

Some by choice, others by chance—*all* by
grace.

THE END

ACKNOWLEDGEMENTS

A huge thank you to my mom who gave this book
flight by telling me over and over again that I had a
story others needed to hear, AND for having faith
that I could do it. Thank you to my dad for your
words one night early in the writing process, "Just
tell your story, Amy." Thank you to each of my
siblings: Jeannie, Todd, Toots (Tami), Justin, and
Darin for letting me share memories of you
throughout the book. Thank you to my three
children, Hayden, Emma, and Maggie for letting me
chase this dream. I hope you will read this book and
understand who I was "way back then" a little better.
A big love to my BFF! To my editor, Katie Carter,
thank you for your support and guidance. A special
heartfelt thanks to all of those friends and family in
my circle of trust who read the first several chapters
of the book for me, sending me emails, text messages
and phone calls with your affirmation – without
which I am not sure I could have kept going.

And thank you to God for whispering into my heart
the simple word, "write…"

SPECIAL THANKS

I am so grateful for my cleft lip and palate team, all of whom I am deeply indebted to.

T. Ray Broadbent, M.D.

David S. Thomas, M.D.

William Owen, M.D.

Steven H. Broadbent, DMD

Stephen L. Hadley, DDS

Utah State University Speech Pathology Department

Primary Children's Hospital, Salt Lake City, UT

LDS Hospital, Salt Lake City, UT

ABOUT THE AUTHOR

Amy Jo Wilde is a motivational speaker and author living in Utah. She frequently contributes to KSL.com, Deseret News and Mormon Times. Amy Jo was given an award for excellence in writing from KSL/Deseret Digital, and has published over 60 articles including coverage of the Sundance Film Festival. She is passionate about helping women find their inner beauty and an advocate for mothers of babies born with birth defects.

The Rebels, the early years, 1983

Jeannie, Todd, Amy Jo, Katie

Darin, Jeannie, Amy Jo, Justin, Toots, Todd

Todd, Justin, Toots, Darin, Jeannie, Amy Jo

white bees

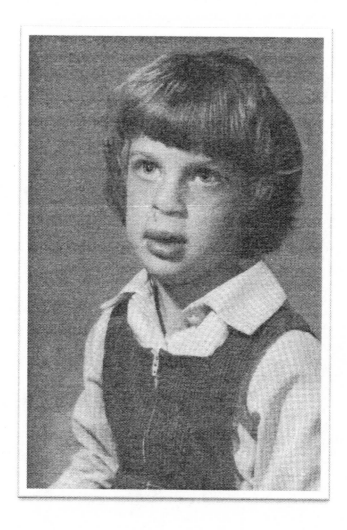

white bees

white bees

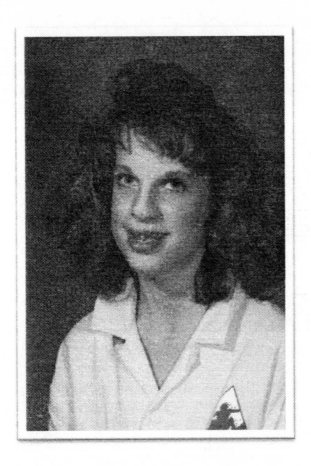

white bees

"I'll love you forever, woman!"